The Fruits of Opportunism

The Fruits of Opportunism

Noncompliance and the Evolution of China's Supplemental Education Industry

LE LIN

The University of Chicago Press
Chicago and London

The University of Chicago Press, Chicago 60637
The University of Chicago Press, Ltd., London
© 2022 by The University of Chicago
Published 2022
Printed in the United States of America

31 30 29 28 27 26 25 24 23 22   1 2 3 4 5

ISBN-13: 978-0-226-82097-2 (cloth)
ISBN-13: 978-0-226-82151-1 (paper)
ISBN-13: 978-0-226-82150-4 (e-book)
DOI: https://doi.org/10.7208/chicago/9780226821504.001.0001

Library of Congress Cataloging-in-Publication Data

Names: Lin, Le, author.
Title: The fruits of opportunism : noncompliance and the evolution of China's
    supplemental education industry / Le Lin.
Description: Chicago : University of Chicago Press, 2022. | Includes bibliographical
    references and index.
Identifiers: LCCN 2022004653 | ISBN 9780226820972 (cloth) | ISBN 9780226821511
    (paperback) | ISBN 9780226821504 (e-book)
Subjects: LCSH: Educational tests and measurements—China. | Education—China.
Classification: LCC LB3058.C48 L56 2022 | DDC 370.951—dc23/eng/20220222
LC record available at https://lccn.loc.gov/2022004653

♾ This paper meets the requirements of ANSI/NISO Z39.48-1992 (Permanence of Paper).

In memory of my grandparents

Contents

List of Abbreviations ix

Introduction   1

1 Opportunities for Opportunists: A Theoretical Excursion   20

PART I   When Opportunists Produce Changes

2 Kill Your Competitors   43

3 Be More Aggressive Than Your Employees   68

4 Not Much English Taught at Our English School   90

PART II   How Opportunism Persists amid Changes

5 Kidnapping Kids for Their Own Good   117

6 There Are No Professional Managers in China   137

7 Who Cares about Tuition Money   165

Conclusion   187

Acknowledgments 199
Appendix: List of All SEOs and Data Source 203
Notes 205
References 221
Index 237

Abbreviations

The Education Industry: China's supplemental education industry

ETS:	Educational Testing Service
GRE:	Graduate Record Examination
IELTS:	International English Language Testing System
IPO:	initial public offering
RMB:	Renminbi (the Chinese currency)
SAT:	Scholastic Aptitude Test
SEC:	Securities and Exchange Commission
SEO:	supplemental education organization
TOEFL:	Test of English as a Foreign Language
VIE:	variable interest entity
WTO:	World Trade Organization

Introduction

The wealthy have always had an edge, but the revelation that dozens actually paid to grease their kids' way underscores what many parents feel in their bones: the college admissions process has become an escalating contest where money often wins. In the latest scandal, parents paid bribes of $100,000 to $6.5 million to guarantee their children got into top schools, including Yale, Stanford, the University of Southern California and Georgetown. . . .

Anyone who's gone through the process of watching a nervous son or daughter wrestle with an unopened decision notification can appreciate the appeal of such an arrangement and its unfairness. "We're talking about a scandal about rich people trying to put their finger on the scale," said Chris Falcinelli, founder of Focus Educational Services, a private tutoring firm in Brooklyn that also provides college counseling.

One cooperating witness in the case described the path he was offering wealthy families as a "side door" into college, as opposed to the front door, "which means you get in on your own," he said in the complaint. "The back door is through institutional advancement, which is 10 times as much money."

AMANDA GORDON AND BEN STEVERMAN (2019)

Very few scandals have struck a nerve in so many ordinary American people as did the 2019 college admission bribery case. Rick Singer, the founder and CEO of Key Worldwide Foundation, helped dozens of American and Chinese customers send their children to elite colleges such as Yale and Stanford University. He accomplished this through a "side door": channeling bribes to sports coaches at elite universities, fabricating athletic records for the children of his clients, and securing extra time for them on standardized tests.

This scandal adds fuel to the fire of widespread suspicion regarding fairness and equity in the college admission process. It also alerts Americans of the existence and clout of the supplemental education industry. This industry encompasses a wide variety of supplemental education organizations (SEOs), ranging from the afore-cited Key Worldwide Foundation and Focus Educational Services, to corporate giants such as Kaplan, Berlitz, and Kumon. These SEOs provide myriad outside-school educational services, such as test preparation, after-school tutoring, foreign language training, and application consulting.[1] Given such a diversity of services, the supplemental education industry has several other names, such as the sector of private tutoring and shadow education.[2]

Of course, the extreme malfeasances of Singer and his SEO do not represent the mainstream practices of the supplemental education industry. That said, many studies, investigations, and lawsuits have linked the misconduct of SEOs with an abnormal jump in test scores and the failure and corruption of the formal education system in the countries in which they operate.[3] The outburst of criticism against the supplemental education industry's misconduct in recent years has made one thing clear: this formerly hidden industry has come out of the shadows and become increasingly influential.[4]

There has been a growing interest in understanding the supplemental education industry, but most studies focus on the demand-side story—how the soaring demand for education contributes to the expansion of this industry and how this industry affects student learning, education effectiveness, and social inequality.[5] Despite recent efforts to survey entrepreneurs and organizational strategies of the supplemental education industry,[6] we still know little about the supply-side story: how this industry actually operates and how it came into being.

This book offers a behind-the-scenes glimpse into China's supplemental education industry (hereafter referred to as the Education Industry). With half of the world's top thirty education corporations and seven of the world's ten richest billionaires in education, this industry is one of the largest and most vibrant education sectors on the globe.[7] Nonexistent before the early 1980s, this industry has experienced exponential growth in the last four decades. For example, the market size of supplemental education for K–12 students—one of multiple niche markets within the Education Industry—ballooned from RMB 115 billion to RMB 560 billion in eight years (2010–18), even though the total number of Chinese K–12 students remained largely constant during this period (fig. I.1).[8] In accordance with this market expansion, the annual student enrollment for K–12 SEO classes grew rapidly and surpassed 137 million in 2016.[9]

The expansion of the Education Industry has come with profound social implications on both domestic and global scales. Within China, the industry

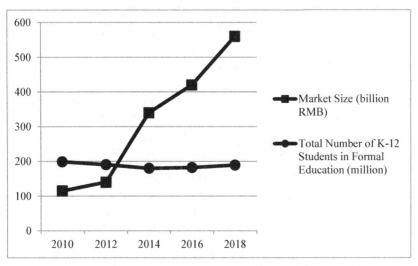

FIGURE I.1. Comparing the Market Size of China's K–12 After-School Tutoring and the Total Number of Chinese K–12 Students in the Formal Education Sector
SOURCES: (1) Deloitte China (2013, 2019); (2) For the total number of elementary and secondary school students (K–12 students), I consulted multiple reports from the Statistical Reports on the National Educational Development by China's Ministry of Education (http://www.moe.gov.cn/jyb_sjzl/sjzl_fztjgb/).

reinforces education inequalities and social stratification. For example, there has been a substantial urban-rural disparity in the student participation rate for SEO classes. At least 50 percent of Chinese K–12 students attended SEO classes every year in the 2010s in provincial capital cities and coastal urban centers, and the participation of K–12 students in SEO classes is as high as 85 percent in megacities such as Beijing.[10] In comparison, the student participation rate in rural areas is much lower. Accordingly, leading SEOs cluster in coastal urban centers, where middle-class and elite families are concentrated. Globally, the Education Industry has changed how Chinese students study abroad and upended the landscape of other countries' higher education systems. For example, it is estimated that by the year 2000 over 70 percent of Chinese students studying in US universities had taken test-preparation classes for study abroad–oriented standardized tests, such as the Test of English as a Foreign Language (TOEFL) and the Graduate Record Examination (GRE).[11]

One of my motivations for examining the Education Industry is to provide sociological clues to a puzzle: How and why has participating in education become an increasingly anxiety-inducing experience for students and their parents even though formal and outside-school educational services are far more available now than was previously the case?[12] For parents and educators around the world, taking an in-depth look at the Education Industry opens the imagination to what could be down the road: How will education look when SEO classes fill children's weekend schedules and when participating in SEO classes becomes an indispensable process in test preparation, college applications, and other critical educational decisions?

My personal experience and observations also prompt a closer look at the Education Industry. As a former teacher and manager in this industry,[13] I witnessed how leading Chinese SEOs, many of which started as small nonprivate entities in dilapidated classrooms with informal practices, morphed into a different species: current market leaders are predominantly private corporations that are operated with a formal managerial hierarchy and have expanded across different regions of the country with directly managed branches.[14] I also experienced firsthand the launching of the first few Chinese SEOs on US stock markets and subsequently the massive influx of global capital into this industry.

With hindsight, the aforementioned development trajectory of the Education Industry might seem to be just another China miracle story. After all, we have encountered so many caterpillar-to-butterfly transformations since China's turn to the market, and many of these transformations were accomplished with strong government support. An examination of the early years of the Education Industry, however, reveals a policy environment that was not so favorable for capitalistic development. This industry grew in the early 1980s as the Chinese state mobilized nonstate societal resources to complement the state-run formal education system (hereafter referred to as the state education system). To keep this system affordable, nonprivate, and not-for-profit, Chinese education policy makers forbade SEOs from being registered as corporate entities, banned SEOs' private ownership, and denied their entry into domestic stock markets. State regulators also mandated that SEO founders had to be senior faculty members and educators associated with the state education system.

In short, the Chinese state encouraged the development of the Education Industry, but the initial rationale of the state was to develop the Education Industry as an extension of the state education system instead of a standalone for-profit industry. The vast majority of Chinese SEOs maintained their legal status as nonprivate and not-for-profit education entities till the early 2000s when many of them were re-registered as private for-profit corporate entities. As such, the Education Industry differs from its counterparts in many other countries in that many Chinese SEOs have undergone extensive transformations, including privatization and marketization, while foreign SEOs have consistently been private and for-profit entities.[15]

The Fruits of Opportunism explores these extensive transformations by asking a question: How and why did China's supplemental education evolve into a for-profit industry dominated by private, nationally operating and globally financed corporations, despite systematic restrictions placed on private ownership, for-profit activities, cross-region expansion, and financial operation in this industry by the Chinese state? In addition to unpacking this industry-level evolution, this book examines the ebb and flow at the organization level: Why have some organizations survived and thrived while others have failed during the phenomenal expansion of this industry?

To answer these questions, this book puts the spotlight on opportunism in the Education Industry.[16] The overall consensus among existing studies is that opportunism occurs when an individual or organization takes advantage of circumstances and/or people with little regard for principles, consequences, or long-term planning.[17] In this book, I use opportunism and opportunistic practices interchangeably in a value-neutral sense: I am more interested in outlining opportunistic practices' noncompliance with specific rules and norms than determining whether these practices are right or wrong. Of rules and norms that often fall into the targets of opportunism, there are three major dimensions: (a) state laws and other formal regulations that are not necessarily specific to any organizational field; (b) informal norms of trust, reciprocity, and cooperation (hereafter referred to as cooperation norms) in economic activities;[18] and (c) norms related to the legitimate ways of organizing activities in a particular organizational field, such as norms of teaching in the Education Industry. Furthermore, this book uses the term *opportunists* to indicate organizations that engage in opportunistic practices systematically.[19]

My analysis draws on in-depth interviews with founders, managers, and teachers of twenty-eight SEOs that were active from 1980 to 2018,[20] the internal archives of these organizations, and my participant observation of their meetings and classes. A thematic finding is that the Education Industry has been ambiguous despite substantial privatization and marketization: it has been unclear whether SEOs are private or nonprivate and whether they are for-profit business firms or not-for-profit social enterprises. This ambiguity manifested itself in not only the gap between SEOs' legal status and their actual operations but also in the fact that the Chinese state has been much more clear about what SEOs should not be than what they should be.

Under this ambiguity, SEOs initially drew on the state education system and the informal economy for resources (e.g., teachers and facilities) and organizational repertoires.[21] In addition, marginal entrepreneurs were early founders of opportunists and opportunists trailed behind other SEOs in terms of resources and legitimacy in the 1980s.[22] Opportunists overcame these disadvantages by introducing resources from the informal economy into this industry and developing opportunistic practices. Furthermore and under ambiguity, state policies that were implemented to contain opportunism often unintentionally benefited opportunists. By the early 1990s, opportunists had occupied market leader positions across this ambiguous industry and maintained their leadership status from then on. Ambiguity rewards adventurers. Although opportunists as a group have kept their leadership status, the competition among opportunists after the mid-1990s presented more nuanced dynamics: those opportunists that were relatively less opportunistic and whose entrepreneurs were more closely connected to the state education system started to gain the upper hand.

I further elucidate how opportunists' market leader status and their opportunistic practices persisted despite the institutionalization of the Education Industry after the early 2000s.[23] The persistence was a result of the lingering ambiguity of this industry, the oscillation of state policies, and the drastic arrival of new resources, such as global capital. Pressured by the changing institutional environment to evolve into nationally operating and globally financed corporations, many opportunists that had been market leaders in the 1990s struggled and stumbled. Nevertheless, a few existing opportunists adapted to the changing environment and continued to lead. A group of new opportunists was also established. On the one hand, these existing and new market leaders were pushing this industry's institutionalization forward. On the other hand, these opportunists unlocked new forms of opportunism. The escalation of opportunistic practices went hand in hand with the institutionalization of the industry. Opportunism is indeed often destructive, but it is also productive to the formation and evolution of a market.

I argue that the rise of opportunists to market leadership and their persistent opportunism in the Education Industry fostered a bottom-up privatization and marketization. In other words, the privatization and marketization of this industry did not unfold primarily as top-down processes that originated from the state or other macro institutions. Initially, there were not only state restrictions on private ownership and for-profit operations but also strong presence of state-affiliated organizations in the Education Industry. Opportunists, as one of the two prototypes of private enterprises, also faced competition from another prototype. But as opportunists outcompeted the other prototype and state-affiliated organizations, they facilitated the retreat of state influence and eliminated alternative development trajectories of this industry. As these opportunists sustained their market leadership, they became rule makers, diffusing their opportunistic practices across the nation, expanding the boundaries of market-oriented operations, and pushing state recognition of a for-profit industry. My empirical chapters also show that although state retreat, globalization, and other supraorganizational changes prepared the ground for the aforementioned extensive transformations, the intraorganizational dynamics of leading opportunists directly triggered the formation of the managerial hierarchy in these organizations and this industry's turn to global financial markets. In short, opportunists acted as the agents for change, steering the course of privatization and marketization from below.

Expansion of Supplemental Education as Organizational Change

The research question of this book concerns the transformation of supplemental education, education privatization/marketization, and organizational change.[24] Let me discuss foundational scholarship relevant to these areas, followed by my proposal to shift the focus of literature from new institutionalism to opportunistic practices in ambiguous industries.

EXPANSION, PRIVATIZATION, AND MARKETIZATION

In the United States, Japan, Canada, and many other countries, supplemental education has been predominantly private and for-profit since its early stages of development (Aurini 2006; Dierkes 2010; Koyama 2010). Although the rise of supplemental education can be viewed as an integral part of worldwide education privatization, literature on supplemental education in the United States, Japan, Canada, and other countries is more interested in its expansion than its privatization. What is special about the expansion of the Education Industry is that it occurred simultaneously with the industry's privatization and marketization and China's market transition. When examining the rise and transformation of the Education Industry, therefore, it is worth including literature on these relevant social processes.

State Neoliberalism as a Top-Down Explanation. A plausible explanation for the simultaneous expansion and transformation is the top-down effort of the state. After the Reform and Opening-Up was unveiled, the Chinese state made education more market oriented than before by retreating from social welfare: under this state neoliberalism, the state rolled back its role in education and health care and shifted responsibilities in these areas to families and individuals (Mok 1997a, 1997b; So and Chu 2012). When it comes to supplemental education, Kwok (2010) identifies the Chinese state's laissez-faire neoliberalism as the engine for the growth of the Education Industry. Zhang and

Bray (2017) also link the boom of China's supplemental education to a state of "micro-neoliberalism"—local governments' policies in decentralizing control of schooling and monitoring performance.

Indeed, the expansion, privatization, and marketization of the Education Industry would not have been possible without the state's retreat. Compared to economic sectors, however, education-related organizational fields have seen much less state support for privatization and marketization.[25] State regulators initially only intended to use the retreat of the state to prepare for a quasi-market sector instead of a for-profit industry (Mok 1997b). Contrary to Kwok's (2010) claim, deregulation and laissez-faire policies—key characteristics of neoliberalism—have not been the Chinese state's governing logic in formal education or supplemental education. In fact, the Chinese state has continuously positioned all education-related organizational fields as socialist public goods.[26] It was with such logic that Chinese state regulators imposed systematic restrictions on SEOs' private ownership, for-profit operation, and listings on domestic stock markets.

The temporal changes and regional disparity of the Education Industry cast further doubt into the state neoliberalism argument. For example, the exponential expansion of the K–12 submarket did not occur during the intensified state neoliberalism of the 1990s but instead ensued during the promotions of the socialist and egalitarian agendas of the early 2000s.[27] A similar pattern is observed in South Korea. Public interest in, and heightened demand for, supplemental education did not result from loosening regulations but instead occurred "every time the government implemented a major reform promoting equal opportunities in education" (Baker 2020). With regard to regional patterns and disparity, southern cities such as Guangzhou and Shanghai have been known for their more developed civil society and more market-friendly policies.[28] But Beijing is the Education Industry's undisputable mecca: not only has the competition been most intense in Beijing's TOEFL/GRE, K–12, and several other major submarkets, but Supernova, Doo & Cool, and many other national market leaders also initially thrived there.

Globalization as a Macro-Level Condition. To the extent that the post-1970s globalization is inherently connected with neoliberalism, decentralization, and deregulation, globalization has been shown as an engine for worldwide education privatization (Apple 2001; Carnoy and Rhoten 2002; Giroux 2002; Stromquist 2002; Maskus and Reichman 2004).

Globalization has also been theorized as a macro-level condition for the worldwide proliferation of supplemental education. While some studies examine globalization as an underlying factor for the recent increase of offshore private tutoring through the internet (Ventura and Jang 2010), others high-

light the global homogenization of formal education as a significant contribu-
tor to the worldwide expansion of formal education's shadow—supplemental
education (Baker et al. 2001; Mori and Baker 2010).

More fundamentally, behind this recent formal education homogenization is the global spread of formal schooling and formal examinations as legitimate institutions since the inception of modernity (Boli, Ramirez, and
Meyer 1985; Meyer, Ramirez, and Soysal 1992; Stevenson and Baker 1992; Bray
2017). With this broadly defined globalization perspective, studies point to
the similarity across nations in the supply of supplemental education (Baker
and LeTendre 2005; Mori and Baker 2010). In addition to its effect on the supply, globalization is also said to have brought about heightened demand for
new education opportunities, such as the increased public interest in school
choice around the world (Dierkes 2008).

The globalization perspective is inspiring for the Chinese case to the extent that the Education Industry also emerged in the wake of the post-1970s
globalization. This industry has become increasingly institutionalized since
the early 2000s and has shown some signs of convergence with the way SEOs
are operated in Western countries. However, this globalization perspective is
inadequate for understanding the distinct development of the Education Industry. As mentioned previously, supplemental education in developed countries such as the United States, Japan, and Canada did not experience privatization or marketization, although privatization of their formal education created
a condition for supplemental education development (Bray 2009). Even in formerly socialist regions, such as eastern Europe and former Soviet Union countries, the supplemental education industry does not share the development trajectory of the Education Industry (Bray and Kobakhidze 2014). State regulators
in those countries gave the green light to SEOs for formal private ownership
and market operation, and the primary engine for the growth of supplemental
education in some of these regions was the income decline of schoolteachers
(Bray 2009).

The emphasis on globalization and cross-nation similarities offers little
help in illuminating my research question that touches on the distinctiveness
of China's supplemental education: whereas SEOs in the United States often
distinguish themselves from formal education by highlighting their small
class size, individually tailored schedules, and interactive classes, the most
popular teaching model in the Education Industry throughout the 1990s and
early 2000s featured large class size, nonflexible schedules, and minimum
teacher-student interaction. In addition, franchising has been adopted as a
popular model for expansion by leading non-Chinese SEOs such as Kumon
and Sylvan Learning Centers (Aurini and Davies 2004), but most of the top

market leaders in China eschewed the franchise model and instead relied on directly managed branch schools for cross-region expansion. Furthermore, the ways in which Chinese SEOs accessed the financial market differ from their counterparts in other countries. For example, both Chinese and South Korean SEOs sought capital from stock markets in the twenty-first century, but the former has been much more active than the latter in overseas stock markets.[29]

By the same token, emphasizing the cultural similarity does not shed much light on the huge disparity in supplemental education across East Asian countries and regions. Admittedly, East Asian countries and regions have all witnessed a strong presence of SEOs, and SEOs in these countries and regions are known for their large classes and charismatic teachers (e.g., Bray 2009; Ng 2009). It is also true that the huge influence of SEOs and the similarities in operation across these regions reflect the deep-seated common values of meritocracy, Confucianism, and desire for prestige in these regions (Kwok 2001; Ventura and Jang 2010; Lee and Shouse 2011; Bray and Lykins 2012; W. Zhang 2014). However, these cultural explanations fall short in making sense of the distinct development trajectory of the Education Industry. Moreover, the cultural explanations have placed the analytical weight on the persistence of traditional values and therefore do not take us far enough in addressing the dramatic changes in the Education Industry in the last forty years.

Economic Considerations. With some overlaps with the neoliberal and globalization perspectives, a series of economic explanations see the participation in supplemental education as a natural extension of the growing demand for education (e.g., Kwok 2001, 2010; W. Zhang 2014). The rising demand has also been shown as the key to understanding the boom of for-profit education in general (e.g., Becker and Posner 2009).

To be sure, the rising demand of Chinese middle-class families and the growth of their purchasing power are indispensable for the Education Industry's soaring development. But these economic explanations cannot help unravel the puzzle of why opportunists founded by marginal entrepreneurs outcompeted other organizations. After all, all organizations faced the same demand spike. Moreover, most economic explanations assume the rising demand for supplemental education as natural and spontaneous, glossing over how, when, and why the demand arose and soared. My empirical chapters document how demand for some supplemental education services is not spontaneous but was instead manufactured, at least in part, by policy swings and SEO strategies.

Another underlying assumption of many economic explanations is that private and marketized SEOs are inherently more efficient, therefore being able to better serve consumers and outcompete other organizational models. My empirical chapters and some existing studies on Chinese SEOs paint a different picture, however. Indeed, a few leading nonstate SEOs, the major candidate for private and marketized SEOs, were indeed highly efficient in recruiting students.[30] But there is no systematic evidence that lends credence to their effectiveness in boosting test scores or enhancing educational gains for students once students' family background and other factors are controlled (e.g., Yu Zhang 2013; Zhang and Xie 2016). More importantly, the concept of efficiency is socially constructed and industry-specific, as Fligstein (1990, 295–302) points out. This is especially true for an ambiguous industry because ambiguity is where "performance criteria conflict and collide" (Stark 2009, 182).

Studies with an attention to macro factors have also used the new institutional theory to make sense of supplemental education (e.g., Aurini 2006).[31] Some of these studies highlight how SEOs imitate each other and copy formal education practices in order to look more legitimate (Mori and Baker 2010), while others emphasize the institutional pressures behind parents' desire to resort to private tutoring and send children to prestigious institutions (e.g., Lee and Shouse 2011). From the new institutional point of view, the Education Industry expanded and evolved not because of the allegedly high efficiency of private and for-profit SEOs but because of the isomorphic pressure—Chinese SEOs increasingly followed the trend in becoming private and for-profit because being organized this way is taken for granted as the legitimate and globally accepted form.

To be sure, the new institutional perspective has demonstrated its merit in understanding the transformation of Chinese enterprises. For example, Guthrie (1999) has shown that Chinese firms have been formalized partly because they have been conforming to Western procedures as a rational approach for operating. Nee and Opper (2012) also begin their analysis with a micro-level new institutional perspective. They claim that private enterprises more compliant with cooperation norms were more likely to succeed when China's normative order shifted from state socialism to market capitalism. These studies adhere to the classic new institutional tenets that organizational changes take place when a rising normative or cognitive order selects a simple and clearly classified organizational form as the new dominant form (e.g., DiMaggio 1991; Haveman and Rao 1997; Ruef 2000; David, Sine, and Haveman 2013).[32]

When it comes to examining the Education Industry, however, some of these new institutionalist tenets do not hold water. First, while new institutionalism stresses how imperative it is for organizations to conform to a single clear normative/cognitive order in order to survive, all Chinese SEOs thrived as ambiguous organizations. Second, while new institutionalism emphasizes the importance of complying with rules and norms, market leaders in this industry since the early 1990s have been opportunist SEOs that were more noncompliant. Third, while new institutionalism often looks at supraorganizational forces as engines of organizational changes, I show how intraorganizational dynamics played an integral role in driving transformations in the Education Industry. Of course, some recent developments of the new institutional theory have attempted to capture more complex and ambiguous institutional environments. As I elaborate in the next chapter, however, these new theories still fall short of inspiring the transition of the Education Industry.

In this book, the significant role of ambiguity brings to the fore a theoretical approach that can be labeled a theory of ambiguity. According to this theory, which is based on a number of loosely connected studies, we should look into unclear arenas as hotbeds for economic, professional, and organizational change (e.g., Stark 2009; Morrill 2017). The next chapter builds on and moves beyond this existing theory of ambiguity. I suggest that these existing studies often focus exclusively on a single dimension of ambiguity, but the Education Industry is ambiguous on two dimensions. Moreover, these existing studies tend to propose hybridizing, blending, coupling, and recombining as the most important mechanisms of change under ambiguity. My theoretical chapter and the findings of my empirical chapters suggest that it is more critical to unpack how different organization models draw on resources and organizational repertoires differently and how such differentiated access affects the competition dynamics among these organizational models.

An Overview of the Methodology

To inquire into the evolutionary dynamics of the Education Industry, I adopt a methodological strategy that combines a historical perspective with qualitative methods, such as in-depth interviews and participant observation. This book is historical not only because it investigates a transformation spanning four decades (1980–2018) but also because I take events' temporal order and their historical contexts seriously.[33]

My case selection starts with picking up submarkets within the Education Industry.[34] I focus on this industry's five major submarkets: (1) the TOEFL/GRE;[35] (2) Graduate School Entrance Examination of China (hereafter referred to as the Chinese Graduate Exam); (3) spoken English; (4) the International English Language Testing System (IELTS);[36] (5) the K–12. These five submarkets are vital not only because they have vast market volume but also because each one has bred nationally influential market leaders.

The fact that the five submarkets boomed in different time periods requires a shift of focus when investigating each period. For example, the submarkets of the TOEFL/GRE, the Chinese Graduate Exam, and spoken English budded in the 1980s and early 1990s. During this period, competition among SEOs only unfolded locally within each submarket. Therefore, it is inevitable to choose one local submarket for closer scrutiny. My inquiries of this period's dynamics focus on Beijing's TOEFL/GRE submarket, where the competition was arguably the most intense and where Supernova—the first nationally dominant SEO—prospered.[37] There will be a shift of focus when I investigate the dynamics after the early 2000s. It was not until then that a nationally integrated Education Industry started to take shape. From the early 2000s on, both the competition within each local submarket and the fight for national dominance among leaders of each submarket intensified. During the same period, new submarkets, such as IELTS and K–12, sprouted with their new leaders. My inquiries of the 2000–2018 period, therefore, capture both the within-submarket and the across-submarket dynamics.

As for the case selection on the organization level, this book draws on twenty-eight SEOs. Twenty of them originated from the five major submarkets mentioned earlier. The rest are drawn from new submarkets, such as online education, that have recently mushroomed. Each one of the twenty-eight SEOs was, or still is, a market leader in a local submarket, a national submarket, or the Education Industry in general.[38] For example, my probe into the competition among opportunists in Beijing's TOEFL/GRE submarket in the 1990s centers on four leaders—Supernova, Pioneers, Cornerstone, and Seven Swords. Among them, Supernova enjoys unparalleled significance not only because it has dominated this local submarket since the mid-1990s but also because it has been a key player in all the five major submarkets since then. Supernova also played the leading role in shaping the teaching, financing, and marketing of the entire Education Industry. When the book shifts to national and cross-submarket competition after the early 2000s, I not only keep Supernova as a key case but also add new market leaders from emerging submarkets, such as United IELTS from the IELTS submarket and Doo & Cool from the K–12 submarket. This book, therefore, is a study of the upper echelon of the Education Industry.[39]

Table I.1 familiarizes readers with the six key SEO cases in the book, their founding year, locations of headquarters, and original submarkets. I offer detailed information about my data sources on these six organizations and the

TABLE I.1. The Six Key SEO Cases in This Book

Name of the Organization	Year Founded	Locations of Headquarters	Original Submarket
Supernova	1991/1993[a]	Beijing	TOEFL/GRE
Pioneers	1992	Beijing	TOEFL/GRE
Blue Ocean	1993	Beijing	Chinese Graduate Exam
Roaring English	1994	Guangzhou	Spoken English
United IELTS	1997/2001[b]	Beijing	IELTS
Doo & Cool	2003	Beijing	K–12

[a] Supernova was registered as an independent SEO in 1993, but it was operated as a division under another SEO from 1991 to 1993.

[b] United IELTS began IELTS test-preparation courses in 2001, but its founder started selling IELTS materials as early as 1997.

Sources: Multiple interviews, internal archives, field notes, and newspaper reports.

rest of the twenty-eight SEOs in the appendix. It is also worth noting that quite a few of these once-leading SEOs have lost their edge over the years or have gone bankrupt. Including these failed SEOs helps overcome the methodological issues of some early organizational studies that are solely based on successful cases.[40] Highlighting the competition among SEOs and a few market leaders' ups and downs, this book is comparative, and yet it is not based on balanced comparison.[41] To protect the identities of my informants and their organizations, I use pseudonyms for all China-based organizations and individuals that are empirically studied in the book.[42]

To investigate these twenty-eight SEOs, I collected primary data (e.g., interviews, archives, and participant observation data) and secondary data on these organizations during my eight-month-long fieldwork in four Chinese cities in 2014 and 2015.[43] After the fieldwork, I followed up with important informants through social media and conducted additional data collection outside of China. For example, I visited a Chinese SEO's office in New York in 2019 and interviewed its founder, managers, and teachers. In 2019 and 2020, I also collected new archives and conducted phone interviews with a few new informants while I stayed in the United States.

My first primary data source is in-depth interviews. I conducted interviews with ninety-five informants: seventy-six interviews were conducted in 2014–15, and the rest were completed during 2019–20. These informants include SEO founders, their family members, shareholders, managers, teachers, consultants, students, and government officials. I used the snowball sampling method in which I asked my informants to identify and introduce additional research participants. More importantly, I purposively targeted specific informants who had significant influence on, or special knowledge of, the Education Industry. For example, I managed to interview twelve founders and cofounders of ten SEOs. In order to pinpoint how Supernova embarked on the New York Stock Exchange as the Education Industry's first case of an initial public offering (IPO), I interviewed eight of Supernova's earliest eleven shareholders as well as a dozen of its former senior managers.

Targeting specific organizations and industry elites is a formidable task, especially given that the Education Industry was initially organized as part of the informal economy. Scant data has been collected and even less is publicly available. In light of this situation, I had to make full use of my insider and prior knowledge as well as my connections with the top leadership of multiple organizations. I relied on my former colleagues and friends to establish initial contacts with new SEOs and submarkets, and then I reached out to targeted informants and others to minimize the reliance on the data access points. This also allowed me to locate some of the most elusive informants of this industry and finish my fieldwork in eight months. My interviews are both structured and semistructured. My interview questions were more structured for interviewees, such as branch school presidents, who shared similar social status or positions. I tailored my interview questions for individual interviewees, especially for those who occupied unique social status or positions. On average, each interview lasted one-and-a-half hours. I also examined the validity of interview data by cross-checking multiple interviews, as several cases of verification in chapter 2 and 3 illustrate.

Archives are another primary source. With permission from top leaders of multiple SEOs, I obtained extensive internal archives, including biographical documents of teachers and managers, official registration records, financial statements, memos, announcements, newsletters, meeting records, photos and class recordings. I gave each archive item a unique number based on its significance and time of collection, and I grouped items of a similar nature in a consecutive order. Of the nearly three hundred internal archive items from six of the twenty-eight SEOs, about two-thirds came from Supernova. This overrepresentation of archives by Supernova and the other five SEOs is not a problem because I do not conduct a balanced comparison across all SEOs. Supernova and the other five SEOs need a closer examination given their profound influence in the Education Industry.[44] The third primary source is ethnographic data collected through participant observation. These data were mostly collected during meetings and special events I attended in 2014 and 2015, although some of them are used to illuminate the social conditions and industry transformation of earlier decades. Undoubtedly, my work experience in the Education Industry inspired this research and guided my fieldwork. But this book does not include any of my work-related information as data.

In addition to these primary sources, I include various secondary data. These data include scholarly studies, reports, newspaper articles, and websites. Secondary data is especially critical for those cases whose primary data are difficult to obtain. To increase the validity of data, I triangulated multiple data sources. For example, I cross-checked primary and secondary data that touched on the same events.

An Outline of the Book

The rest of this book is divided into four parts: a theoretical chapter, two empirical parts, and a conclusion. Chapter 1, the theoretical chapter, develops a theory of ambiguity, a theory of opportunism, and a theory of opportunist-led changes under ambiguity. Readers who are less interested in theories can skip this chapter.

Parts 1 and 2 include six empirical chapters. They are organized around both themes and historical periods: each empirical chapter in part 1 highlights one of the three aforementioned dimensions of rules and norms—formal regulations, cooperation norms, and industry-specific norms—that are often susceptible to opportunism during a specific period before the early 2000s; similarly, each empirical chapter in part 2 unpacks one of the major themes of institutionalization, such as the formalization of managerial career path, during a specific period after the early 2000s. Moreover, these empirical chapters are arranged such that the changing dynamics of multiple submarkets and organizations are woven into the book. To fully capture within-submarket dynamics, the three empirical chapters of part 1 primarily draw on the competition within Beijing's TOEFL/GRE submarket in the 1980s and 1990s. To examine the competition across submarkets and the fight for national supremacy, the three empirical chapters of part 2 look at how the new market leaders of the K–12 and the IELTS submarkets competed nationwide with existing leaders of other submarkets.

Chapter 2, "Kill Your Competitors," explores the deviation from formal regulations in the initial entrepreneurial process in Beijing's TOEFL/GRE submarket from the early 1980s to the early 1990s. I focus on how opportunist SEOs, the nonstate opportunists in the Education Industry, overtook state-affiliated SEOs and other nonstate SEOs as market leaders. Under ambiguity, all SEOs drew on the state education system and the informal economy for resources and organizational repertoires, but the relationship with these two sources varied across different types of SEOs. Opportunist SEOs and their entrepreneurs had tight connections with the informal economy, and they spearheaded efforts to introduce resources from the informal economy into the Education Industry. Opportunist SEOs adopted practices that were more noncompliant with state laws and other formal regulations than other SEOs. These opportunistic practices helped them overcome disadvantages in resources and legitimacy. The ambiguity of the Education Industry also unintentionally turned state regulations that were implemented against opportunism into advantages for opportunist SEOs. As nonstate opportunists became market leaders and state-affiliated SEOs lost steam, state influence in this industry dwindled.

Chapter 3, "Be More Aggressive Than Your Employees," focuses on another dimension of opportunism—noncompliance with cooperation norms—during the same historical period as the previous chapter. With a focus on the power dynamics between teachers and entrepreneurs, I document how the distinct institutional environment and the ambiguity of the industry led to volatile employment relationships and widespread teacher opportunism. Comparison of different SEOs' responses to teacher opportunism makes clear that opportunist SEOs were more likely to survive such opportunism than other forms of SEOs. Opportunist SEOs were more capable of fending teacher opportunism with coercive and noncoercive opportunistic practices. Some entrepreneurs of opportunist SEOs even developed arrangements to make teachers more replaceable, thus reducing teachers' bargaining power and the risk of teacher opportunism. As opportunist SEOs became the only candidates for private enterprises in this industry, they further expanded their influence in setting the course of privatization and marketization.

Chapter 4, "Not Much English Taught at Our English School," analyzes the third dimension of opportunism—breaking away from the existing teaching norms—during the mid- and late 1990s. I ask how and why only some leading opportunist SEOs in Beijing's TOEFL/GRE submarket developed new teaching models. I first describe how marginal entrepreneurs who had work experience in the state education system were more likely to shift the focus of opportunism from violating regulations to revolutionizing teaching norms. Then I turn to a more dynamic analysis of how Supernova, then an emerging dominant player in the TOEFL/GRE submarket, crafted a new teaching model. Under this new teaching model, the norm transitioned from teaching English to coaching test-cracking skills and, further, to instilling motivational, nationalist, and entertaining discourses in students. I further explicate how Roaring English—another opportunist SEO and a market leader in the spoken English submarket—developed a similar new teaching model and how its success largely fits the pattern of the Supernova case.

Chapter 5, "Kidnapping Kids for Their Own Good," connects the first and second parts of the book by reorienting our attention to the sustained success of opportunist SEOs as well as the persistence of opportunism after the early 2000s. I start with the environmental changes on the supply side, such as the state's growing tolerance for private education and the lingering ambiguity in the Education Industry. I highlight how some existing leading opportunist SEOs were able to sustain their market leadership positions. I also document how new SEOs in the K–12 submarket were established and how successful managers and business individuals replaced educators and socially marginalized individuals as this industry's new entrepreneurial group.

Then this chapter chronicles how education policy oscillation and other environmental changes on the demand side fostered the development of new opportunistic practices. Many newly established SEOs, although developing new teaching models to fit the characteristics of K–12 students, indirectly defied formal regulations. The result was the rise of new opportunist SEOs in K–12 supplemental education programs as well as making the K–12 submarket the largest in the Education Industry.

Chapter 6, "There Are No Professional Managers in China," unravels the coevolution of the rise of non-kinship-based managers in the Education Industry and SEOs' cross-region expansion during the 2000s and 2010s. I identify three tracks of coevolution: fast track, slow track, and exception track. New K–12 market leaders and especially Doo & Cool, born in an environment rich in formal managerial hierarchy and relevant organizational repertoires, rode on the fast track to rapidly expand to other cities with directly managed branch schools. In comparison, many leading opportunists that survived the 1990s were stuck in their family business structure, which hindered their empowerment of non-kinship-based managers and these SEOs' cross-region expansion strategies. These opportunist SEOs relied on franchise and other forms of local partnership, but the reliance on these approaches made them susceptible to local collaborators' opportunistic practices. In turn, the failed cross-region expansion of these market leaders impeded the development of their managerial teams. Among existing opportunist SEOs that survived the 1990s, Supernova treaded on an exception track. One of the earliest SEOs that walked out of the family business structure, Supernova built a decentralized network of directly managed branch schools across China. This decentralized model, together with opportunistic practices by branch school presidents and Supernova founder's response, constituted a bottom-up development of managers.

Chapter 7, "Who Cares about Tuition Money," dives into how the upper echelon of the Education Industry became globally financed from the mid-2000s to the late 2010s. I flesh out details on the first wave of IPOs on overseas stock markets. I show that this first wave unfolded only partially as a selection and institutionalization process, as most of these IPOs were responses to, and imitations of, the very first IPO case of this industry—Supernova's IPO. Despite the visible roles of institutional actors and supra-organizational forces, Supernova's IPO was also driven by its adaptation and intraorganizational dynamics. The first wave of IPOs spurred an inpouring of global capital, contributing to a financial standardization process as well as an escalation of opportunism. This escalation included the emergence of new opportunistic practices and the resurfacing of old ones.

The conclusion answers questions presented in this introduction and summarizes findings of the empirical chapters. I further discuss the policy implications of my findings as well as the takeaways on ambiguity and opportunism beyond the Education Industry. The last part of this chapter extends the findings to broader theoretical inquiries on institutional and organizational changes.

Opportunities for Opportunists:
A Theoretical Excursion

Societies have never been sufficiently institutionalized to prevent interstitial emergence.

MICHAEL MANN (1986, 16)

I insist that the original sin [of Chinese private enterprises] is a disease caused by the predicaments and dilemmas in the institutional arrangements.

FENG LUN (2017, 12)[1]

This chapter examines how ambiguity serves as a condition under which opportunism thrives as well as how opportunists orchestrate organizational changes under ambiguity. This excursion is a theoretical endeavor that includes a theory of ambiguity, a theory of opportunism, and a theory of organizational changes. Since this book focuses on the organizational transformations of SEOs, I will primarily engage with literature in organization studies. Most of my cases and data come from the Education Industry, although I also draw on other industries and countries for examples. In doing so, this chapter does not attempt to build a general model or causal mechanism. Rather, my efforts are centered on disentangling theoretically informed processes.

I begin by theorizing two-dimensional ambiguity as a distinct type and consider the two social sources for this type of ambiguity: a giant state system and the informal economy. The second section of this chapter focuses on opportunism, opportunist organizations, and their entrepreneurs. I identify social conditions under which opportunism flourishes. I also connect the literature of opportunism to studies of market transition, and I highlight how socially marginalized individuals are ideal candidates for leading opportunist organizations. The third section theorizes opportunist-led organizational changes under ambiguity. The focus of this section is on clarifying the processes of change and the direction of change.

Theorizing Ambiguity: Introducing Two-Dimensional Ambiguity

New institutionalism is a prominent theoretical paradigm for understanding organizations in general and education organizations in particular. Since its breakthrough in the late 1970s, new institutionalism has been widely used to account for continuity and change in organizations, as well as constraints of social structures (Scott and Davis 2003; Thornton, Ocasio, and Lounsbury 2012, 7).

New institutional studies espouse the assumption that organizations conform to a single well-defined normative and classification order. Complex and ambiguous organizations, according to new institutionalists, will face legitimacy crisis and penalty from the institutional environment (e.g., Zuckerman 1999; Zuckerman et al. 2003). Accordingly, new institutional studies contend that organizational changes often take place when a rising institutional template selects a clearly classified organizational form as a new dominant form (e.g., DiMaggio 1991; Haveman and Rao 1997; David, Sine, and Haveman 2013).

Throughout the years, new institutionalism has been criticized for not being attentive enough to agency, power, and conflict (Friedland and Alford 1991; Stinchcombe 1997; Clemens and Cook 1999), for being sensitive to imitation but not as clear about the initial emergence to be imitated (Clemens 1993; Padgett and Powell 2012), and for emphasizing formal rules but ignoring circumventing rules as an important source of change and innovation (Fligstein 1990, 2002).

Within the broad institutional framework, several growing strands of literature have attempted to address these criticisms and revitalize new intuitionalism. One area of research looks at institutional complexity, which builds on the recent development of institutional logics.[2] Institutional logic perspectives develop new institutionalism by moving beyond the latter's premise about a "simple coherent institutional template" within a given organizational field (Pache and Santos 2013, 973). According to the institutional logic perspective, it is common for organizational fields to be governed by multiple and even contradictory institutional logics (e.g., Thornton, Ocasio, and Lounsbury 2012, 5–10). What organizations often face, therefore, is the multiplicity of institutional templates (Dunn and Jones 2010). This multiplicity of institutional logics is the basis for institutional complexity (Greenwood et al. 2011; Besharov and Smith 2014; Ramus, Vaccaro, and Brusoni 2016). Since research

TABLE 1.1. Organizations with Clear or Ambiguous Ownership and Marketability

Dimensions	Clear Marketability	Ambiguous Marketability
Clear Ownership	For-profit business enterprises with clear ownership	Social-business hybrid enterprises with clear ownership: e.g., microfinance (Battilana and Dorado 2010), work integration (Pache and Santos 2013)
Ambiguous Ownership	Chinese township and village enterprises (Nee 1992; Tsai 2007), Hungarian "recombinant model" (Stark 1996)	China's SEOs, hospitals in China's specialty health-care industry

on institutional complexity has shifted the emphasis from a single coherent institution to complex and ambiguous institutions, these studies share similarities with the theory of ambiguity.

Compared to studies of institutional complexity, the theory of ambiguity edges further away from new institutionalism. A loosely connected body of literature, the theory of ambiguity questions the prevalence of sufficiently institutionalized fields and instead considers ambiguity, interstices, and things-of-boundaries as hotbeds for organizational changes (e.g., Mann 1986, 15–16; Abbott 2001, 261–279; Stark 2009). This theory uses various labels, such as ambiguity (Lester and Piore 2004; Stark 2009), ambiguity/multivocality (Padgett and Ansell 1993), interstices (Fligstein and McAdam 2012, 87; Morrill 2017), hybridity (Padgett and Powell 2012), and boundary-in-between (Eyal 2011; Medvetz 2012), to highlight ambiguous and poorly institutionalized social conditions in fostering changes.

Despite the insight of existing literature on ambiguity and institutional complexity, each study focuses on only a single dimension of ambiguity. Table 1.1 includes two common types of single-dimensional ambiguity. One type, as seen in the lower left cell, characterizes ambiguity on the dimension of ownership. In the context of China's market transition, organizations with this kind of ambiguity are for-profit business enterprises whose ownership structures are unclear. For example, Chinese township and village enterprises in the 1980s and early 1990s were often registered as collectives but their de facto control arrangements were unclear (e.g., Nee 1992; D. Li 1996; Tsai 2007; Xu, Lu, and Gu 2014). In other words, inquiries about their ownership cannot be reduced to the dichotomy of state-owned versus private enterprises or simply the state versus the market logic (Bruton et al. 2015). Ambiguity of ownership was also common during the postsocialist transition of eastern Europe, where ownership-ambiguous enterprises took a variety of forms, from transposing informal economy into state enterprises to recombining state logics with private logics (e.g., Stark 1996, 2009).

Table 1.1 features another type of single-dimensional ambiguity: ambiguity on the dimension of marketability. Organizations facing such ambiguity have clear ownership structures, but it is unclear whether they are for-profit business organizations or nonprofit social enterprises. Outside of China, such ambiguity is most visible in hybrid organizations that navigate between the for-profit market logic and the nonprofit social responsibility logic (e.g., Battilana and Dorado 2010; Pache and Santos 2013; Smith and Besharov 2019). Recent studies on Chinese associations and foundations also outline a similar ambiguity where organizations are struggling between social missions and market/financial logics (e.g., Yan, Ferraro, and Almandoz 2018).

To date, we know little about industries where organizations are ambiguous in both ownership and marketability, as illustrated in the lower right cell of table 1.1. I call this two-dimensional ambiguity. As we see in the next section, such ambiguity originates from the state and the informal economy influencing organizations with different institutional demands and supplying organizations with different organizational repertoires, thus pulling organizations in two opposing directions. In the Education Industry, this ambiguity is manifested in the fact that different stakeholders of Chinese SEOs—state regulators, private entrepreneurs, employers, and consumers—have had different perceptions about what SEOs are and how SEOs should operate.[3] For example, state regulators have positioned SEOs to be nonprivate and not-for-profit, but a large number of private entrepreneurs have been operating their SEOs as private and for-profit enterprises. Moreover, organizations within the Education Industry have drawn on the state education system and the informal economy for resources and organizational repertoires, furthering the ambiguity of this industry.

It is not uncommon for an industry under two-dimensional ambiguity to experience ambiguity along additional dimensions. For example, some might claim that the Education Industry has also faced ambiguity on the dimension of formality: it is unclear whether SEOs are formal or informal organizations. Having said that, theorizing ambiguity only in terms of ownership and marketability keeps my framework parsimonious. Moreover, ambiguity on these two dimensions, especially when combined with social actors' interpretation of the situation in favor of their own interest, has played a more significant role than other ambiguous factors in creating confusions and chaos. For example, six senior professors retired from the state education system and, as founders of Nova Academy—an SEO founded in 1984 in Beijing—had signed a contract to sell their SEO. Two of them later annulled the deal, however, claiming they could not transfer a social enterprise of which they did not have legal ownership (Informants No. 16, No. 26). This chaotic situation resulted primarily from the ambiguity in the dimensions of ownership and marketability.

The Education Industry is not the only Chinese industry that has faced two-dimensional ambiguity. A number of industries that grew out of China's socialist public goods (e.g., education and health care) have been stuck in the same kind of ambiguity. By growing out, I am referring to the process in which new industries prospered on the peripheries of socialist public goods and later experienced substantial privatization and marketization.[4] Besides the Education Industry, China's specialty health-care industry mushroomed on the periphery of China's state-run health-care sector. This industry is represented by specialty hospitals, such as those focusing on sexually transmitted diseases. Hospitals in this industry were all ambiguous in terms of ownership and marketability. By 2018, this industry had not walked out of ambiguity but had been substantially privatized and marketized. In other words, the Education Industry and the specialty health-care industry shared a similar pathway: vibrant private sectors flourished in an area of socialist public goods. In table 1.1, this pathway reveals itself as a route from the lower right cell to the upper left.

SOCIAL SOURCES OF TWO-DIMENSIONAL AMBIGUITY

Two-dimensional ambiguity does not come from nowhere. It is buttressed by social sources. By social sources, I am referring to the social institutions that make institutional demands on organizations and supply these organizations with organizational repertoires. These social institutions are also likely the pools from which ambiguous organizations draw their organizational repertoires and resources. For the Education Industry and China's specialty health-care industry, their two-dimensional ambiguity has two social sources: a colossal state system and the informal economy. In the following, I use the Education Industry to illustrate the two social sources.

The state education system is one of the two major social sources for the Education Industry's ambiguity. State regulators mandated how SEOs should operate. State regulators initially aimed to develop the Education Industry as an extension of the state education system instead of as a for-profit industry. Accordingly, regulators demanded that founders be senior educators, that SEOs be registered as educational entities and that local education bureaus regulate SEOs. These regulations laid the foundation for the formal status of SEOs as nonprivate and not-for-profit educational organizations. In addition,

SEOs directly borrowed organizational repertoires from state education institutions. The next chapter shows how in the beginning all SEOs followed the approach used by state universities to teach classes and recruit students.

In contrast, the informal economy prescribes organizations with a different set of institutional demands and organizational repertoires. Private education in general, and supplemental education in particular, are often organized around the following organizational repertoires of the informal and underground economy (Portes and Sassen-Koob 1987): (a) non-legally regulated, non-contract-based, and part-time employment; (b) part-time entrepreneurship; (c) cash transactions; (d) tax evasion; and (e) other informal structures and procedures, such as no registration, heavy reliance on family operation, and lack of managerial hierarchy. In other words, there seems to be a natural affinity between SEOs and the informal economy that is predominantly private, for-profit, and often underground.

Chinese SEOs have been subject to the gravitational pull of the informal economy. All SEOs in the 1980s and early 1990s employed state university faculty members on a part-time and noncontract basis. Except for some senior faculty members retired from state universities and working as full-time entrepreneurs, the vast majority of SEO founders were part-time entrepreneurs whose full-time jobs were in the state education system. In short, few people considered a job in the Education Industry a career. With regard to structures and procedures, no SEO started with a formal structure or a managerial team. Every early non-state-affiliated SEO examined in this book started as the founder's family-operated organization. For many other countries, the informal economy has also been prescribing SEOs with institutional demands and organizational repertoires. For example, SEOs in Japan are mostly small, informal businesses (Dierkes 2010). In the United States, even corporate giants such as Kaplan started as informal home tutoring.

In terms of resources, the state and the informal economy are the two foundations on which two-dimensional ambiguity is built. In the Education Industry, all SEOs in this book initially employed faculty members from state universities and rented classrooms from nearby state education institutions. Additionally, the SEOs depended on the state-run formal education sector for students, and accordingly, the SEOs were located in areas proximate to one or more state universities. Furthermore, entrepreneurs relied on their access to state universities for critical information. Very often entrepreneurs' initial knowledge about the Education Industry as a business opportunity also came from their experience in, or connection with, the state education system.[5] This is why many SEO founders, including those who had not worked in the state education system prior to entrepreneurship, preferred to partner with someone who had a background in the system—so that these founders could obtain relevant information.

The informal economy was the other source of resources under two-dimensional ambiguity. In terms of personnel, people who had been employed part-time in the informal economy were introduced to the Education Industry as staff and teachers. The next chapter shows that opportunist SEOs had closer connections with the informal economy than other models of SEOs. In this regard, opportunists played the pioneering role in introducing personnel and other resources from the informal economy. For example, opportunist SEOs such as Supernova and Blue Ocean were among the first to employ workers laid off from state-owned enterprises as classroom janitors, migrant workers as marketers, and street vendors as teachers.

CHARACTERISTICS OF TWO-DIMENSIONAL AMBIGUITY

This section sets out to understand the characteristics of two-dimensional ambiguity by comparing it with other forms of ambiguity. Ambiguity is associated with challenges of illegitimacy discounts.[6] One-dimensional ambiguity imbues organizations with crisis, tension, and conflict (e.g., Glynn 2000; Battilana and Dorado 2010). In the market transition context of China, nonstate organizations, such as many township and village enterprises, are often the prototypes of private firms, and they used to be ambiguous in terms of ownership. Compared to state-owned enterprises, nonstate organizations possessed lower status, had less access to financial resources, and suffered from illegitimacy discount and stigma.[7]

In comparison, nonstate organizations under two-dimensional ambiguity were subject to additional illegitimacy discounts. In the Education Industry, these additional illegitimacy discounts include:

(a) Market access discounts: Given state regulations on founders' social backgrounds, noneducators, nonstate educators, and junior faculty/educators within the education system were forbidden to enter the market.
(b) Survival discounts: State requirements on the not-for-profit status of SEOs led to a paranoia that caused the public to view SEO entrepreneurs as money grabbers. The next chapter fleshes out details on how such paranoia jeopardized nonstate SEOs' initial survival.

What is behind these additional illegitimacy discounts is a distinct state governing logic. Under one-dimensional ambiguity on ownership, the governing logic is clearly economic: for China's township and village enterprises, it has never been a question that these enterprises are, and should be, governed as business enterprises, even though it is unclear whether they are private or not. But for industries facing two-dimensional ambiguity, state regulators are only sure that organizations in these industries should be neither private nor for-profit. In other words, the state governing logic here is not what organizations are but what they are not.

Associated with this distinct state governing logic are two characteristics of two-dimensional ambiguity: state fragmentation and underdeveloped market institutions. State fragmentation refers to unclear boundaries, overlapping territories, or turf wars among multiple state agencies.[8] Admittedly, many economic sectors during China's market transition were regulated by multiple state agencies and were thus subject to state fragmentation. For most industries and most ownership-ambiguous organizations, however, it is usually clear which agency is the primary regulator for a particular issue. For example, taxation of any for-profit industry falls under the jurisdiction of the tax bureau. For the Education Industry, however, it is unclear whether it is the tax bureau or the education bureau that should determine tax-related issues due to the aforementioned distinct state governing logic. This highly fragmented situation provides abundant room in which organizational actors can maneuver and interpret state regulations in their favor. My empirical chapters discuss how this situation grants comparative advantages for those who are less compliant with regulations.

By underdeveloped market institutions, I am referring to the situation in which social institutions necessary for the functioning of markets, such as private ownership and corporate governance, are missing or lacking.[9] In the early 2000s when a few leading SEOs were considering IPOs, not only was formal private ownership missing in the Education Industry, but the vast majority of SEOs also did not even have a corporate structure. As a result, even the most successful entrepreneurs in this industry had much less exposure to, and knowledge of, financial operation than did entrepreneurs in other for-profit industries.

Theorizing Opportunism and Portraying Opportunists

The introduction of this book conceptualizes opportunism as taking advantage of circumstances and/or other social actors with little regard for principles, consequences, or long-term planning. Theorizing opportunism this way is in accordance with a diverse body of dictionaries as well as scholarly studies on opportunism.[10] For example, Oliver Williamson (1975, 1993) considers opportunism principle-less when he defines opportunism as "self-interest seeking with guile." Opportunistic practices, according to him, are based on distrust and deception (Williamson 1975, 1993).[11] Werder (2011) defines opportunism more broadly as a departure from fair transactions. While economic sociologists disagree with economists on many fronts, the former group generally agrees with the latter when it comes to opportunism: opportunism constitutes a challenge to the morality of human society (e.g., Granovetter 1995; Abolafia 1996).

My conceptualization of opportunism, though in general agreement with these studies, differs from their approach in two significant ways. First, my approach does not infer intention of opportunists. It is difficult, if not impossible, to empirically confirm whether an individual or organization conducts an action with the intention to serve only one's self-interests. An individual's self-interests are often plural and sometimes contradictory with one another, as one's long-term self-interest might collide with his or her short-term interest. The self-interest of organizations is even more complex. Thus, this book is more interested in how opportunists take advantage of others than whether opportunists do so in order to serve their self-interests. Second, most existing studies hold a negative value judgment toward opportunistic practices, but such practices are examined in a value-neutral sense in this book.

Since opportunism is defined in relation to principles, it is informative to categorize opportunism based on the specific rules and norms from which opportunistic practices deviate. When examining interfirm exchanges in emerging markets, Yadong Luo (2006, 123) classifies opportunistic practices into strong and weak forms. The former refers to those practices that break laws, regulations, and other explicitly codified norms; the latter involves actions that violate implicit but shared norms within a group. My classification, as shown in the introduction, is by and large consistent with Luo's approach. I break down opportunistic practices into three types: (a) practices that deviate from state laws or other formal regulations that are not specific to any particular organizational field; (b) practices that aim to take advantage of others and thus violate cooperation norms; (c) practices that break from existing shared norms of operation in a specific organizational field.

A few caveats are needed here. With regard to noncompliance with laws or regulations, some might argue that noncompliant practices during China's early market transition were not necessarily opportunistic because many laws and rules were either outdated or unfit for the market economy. Indeed, legal codes in China's economic sector were markedly different before and after the kickoff of Deng Xiaoping's reforms in the late 1970s (Sun 2019). But there was also tangible continuity in terms of logics and names of legal codes in economy (ibid.). Actions that involve physical harm to others, such as murder, have also been similarly punishable in nature, if not in the same degree, across different periods of time. More importantly, it is not a problem labeling practices that deviate from outdated laws as opportunistic to the extent that laws are not considered inherently legitimate and opportunism is defined in a value-neutral sense.[12] After all, both conformity and nonconformity are parts of organization routines (Vaughan 1999).

As for the third type of opportunistic practices—noncompliance with norms of a specific field, some of these noncompliant practices might be more opportunistic and others less so. Indeed, conceptualizing opportunism this way presupposes a substantial overlap between opportunism and innovation. After all, innovation perceived in the Schumpeterian tradition is no different from destruction or deviation. Having said that, not all innovations are opportunistic, at least not in the same degree. For example, chapter 4 describes how leading opportunist SEOs developed new teaching models, and we can observe that not all new teaching models are equally opportunistic. Some new approaches to guiding TOEFL/GRE preparation encourage using mnemonics skills to memorize vocabulary, while other approaches advocate for earning high TOEFL listening scores without having to comprehend the conversations in the listening part (L. Wu 1998). Comparatively, the latter approach is more opportunistic in the sense that it is more lacking in long-term planning, and it moves further away from the original goal of the TOEFL—measuring English language proficiency.

It is useful to clarify the relations between opportunism and other allegedly objectionable practices—malfeasance, predation, and corruption. To the extent that organizational malfeasance concerns illegal activities or practices that defy cooperation norms, there are some similarities between opportunism and malfeasance.[13] Opportunism is also related to other economic wrongdoings, such as predation. Opportunism is frequently observed during rapid social changes, and so is predation, which I elaborate on in the next section. For example, cutthroat and ruthless predatory practices pervaded the United States in the nineteenth century when "there were no rules governing competitive behaviors" (Fligstein 1990, 21). Such predatory practices, though not necessarily in violation of rules because of the nonexistence of relevant rules, are opportunistic in the sense that they took advantage of competitors and business partners.

Despite these similarities, there are nuanced differences between these terms. For example, corruption violates state regulations, but this term is most often used to indicate the misuse of public office for private gains (e.g., Treisman 2000). In China, many behaviors under clientelist relations violate state regulations, but these behaviors may very well be in accordance with cooperation norms between transaction partners (e.g., Wank 2001).

OPPORTUNITIES FOR AND LEADERSHIP OF
OPPORTUNISTS DURING MARKET TRANSITION

This section contextualizes social conditions under which opportunism prevails. Opportunistic practices tend to be more visible when there is lax regulation and when the risk of penalty for violation is low (Akerlof and Romer 1993; Fligstein and Roehrkasse 2016). In addition, there are three social conditions that are particularly conducive to opportunistic practices: (a) rapid and broad social changes, such as the market transition of China and eastern European countries; (b) abundance of resources and especially sudden influx of resources, such as a spike in demand and entrance of financial capital; (c) ambiguity in product standards and/or consumers' unfamiliarity with measures of product quality. Each one of these three conditions encourages opportunism in its own way: while broad social changes are often associated with uncertainty and chaos in fundamental market institutions such as ownership, an abundance of resources encourages twisted competition that discourages product quality upgrades. Ambiguous industries such as the Education Industry and the specialty health-care industry abound with all three conditions.

Since transition economies often experience rapid social changes, demand surge, and inexperienced consumers simultaneously, it is unsurprising that transition economies abound with opportunistic practices (e.g., Mehlum, Moene, and Torvik 2003; Y. Luo 2006). It is also common for transition economies to witness frequent and radical policy changes, which further prepare the ground for opportunism. Moreover, a vibrant informal economy often finds its place in transition economies, and it tends to spawn opportunistic and predatory practices (Rona-Tas 1994; Feige 1998, 21–33). During the 1980s and 1990s when Deng Xiaoping's economic reform had just taken off, the aforementioned conditions were ripe and opportunism flourished.

Transition economies also serve as a favorable condition for opportunists to climb to market leader positions. Chapters 2 and 3 will draw on the Education Industry to illustrate how opportunist SEOs founded by marginal entrepreneurs outcompeted other more compliant SEOs that were established by entrepreneurs with better connections. These findings challenge the conclusions of multiple studies on the status of organizations during China's market transition. Most notably, my findings cast doubt on Victor Nee and Sonja Opper's (2012) claim that enterprises more compliant with cooperation norms are likely to thrive, while noncompliant ones are likely to fail. Anecdotes and stories about Chinese entrepreneurs lend support to my findings. For example, the quote I cited at the outset of this chapter by Feng

Lun, a famous private entrepreneur from China, suggests the indispensability of "sin"—amoral and illegal practices—in the success of private enterprises. That Feng's success stories were drawn from the real estate industry indicates that the advantage of opportunists during the market transition is not limited to the Education Industry.

My findings about the success of nonstate opportunists also move beyond the claim of the significance of connections during market transition. Experts familiar with China's market transition readily presuppose the central role of social and political networks in economic actions in China (e.g., Boisot and Child 1999; Burt and Opper 2017). Some studies further argue that firms with solid ties to the state perform significantly better than others (Peng and Luo 2000; Hongbin Li et al. 2008; Haveman et al. 2017). Mike Peng and Yadong Luo (2000), for example, contend that business-state ties, either in the form of having former state bureaucrats as top executives or building reliable relationships with current officials, help firms access key resources, such as bank loans.

MARGINAL ENTREPRENEURS AND THE MARKET TRANSITION

Feng's quoted words on the sins of private entrepreneurs and their successful enterprises also point to the importance of examining the link between individuals and organizations. The rest of this chapter and subsequent empirical chapters substantiate the affinity between marginal entrepreneurs and opportunist organizations. Here let me begin by clarifying who marginal entrepreneurs are and how they perform in the context of China's market transition.

Marginal entrepreneurs are those who are excluded by the state from entering a market. In the context of the Education Industry, they are noneducators, educators outside of the state education system, and junior educators in the system. Conceptualized this way, the term *marginal entrepreneurs* in this book shares similarities with previous studies but is also different. With regard to the similarities, both previous studies and this book emphasize socially peripheral and low-status actors or actors on the margin of a particular field. For example, Haveman, Habinek, and Goodman (2012) highlight the role of "entrepreneurs from the social periphery" in the formation of the US magazine market. With regard to the role of marginal actors in more professionalized fields, Kellogg (2011, 9) draws on reforms in the US hospitals and suggests that "actors who can most readily initiate changes are those on the periphery of an industry." As for studies on China's market transition, scholars use *marginal entrepreneurs* to indicate the socially peripheral statuses of early private entrepreneurs (e.g., Tsai 2007, 50; Nee and Opper 2012, 33). The major distinction in my conceptualization is that the marginality of marginal entrepreneurs is primarily attributable to state regulation.

Although no marginal entrepreneur in this book was a cadre or a social elite, some of them tend to have relatively higher social status than others. In line with this observation, I categorize marginal entrepreneurs into two groups: highly marginal and moderately marginal entrepreneurs. In the Education Industry, neither group met state regulators' requirements on SEO founders. Nonetheless, there is a pronounced difference between the two groups: entrepreneurs in the former group had not had any work experience in the state education system before their entrepreneurship, while people in the latter group had. Unsurprisingly, people in the former group tend to have received less education and have lower social status than the latter. In other words, the highly marginal entrepreneurs were not only denied market entry but were also socially marginalized.

The significance of socially marginal individuals across industries in the early stage of China's market transition needs to be comprehended in its historical context. That was a special period of time that ensued at the end of the Cultural Revolution, a tumultuous time when economic and education orders were razed to the ground. Even in the more developed urban areas, there were millions of unemployed youth who were excluded from the state *danwei* system, the only major employer system across China at that time (Shirk 1993, 42). In other words, a vast number of urban youth were uneducated and unemployed, and therefore on the margin of the society in the early 1980s. It is not exaggerating to claim that the supply of socially marginal individuals was abundant in this special period of time.

These socially marginal individuals were a revolutionary force during the market transition. A series of studies document how socially marginalized individuals served as the earliest private entrepreneurs during China's market transition. For example, Yasheng Huang (2008) lists a number of first-generation private Chinese entrepreneurs who possessed low social status. He even directly attributes China's thriving market capitalism to the entrepreneurship of marginal figures from rural regions. In addition, a series of surveys confirmed that most early private entrepreneurs, including individual businessmen (*getihu*), were made up of unemployed youth, the formerly imprisoned, migrant peasants, and other marginal figures (e.g., Gold 1990; Davis 1999; Wu and Xie 2003).

Despite their recognition on the short-term prosperity of many socially marginal individuals, existing studies generally paint a pessimistic picture for the long-term potentials of these entrepreneurs. According to Szelenyi and Kostello (1996), the market entrance and initial success of socially marginalized individuals are simply due to the fact that they did not have much to lose. Thus, the two scholars predict the rise of these entrepreneurs to be transitory. Such pessimistic prediction of socially marginal individuals is echoed in studies on the social stratification of individuals during China's market transition. For example, Rona-Tas (1994) contends that low-status individuals will not be able to change their fates and elevate themselves from the last to the first. As market reform deepens, according to Wu and Xie (2003), socially marginal individuals would give away their high status to former cadres and/or well educated people.

The prospect of socially marginalized individuals is depicted as even bleaker in some other studies that prioritize political connections and education. These studies do not even recognize the short-term prosperity of socially marginalized individuals because former party and government cadres are more capable of benefiting from their political connections and positional power (Oi 1992; Parish and Michelson 1996). Still a few other studies demonstrate a more complicated route: former cadres might initially trail behind, but they can easily transition into new elites once they become entrepreneurs, especially by utilizing their access to education (Rona-Tas 1994; Zhou 2000). In sum, none of these studies would have predicted the success of socially marginalized individuals.

My analyses in subsequent chapters, although with some findings in support of these existing studies, propose new directions in understanding marginal entrepreneurs. With regard to supportive findings, I show that the highly marginal entrepreneurs indeed had ephemeral successes, especially when compared to the moderately marginal. In addition, this book finds that among opportunist organizations, those that were founded by state-affiliated moderately marginal entrepreneurs outcompeted those operated by highly marginal entrepreneurs. Among marginal entrepreneurs, it was those less marginal who enjoyed successes for a longer time.

With regard to new directions for studying marginal entrepreneurs, my empirical chapters reveal the following patterns: (a) marginal entrepreneurs as a whole enjoyed sustained successes from the early 1990s to 2010s, at least in the Education Industry and other industries under two-dimensional ambiguity; (b) marginal entrepreneurs on average had closer connections with the informal economy than did other entrepreneurs, which was associated with marginal entrepreneurs' systematic adoption of opportunistic practices; (c) marginal entrepreneurs prevailed not because they had nothing to lose, but because marginal entrepreneurs resorted to opportunistic practices and because opportunism was effective under ambiguity.

Opportunist-Led Changes under Ambiguity: Processes and Directions

PROCESSES OF CHANGES

Drawing on the Education Industry and the specialty health-care industry in China, this section reveals two specific processes of opportunist-led organizational changes.

Competition Dynamics under Two-Dimensional Ambiguity. Under two-dimensional ambiguity, the competition dynamics of opportunists—both the competition between opportunists and other organizations and the competition among opportunists—play an integral role in driving organizational changes.

Existing theories of ambiguity have spilt much ink on the issue of organizational changes. Many studies outline blending, hybridizing, formalizing, collaborating, and various coupling strategies as organizations' effort to facilitate changes under ambiguity (e.g., Stark 2009; York, Hargrave, and Pacheco 2016; Ramus, Vaccaro, and Brusoni 2017). These studies share the assumption that a group of relatively homogeneous organizations use similar strategies to respond to, or benefit from, ambiguity. There has been a lack of attention to the heterogeneity of organizations or the competition among organizations under ambiguity. Admittedly, some studies within the institutional framework recognize the diversity of organizations under ambiguity and some studies have even examined the competition among multiple models (e.g., DiMaggio 1991; Haveman and Rao 1997; Pache and Santos 2013). However, these studies attribute the consequences of intermodel competition mostly to macro and supraorganizational institutional changes, glossing over how the competition dynamics is a function of diverse organizational models maneuvering in the ambiguity.

This book features the distinct competition dynamics under two-dimensional ambiguity. Let me use the Education Industry to illustrate the three paths through which this competition dynamics unfolds. First, under two-dimensional ambiguity, different organizational models engage with and make use of the state education system and the informal economy differently. As chapter 2 elaborates, multiple organizational models coexisted in the Education Industry in the 1980s and early 1990s, and they were all ambiguous on the dimensions of ownership and marketability. Despite their similarity in being ambiguous, these different models had disparate levels of connections with the state system and the informal economy.

Opportunists, as a type of nonstate organization, had closer connections to the informal economy than others. To the extent that the informal economy breeds predatory practices (Feige 1998, 21–33), opportunists' close connections with the informal economy enabled them to transpose resources and repertoires of the informal economy into opportunistic practices. As chapters 2 and 3 show, these practices not only empowered opportunists to overcome their disadvantages in resources and legitimacy but also helped these organizations systematically weaken the bargaining power of teachers. Weakening teachers' bargaining power and making them more replaceable were consequential steps to prevent them from exiting organizations and launching their own entrepreneurial enterprises.

Second, under two-dimensional ambiguity, state regulations and sanctions aimed at curtailing opportunism often unexpectedly enhanced the competitiveness of opportunists. The next chapter describes several specific processes in this regard. For example, one of the processes concerns how, given the tight connections between the state education system and state-affiliated SEOs, state regulations against opportunism were often carried out most effectively on the more compliant state-affiliated organizations.

The third path concerns the competition among opportunists. The institutionalization process during the market transition tends to favor those moderately marginal entrepreneurs who had worked within the state education system. Although these marginal entrepreneurs also participated in opportunistic practices, they acted faster than highly marginal entrepreneurs to phase out explicitly rule-breaking practices and shift their opportunistic practices to revolutionizing teaching norms.

Along with these three paths and against the backdrop of market transition, the Education Industry witnessed the fleeting market leadership of state-affiliated organizations and the subsequent rise of nonstate opportunist organizations. As the market leadership of opportunists was sustained, the competition within the group of opportunists occupied the center stage, and opportunists led by moderately marginal entrepreneurs outcompeted other opportunists led by highly marginal entrepreneurs. Apparently, these patterns of changes are different from those outlined in earlier studies of ambiguity. Having said that, blending and hybridizing are still relevant in the evolution of the Education Industry. As we shall see in the next chapter, all SEOs blended organizational repertoires of the state education system and the informal economy into novel practices, although nonstate opportunists and state-affiliated SEOs employed different blending strategies.

These patterns of changes are observable in other industries facing two-dimensional ambiguity. Take China's specialty health-care industry as an example. Although state-affiliated hospitals initially dominated the field, market leaders shifted to nonstate hospitals founded by the so-called barefoot doctors—marginal entrepreneurs who had had no professional medical training and had worked as migrating medicine peddlers in rural areas prior to their entrepreneurship (R. Huang 2018). Many of them, especially those who came from one particular region in China's Fujian province, built giant hospital chains by adopting opportunistic practices. These hospitals used fake physician licenses, promoted unwarranted cure rates, and caused a high volume of medical accidents with their malpractices (Yao 2016; R. Huang 2018).

Despite their opportunistic practices, these nonstate hospitals outcompeted state-affiliated ones. Those Fujian-originated nonstate opportunists were so successful that they now make up "eight out of every ten Chinese private hospitals" (R. Huang 2018). As time moved on, the competition within the group of opportunist hospitals took the center stage. Opportunist hospitals that were founded by moderately marginal entrepreneurs and engaged in less explicit rule-breaking activities transitioned into new market leaders. They were also the earliest to become formalized and embark on stock markets.

In both the Education Industry and the specialty health-care industry, the longevity of nonstate opportunists had a long-lasting impact on the privatization and marketization of these industries. To begin with, the rise of nonstate opportunists pushed out the influence of the state. In both industries, nonstate opportunists cannibalized state-affiliated organizations by taking away the latter's employees and consumers. As state-affiliated organizations lost steam, state regulations and organizational repertoires employed by these organizations lost their ground. State influence, achieved through resource and reputation advantages, also declined significantly in these industries.

Second, the success of nonstate opportunists was associated with the diffusion of opportunistic practices, making opportunism the new rule of the game. In the Education Industry, for example, state regulators initially banned cross-region expansion. State-affiliated SEOs rarely engaged in cross-region expansion. As nonstate opportunists climbed to market leader status, they quickly established branch schools in different regions and promoted this practice across submarkets. As this practice was widely adopted, the formation of a nationally integrated industry accelerated. This occurred despite the state effort in keeping the competition of the Education Industry within a few small local submarkets.

Last but not least, under two-dimensional ambiguity the diffusion of these opportunistic practices was often hidden to state regulators. As the end of chapter 2 shows, under two-dimensional ambiguity state regulators were more aware of opportunism by state-affiliated SEOs. Opportunism by nonstate opportunists, especially opportunistic practices beyond any single city or district, often escaped the radar of regulators. Li Su, a former consultant to the Education

Industry, shares a revealing example. As Li (2009, 331) recalls, "I went to a top official at the Ministry of Education to brief him about Supernova. When he heard from me that Supernova enrolled 300,000 students last year to Beijing [from all over the country], he could not at first believe it and then cast strong doubt. He thought it was a unique phenomenon in a unique period of time and therefore ephemeral."

In this account, the top official at the Ministry of Education was surprised when he first heard about Supernova's exorbitant enrollment number in the late 1990s, even though Supernova had recruited students from across China for several years. This official also found Supernova's nationwide popularity unbelievable and transient, partly because the Ministry of Education and education bureaus—the state-level and local-level regulators—had forbidden cross-region expansion. SEOs, according to officials' knowledge, had operated as local education organizations only serving local students. What SEOs had done in terms of nationwide expansion went unnoticed.[14]

The theme of competition continues in part 2 of this book. This part further discusses the competition and ups and downs among three groups: (a) opportunist SEOs that survived the competition of the 1990s but faced difficulties in adapting to environmental changes after the early 2000s; (b) opportunist SEOs that survived the competition of the 1990s and were able to adapt and lead new changes after the early 2000s; and (c) opportunist SEOs that were established after the early 2000s with more formalized structures and procedures.

Selection and Adaptation of Opportunists. Empirical chapters of this book, especially the three chapters making up part 2, revive the selection-versus-adaptation debate. The debate about whether organizational changes are governed by selection (i.e., the founding of new organizations) or adaptation (i.e., survival and transformation of existing organizations) is a classic topic in organizational theory. Whereas earlier works use in-depth case studies to highlight the adaptation of individual organizations (e.g., Cyert and March 1963; Thompson 1967; Miles 1982), organizational studies since the late 1970s have turned toward selection as a more promising theoretical direction (e.g., Hannan and Freeman 1977, 1989; Carroll and Hannan 2000).

To be sure, selection and adaptation can be complementary to each other (Astley and Van de Van 1983; Aldrich 1999; Levinthal and Posen 2007; Peli 2009). But prominent organizational theories since the late 1970s, particularly new institutionalism and population ecology, all contend that the succession of dominant organizational forms is largely a function of selection—the founding of new organizations and a rising normative system favoring these new organizations. According to these theories, the adaptability of organizations is highly unlikely due to the ubiquity of structural inertia (Hannan and Freeman 1977, 1989).

This book sheds new light on this debate by examining the trajectories of opportunists. Part 2 provides new empirical data to support the existing literature's conclusion about the significance of selection and the difficulty of adaptation. For example, chapter 6 shows that the rise of non-kinship-based managers in the Education Industry, as well as the related formalization process, largely resulted from the founding of new organizations rather than from the transformation of existing opportunists. Chapter 7 also illustrates how a new institutional environment prepared the ground for the first wave of IPOs in the Education Industry.

Moreover, I found that it was extremely difficult for existing opportunists to adapt to environmental changes, especially when the business environment had been increasingly institutionalized. The Education Industry since the early 2000s presents an example. SEOs were under tremendous institutional pressure to move away from the control of founders' families. But the majority of opportunist SEOs that had been market leaders before the early 2000s struggled to dismantle their family control structures. Entrenched family control and rampant opportunism in local collaborations hindered the cross-region expansion of opportunist SEOs.

Despite all these difficulties, the adaptation of opportunists proves to be not impossible.[15] Part 2 takes a close look at the transformation of Supernova as a rare case of adaptation. In the early 2000s, Supernova moved out of its family control and built a powerful team of non-kinship-based managers. Supernova was also the first Chinese SEO to be publicly listed. Most notably, this IPO was accomplished even though the market institutions needed for financial operation were absent. When these market institutions were underdeveloped, institutional pressures were insufficient to push the first IPO forward. I show that the first IPO was largely the fruit of adaptation, not selection.

Chapter 7 streamlines the process of Supernova's IPO and traces the drive of the adaptation to Supernova's intraorganizational conflict. Supernova's tense intraorganizational conflict represents a common phenomenon under ambiguity: in China and other transition economies, ambiguous ownership is associated with widespread internal conflicts among business partners regarding profit distribution, ownership transfer, and share distribution (Francis 1999; Su, Xu, and Phan 2008). In the Supernova case, intraorganizational conflict facilitated the IPO via two processes: deadlock and professionalization. When conflict reached a protracted stalemate and all alternative solutions were exhausted, the IPO as a solution to intraorganizational conflict

OPPORTUNITIES FOR OPPORTUNISTS

started to make sense to shareholders. In terms of professionalization, the intraorganizational conflict among multiple factions in Supernova spurred a shift of trust from relatives to professional financial managers, paving the way for the IPO.

Last but not least, the Supernova case illustrates how the adaptation of a leading opportunist triggered industry-level organizational changes. After Supernova went public on the New York Stock Exchange, its major competitors followed suit, and they also targeted overseas stock markets for IPOs. Among SEOs that had initiated IPOs by 2010, as chapter 7 shows, the majority of successful IPOs were done by SEOs established after 2000 rather than opportunist SEOs that survived the 1990s. Newly established SEOs were born with structures and procedures that were more prepared for listings on stock markets. In other words, it was an adaption-induced selection process. After a dozen Chinese SEOs embarked on global stock markets, the Chinese state felt obliged to change its policies. In the early 2010s, the Chinese state finally gave the green light by acquiescing to the first public listing of an SEO on the domestic stock market. However, as shown, this policy adjustment did not occur as state-led reform from above but rather as an organization-led change from below.

DIRECTIONS OF CHANGE

The findings of this book seem to point to a unidirectional development trajectory for industries under two-dimensional ambiguity: China's supplemental education and specialty health-care sectors have evolved into for-profit industries dominated by nonstate opportunists. In addition, it seems that leading organizations in these industries have become more institutionalized and formalized since the early 2000s.

Notwithstanding the institutionalization and formalization, the development trajectory of these industries is not unidirectional. Institutionalization and formalization do not necessarily mean the decline or disappearance of opportunism. In fact, there was an escalation of opportunism in the Education Industry as leading SEOs advanced toward being more institutionalized and formalized. For example, leading SEOs' financial operations have become more standardized and formalized as more SEOs were listed on global stock markets. Nevertheless, old and new opportunistic practices sprang up during the same time. Inflow of new resources, lingering ambiguity, and oscillating state policies undergirded the persistence and escalation of opportunism. Take the inflow of resource for example. Domestic and global capital poured investments into this industry after Supernova was successfully listed on the New York Stock Exchange in 2006. As financial resources inundated this field, new and existing opportunists became less interested in improving educational services and more interested in fishing for venture capital.

My findings on the coevolution of institutionalization and opportunism escalation echo the caution about not characterizing the Chinese market as "approximate [to] an ideal-typical market image" (Parish and Michelson 1996; Wank 2001, 13). Undoubtedly, findings of my research and existing studies suggest that Chinese enterprises are, overall, inching toward the more formalized model commonly seen in Western countries (e.g., Meyer et al. 1997; Guthrie 1999). But as Wank (2001) observes, the Chinese approach to market operation—in which trust and reciprocity revolve around close partners rather than rules for distant acquaintance—is not inherently absent of rationality. It is not necessarily true that the transition from the less rational to the more rational has taken place. This casts doubt on Nee and Opper's (2012) unidirectional claim that norm-complying practices replaced opportunism after market capitalism took roots in China.

PART I

When Opportunists Produce Changes

Kill Your Competitors

The probability that a man or a group of men will be motivated to start an organization is dependent on the social structure and on the position of men within it.

ARTHUR STINCHCOMBE (1965, 147)

In those years [of the 1980s and 1990s], whether founders had problems entering an industry depended on their social background, not economic background.

(INFORMANT NO. 4)

Think of one of the top US universities. If we were to examine its list of top donors, we are likely to discover names of financial tycoons, technology gurus, and well-known families in oil, steel, and railroad industries. But the lists of top donors for Chinese universities present different patterns. A noticeable pattern is the cluster of top donors from the Education Industry. For example, entrepreneurs from this industry frequent the donor list of Capital University, one of China's top three universities. Several high-profile donations for Capital University, including its largest financial contribution to date,[1] come from alumni entrepreneurs who built giant SEOs.

One of these donors is Su Leidong, the founder of Supernova Inc. Today, Su is widely known as the godfather of overseas education, the spiritual mentor of Chinese youth, and one of the richest teachers in China. Three decades ago, prior to his entrepreneurship, Su was only a recent undergraduate alumnus and a lecturer of English at Capital University. Shortly after, he had to quit the job due to a conflict of interest with the department chairperson who was running the department's SEO.[2] After he left Capital, he initially could not establish his own SEO because he did not meet the state requirement on founder profiles. He had to circumvent this requirement to enter the market.

Su is far from the only SEO entrepreneur who grew from unqualified to unstoppable. A large number of SEO entrepreneurs share similar life trajectories: they were initially denied access to the Education Industry by the state and many of them had low social statuses, but they later steered their SEOs to be market leaders. These rags-to-riches stories are counterintuitive because this was an industry where state regulators set stringent restrictions for private entrepreneurs and where state-affiliated organizations once enjoyed unparalleled privilege in teachers, facilities, and reputation.

This chapter uncovers how opportunists founded by marginal entrepreneurs grew to become market leaders between the 1980s and the early 1990s. Special attention is given to opportunistic practices in terms of noncompliance with state laws and other formal regulations. Conducting these noncompliant practices usually involves taking advantage of competitors, business partners, and consumers. These practices were essential to the rise of opportunist SEOs as a group. Although opportunism in teaching also mattered for survival and success, most SEOs used similar teaching approaches in the 1980s and early 1990s. Deviation from existing teaching norms and the sprouting of new teaching models did not become visible until the mid-1990s when the intramodel competition among opportunist SEOs intensified.

This chapter primarily features Beijing's TOEFL/GRE submarket.[3] I first introduce the social context and the succession of market leaders among three organizational models—state SEOs, intellectual SEOs, and opportunist SEOs. The second and the third models were registered as nonstate SEOs, the prototypes of private enterprises in the Education Industry. Under two-dimensional ambiguity, opportunist SEOs blazed the trail for introducing resources to this industry from the informal economy and for blending organizational repertoires of the informal economy with those of the state education system. Unsurprisingly, opportunist SEOs adopted opportunistic practices more systematically than did the other two models.

This chapter documents a variety of opportunistic practices opportunist SEOs adopted, such as using force to deter competitors and secure advertisement space. I illustrate how these opportunistic practices helped opportunist SEOs overcome disadvantages associated with two-dimensional ambiguity. Furthermore, under two-dimensional ambiguity state regulations against opportunistic practices unintentionally made opportunist SEOs more competitive. As opportunist SEOs outcompeted state-affiliated SEOs, state influence dwindled in the Education Industry. The rise of opportunist SEOs and the retreat of the state also made opportunistic practices the new rules of the game, setting the initial course of this industry's privatization and marketization.

The Context and the Competitors

The Education Industry took off in the late 1970s when Deng Xiaoping's market reforms were unveiled. From the 1950s to the late 1970s, when China was experiencing the high tide of socialism, education was monopolized by the state.[4] The Chinese state confiscated all private schools in the 1950s. During the Cultural Revolution, which lasted from 1966 to 1976, all forms of education were in jeopardy: even the formal education system and the College Entrance Examination were suspended, not to mention supplemental education programs.

In the early 1980s,[5] all this changed. Although all formal K–12 schools and higher education institutions were still in the hands of the state, the state began to allow private individuals to establish and operate nonstate SEOs. The state's primary rationale for involving private individuals was to marshal nonstate resources and educate the large number of uneducated and unemployed youths in the aftermath of the Cultural Revolution, according to three retired faculty members from state universities and veteran entrepreneurs who started working in the Education Industry in the 1980s (Informants No. 10, No. 11, No. 16). When the Cultural Revolution came to an end, a large number of young people returned from rural areas and were looking for jobs in cities. As the education order was restored, the number of students who participated in the College Entrance Examination and the Chinese Graduate Exam kept increasing. In the 1960s and 1970s, overseas study programs were suspended and Russian was the only foreign language available for Chinese students. As China re-opened its gate to the world in the late 1970s, there was a revival of interest among Chinese people in English and other foreign languages. In sum, the state's welcoming stance to private entrepreneurs was a response to a substantial demand uptick in all areas of education.

Although the state gave private individuals the opportunity to operate SEOs, its initial intention was to develop supplemental education into an extension of the socialist education system, not a for-profit industry. Accordingly, all SEOs were asked to register as educational entities under the supervision of district-level education bureaus of each city.[6] To put SEOs into the hands of senior educators, education bureaus stipulated that only professors/educators from the state education system with titles of associate level or above could be qualified as founders. Education bureaus also required that the current or former employers of potential founders—state universities and schools—needed to issue a letter of approval for founding SEOs. Education bureaus even made it clear that there was a list of don'ts. For example, SEOs were not allowed to expand to another district or city. Registering SEOs as corporations or listing them on stock markets was unthinkable at that time.

Accompanying the spike in demand was a surge of new SEOs. In Beijing, Haidian District became the center for the SEO boom because, with over thirty state universities located in the area, there was easy access to state resources. This district's first SEO was founded in 1982; by 1990, the number had increased to 87 and to 190 by 1992 (H. Wang 1993). In accordance with student interest in test preparation and foreign languages, over 50 percent of SEOs that were founded in Beijing in the 1980s targeted these academic areas, whereas 30 percent fell into vocational training such as sewing, typing, and accounting; the rest were targeted to various art forms, such as music and painting (Wen 1983).

Supplemental education related to overseas studies and English was one of the hot spots of demand and supply. The ever-growing interest in the West and the booming demand for English contributed to the US-oriented "study-abroad fever" (Zhao 2001, 130): there was a fast and significant surge in the number of Chinese students studying in higher education institutions in the United States from the 1980s on. As table 2.1 shows, this number increased from 1,000 in 1980 to 33,390 in 1990, helping China climb from the number eighteen to the number one country of origin of foreign students in the United States within a decade.[7]

As the number of Chinese students enrolled in US universities kept its upward trajectory, US universities imposed stricter policies regarding language proficiency. More and more US universities required TOEFL scores for admission, and the number of Chinese TOEFL test takers increased from 723 in 1981 to over 40,000 in 1989.[8] More students attending US universities also meant that the competition among applicants intensified. Having a satisfactory TOEFL score increasingly became a necessary requirement for a

TABLE 2.1. Overseas Chinese Students in the United States, 1980–90

Academic Year	1979–80	1981–82	1983–84	1985–86	1987–88	1989–90
Number of Chinese Students	1,000	4,350	8,140	13,980	25,170	33,390
Ranking among Countries of Origin	N/A	18	12	7	2	1

Sources: Institute of International Education (1980–1990)

TABLE 2.2. The Shift of Top Market Leaders in Beijing's TOEFL/GRE Submarket

	Early to Mid-1980s	Early 1990s
Top Market Leaders[a]	Capital University SEO (state SEO)	Seven Swords (opportunist SEO)
	Central College SEO (state SEO)	Supernova School[b] (opportunist SEO)
	Questing School (intellectual SEO)	Pioneers School (opportunist SEO)
		Cornerstone School (opportunist SEO)

[a] This table includes all SEOs that once occupied the top three statuses in a given era. The right column features the era when four brands had such statuses. SEOs within each column are not ranked. Sources: Lu (2002), multiple interviews, and archives
[b] From 1991 to 1993, Supernova was known as Nova Academy's division on English. I will show that Supernova had a complicated structure then and it was like an opportunist SEO inside an intellectual SEO. After 1993, Supernova School became an independent SEO. Since Supernova's complicated structure only lasted for two years and it met most of the criteria of an opportunist SEO for most of the time, I put it in the category of opportunist SEOs.

successful application. This is especially true if students needed financial aid from US colleges. Chinese students even developed the idea that the TOEFL was one of the most important determinants for studying abroad. The demand for higher scores surged and test-preparation courses flourished. Adding fuel to the fire, the 1989 Beijing Student Movement provided a direct boost to the number of TOEFL/GRE test takers.[9]

In Beijing's feverish TOEFL/GRE submarket, there was a shift among the three organizational models—state SEOs, intellectual SEOs, and opportunist SEOs—in leading the market from the 1980s to the early 1990s.[10] As we can see from table 2.2, while state and intellectual SEOs led in the early and mid-1980s, opportunist SEOs occupied all market leader positions by the early 1990s.

In the early and mid-1980s, state SEOs, affiliated with state universities, sprang up as the earliest market leaders. The leading state SEOs were primarily those that were associated with top state universities, such as Capital University and the Central College of Foreign Languages. As we can see from table 2.2, SEOs affiliated with these two universities—the Capital University SEO and the Central College SEO—rose to the top in Beijing's TOEFL/GRE submarket soon after they opened their doors to the public.

The ways in which state SEOs were affiliated with their host institutions varied substantially (Y. Wu 2007). In general, the affiliation means being listed under state universities' names, being partially funded by universities, and being led by university administrators or veteran professors. For some state SEOs that were relatively independent from their host institutions, their leaders could entitle themselves to a large sum of money after contributing a certain proportion of their tuition revenue to the host university or a particular academic department.

State SEOs benefited from high-quality teachers, modern facilities, and the exceptional reputations of state universities among Chinese students. State SEOs affiliated with elite universities also benefited from their prime locations since the earliest TOEFL/GRE test centers were mostly located on the campuses of these elite universities. Given the tight connections between state SEOs and their host institutions, many SEO leaders reserved teaching positions only for senior faculty members from host institutions and/or junior ones who were popular among students. At a time when most faculty members were equally poor, teaching at SEOs was considered a precious opportunity to moonlight.[11]

Today's students and observers who are used to the success of nonstate SEOs can hardly imagine the towering statuses of state SEOs four decades ago (Y. Wu 2007). Leading state SEOs, such as the Central College SEO, recruited students so easily that students had formed in long lines before these SEOs made any advertisement (ibid.). Some entrepreneurs of nonstate SEOs also acknowledged the advantages of state SEOs. In his memoir,[12] Supernova founder Su Leidong described the supreme reputation and popularity of the Capital University SEO among students as follows:

> The Capital University SEO was even more magnificent [than other nonstate SEOs]. It was located in those buildings of historic charm. Anyone who gave it a look would know that this SEO had great capacity and high quality. Among those students who went for consultation, there were very few who were not impressed [by the SEO] and they would all sign up for classes. . . . People would not hesitate to pay their money. They knew that, within the Capital campus, there would be no running away [with their money by SEO founders]. Even if there were running away [of founders], Capital University was still there. After all, people had unparalleled trust in the reputation and authority of Capital University.
>
> (Supernova Archive No. 5, 53)

The second model, intellectual SEOs, also emerged as a key player in the 1980s. Mostly registered as nonstate SEOs, intellectual SEOs were founded and operated by senior professors from state universities. Not officially affiliated with state universities, intellectual SEOs were a prototype of private enterprises. Questing School serves as a good example. A retired professor from the state-led Central Academy of Sciences established Questing in 1984.

By the mid-1980s, Questing had become one of the top three market leaders. According to a veteran teacher who had taught in multiple SEOs since the 1980s, Questing was "where Beijing's supplemental education revolution started" (Informant No. 65). Another intellectual SEO that emerged as a leader during this time was Nova Academy. Six faculty members retired from the state education system founded Nova Academy in 1984. Although from 1991 to 1993 its division on English had a complicated structure that included many characteristics of an opportunist SEO, Nova Academy in general was an intellectual SEO.

The majority of intellectual SEO entrepreneurs were professors who had retired from state universities (e.g., Wen 1983). This is unsurprising because education bureaus demanded that SEO founders be senior educators. To mobilize societal resources to complement the state education system, according to three Nova Academy top leaders and their memoirs, state regulators called on retired professors and educators to "contribute their remaining energy" (Informants No. 10, No. 11, No. 16; Nova Academy Archives No. 14, No. 15). Compared to junior faculty members and educators, retired professors and educators tended to possess higher titles and more free time. As a result, retired professors made up the major entrepreneurial force for intellectual SEOs. These retired professors were familiar with, and had rich connections in, state universities.

In the late 1980s, the third model, opportunist SEOs, entered the market. A pronounced characteristic of these SEOs is that they engaged in opportunistic practices more systematically than did the other two models, as I elaborate in the next section. Opportunist SEOs were also registered as non-state SEOs. They were the other prototype of private enterprises in this industry. The founders of opportunist SEOs were all marginal entrepreneurs. The state's stringent requirements on founders' social background denied them access to the Education Industry.

These marginal entrepreneurs included two groups of people: highly marginal entrepreneurs who had not had any work experience in the state education system before founding their SEOs, and moderately marginal entrepreneurs who had previously held peripheral or junior positions in this system prior to or during their entrepreneurial activities. Individuals in the first group used to be peasants, migrant workers, laid-off workers, and private businessmen. Not a single highly marginal entrepreneur in Beijing's TOEFL/GRE submarket had received a college education before his or her entrepreneurship. In any case, neither the first nor the second group met the state regulators' requirement on SEO founders.

By the early 1990s, as table 2.2 shows, opportunist SEOs had secured all top-three positions. Around 1990, Seven Swords had a fleeting glory of enrolling over a thousand students, but it soon surrendered the market leader position to the Big Three: Pioneers, Cornerstone, and Supernova.[13] These three SEOs went beyond Seven Swords and established themselves as the new leaders in Beijing's TOEFL/GRE submarket. In sum, the market leader positions in this submarket shifted from state SEOs (Capital University SEO and Central College SEO) and intellectual SEOs (Questing and Nova Academy) to opportunist SEOs (Seven Swords, Supernova, Pioneers and Cornerstone) within a decade.

The same shift of market leadership is observable in the Chinese Graduate Exam and spoken English submarkets. In addition, the leadership of opportunist SEOs continued after the mid-1990s across these markets. Even in the 2010s, the national leaders in TOEFL/GRE and Chinese Graduate Exam submarkets were still mostly opportunist SEOs. State and intellectual SEOs have never returned to the top positions.

The Three Models under Two-Dimensional Ambiguity

The Education Industry was highly ambiguous in the 1980s and 1990s: all SEOs were ambiguous in terms of whether they were private and for-profit. This ambiguity lingered after the 2000s despite substantial privatization and marketization of this industry.[14] Although in the 2000s the state showed greater tolerance toward privatization and marketization than before, state regulators kept applying such labels as "public enterprise" and "socialist education enterprise" to education in general and nonstate education in particular (Tao and Wang 2010, 31). During my fieldwork in 2014, a former Supernova star teacher who is a current investor in the Education Industry described the never-fading ambiguity this way,

> What is the business of the Education Industry? It is not education. Its business and education are two different things. The Education Industry has no position in our economy and society. No clear status. Do you call an SEO a corporation? Not necessarily. It is very complicated. Even now there is still no clear government policy on what it is.
>
> (Informant No. 5)

As mentioned in the last chapter, the Education Industry's two-dimensional ambiguity originated from the fact that the state and the informal economy pulled this industry in opposing directions. On the one hand, state regulators maintained that all SEOs should be nonprivate and not-for-profit. The formal and legal statuses of SEOs, therefore, were nonprivate and not-for-profit educational organizations. On the other hand, the affinity of this industry with the informal economy allowed most entrepreneurs to operate their SEOs more or less as private and for-profit enterprises. These entrepreneurs referred to themselves as individual businessmen (*getihu*). They enjoyed full autonomy in internal control, hiring/firing, and other strategic decisions. Even some state SEO founders considered themselves partial owners because they were entitled to financial return instead of salary. Having said that, the fact that SEOs were ambiguous meant that private entrepreneurs could not enjoy the rights to which private owners in other for-profit industries were entitled. For example, it was unclear who could claim the remaining assets of an SEO when it was to be dissolved.[15]

In addition to state regulators and entrepreneurs, other stakeholders of this industry also had diverse perceptions about what SEOs were. For customers, what SEOs are has long been unclear and confusing. When problems arose, therefore, customers tended to interpret a situation in favor of their own interest. Ambiguity provided room for multiple interpretations. The confusing situation continued into the 2010s. For example, a group of parents complained to the Haidian Education Bureau in June 2014 because their children signed up for classes with an SEO, but the founder of the SEO absconded with their money. These parents demanded that the education bureau organize free makeup lessons for their children. On June 10, 2014, the education bureau convened a meeting and called on three large SEOs to attend. Before the meeting started, a manager from one of the three SEOs discussed the situation privately with me. He predicted that the education bureau would cater to all parent demands because Chinese government officials were afraid of people "escalating a situation and making a scene (*ba shiqing nao da*)" (field notes, 6/10/2014).

During the meeting, an education bureau official and two managers from the other two SEOs agreed that all parties should work together to accommodate parent needs. But the reasons they invoked were based on the ambiguity of the industry. According to them, the SEO whose founder absconded had two entities—a corporate entity registered under the Administration of Industry and Commerce[16] and a school entity under the education bureau. While the parents did not request compensation from the Administration of Industry and Commerce, the parents claimed that the education bureau bore the responsibility for makeup lessons because SEOs were educational entities under the supervision of state education departments. The education bureau official and the three managers agreed that the parent demands were not inappropriate given the ambiguity of the industry. To put the complaint to an end, the education bureau official urged the three SEOs to accept the protesters' children as students and the three SEOs agreed to provide free makeup classes to these students.

Organizations in the Education Industry were not only under the influence of the state education system and the informal economy but also drew on the two social institutions for resources and organizational repertoires. Although all SEOs actively engaged with the two social institutions, the ways in which the three organizational models accessed the state education system and the informal economy were different. All three models used teachers and venues from the state education system. But state and intellectual SEOs on average enjoyed better access to these resources than did opportunist SEOs. Except for some opportunist SEOs, such as Supernova and Pioneers, whose founders had worked in the state education system before their entrepreneurship, many opportunist SEOs lacked access to high-quality teachers, free venues, and advanced facilities at state universities.

Opportunist SEOs spearheaded the effort to seek resources from alternative routes. They resorted to the informal economy for staff and teachers. Before the emergence of opportunist SEOs, state and intellectual SEOs could rely only on junior faculty and family members to serve as administration and marketing staff (Informants No. 10, No. 11, No. 24). Opportunist SEOs brought in those who were associated with the informal economy—people who were employed part-time by the underground economy, who established their own small businesses and who were laid off by state enterprises. For example, Supernova was a trailblazer in using laid-off workers as classroom janitors (Informant No. 9). Later, it also employed a street vendor (who was also a high school dropout) as a GRE teacher (Lu 2002).

College students who had been involved in part-time employment elsewhere were another major group brought into the Education Industry from the informal economy. Cornerstone and Seven Swords, two prominent opportunist SEOs in the early 1990s, drew heavily on college students as their marketers. Cornerstone was able to build a team of part-time marketers by recruiting students who had prior experience in marketing or sales (Informant No. 21).

Opportunist SEOs in the Chinese Graduate Exam submarket acted similarly. Blue Ocean was a leading opportunist SEO in this submarket. One of its founding members recollected how Blue Ocean built a vast network of marketers by employing college students all over Beijing:

> We employed students from thirty to forty colleges. We gave students thousands of flyers and they could help us distribute these flyers one dorm after another. These students lived in those dorms too. We asked them to write their names, dorm numbers and contact information [on the flyers]. Prospective students could sign up for classes in the dorms of these distributors! Do you know what the advantage is for doing so? This lowered my cost in the first place. Also, there is trust among these students. This is especially helpful

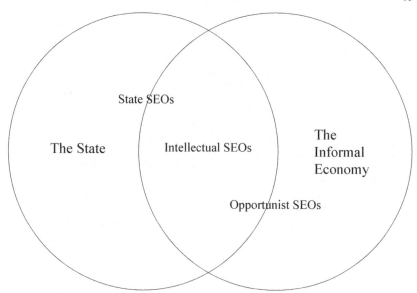

FIGURE 2.1. The Differentiated Access to the State and the Informal Economy among the Three Organizational Models

if you find someone from the Student Union or other similar organizations. You know, it is great to have distributors who have influence among students. Sometimes in one college these guys could give me over a million RMB worth of tuition revenue.

(Informant No. 8)

It was also common for opportunist SEOs to involve unemployed youths, migrant workers, and even local gang members for marketing. Blue Ocean, for example, used other industries' informal laborers, such as migrant workers in construction, as flyer distributors (Informant No. 8). One of its flyer distributors who had come from a rural area later even became the founder of Blue Wings, another opportunist SEOs that is now one of Blue Ocean's strongest competitors.

One reason opportunist SEOs were able to introduce resources from the informal economy was because state and intellectual SEOs were connected with the state education system more tightly, while opportunist SEOs had closer connections with the informal economy. Because of this close connection, opportunist SEOs were the earliest and, for a long time, the only type of SEO that introduced tangible resources from the informal economy. Figure 2.1 visualizes the differentiated access to the state and the informal economy among the three models of organizations.

Opportunist SEOs' closer connection with the informal economy was manifest in the fact that many marginal entrepreneurs had social ties with, or experience in, the informal economy. This is the case for the founders of Cornerstone, Seven Swords, and Supernova. The founder of Cornerstone had experience in the informal economy. Before establishing Cornerstone with her sister, she was laid off from a state enterprise and then became a private businesswoman (Informants No. 21, No. 61). The founder of Seven Swords also participated in a variety of small businesses before joining in on the study abroad fever (Informants No. 21, No. 61). Su Leidong commented on these founders and their SEOs:

> These SEOs were not founded by educated people but founded by people outside of the state education system,[17] such as laid-off workers and private businessmen who had the goal to make money. They just got together, rented a few classrooms and hired several teachers. Then their SEOs were good to go.
>   (Supernova Archive No. 5, 58)

Su himself accessed the resources and organizational repertoires of the informal economy through his family members. His mother was among the earliest private entrepreneurs in China after Deng Xiaoping's reforms unlocked new economic opportunities. She actively engaged in the informal economy when she came to visit Su when he was still a student at Capital University. A former senior manager and early shareholder at Supernova recalled,

> Su has a sharp mind [on business]. His mother definitely influenced him. You know, their hometown is a village in a coastal province in Southern China and this province was one of the earliest places for openness and reform after [Deng Xiaoping's] Tour of the South. Every family [in their village] used a small punch to make silicon steel sheets. You know, handmade silicon steel sheets. His mom was one of the earliest to do this. . . . Every time his mom came to visit him from Southern China, she would bring a lot of clothes that were not yet fashionable in Northern China. When she came, she would set up a vendor at the campus center in Capital University to sell those clothes.
>   (Informant No. 9)

In comparison, no founder/cofounder of the two intellectual SEOs I studied—Questing and Nova Academy—participated in the informal economy themselves. They were all senior educators, and they insisted that people in charge of SEOs ought to be educators. As a former entrepreneur at Nova Academy said, "There are other SEOs that were operated by non-educators. At Nova, we make sure that only educators are running our school" (Informant No. 16).[18]

Despite the fact that not a single one of its six cofounders (composed of three couples) directly participated in the informal economy, Nova Academy was in fact an exception among intellectual SEOs in that at least one family member of two of the cofounders was an avid participant in the informal economy. The son of one of the founding couples sold handicrafts as a vendor and became richer than his parents, making more money in a month than they did in one or two years, which astonished them and catalyzed their decision to embrace the market and establish an SEO (Informant No. 26). This son also gave his parents the capital needed for founding the SEO. In a time when the majority of Chinese were equally poor, a relative with direct experience in the informal economy was helpful in not only providing a push but also offering the initial capital.

Despite this type of exception, state and intellectual SEOs on average had less connection with the informal economy than did opportunist SEOs. As a result, intellectual and state SEOs lagged behind opportunist SEOs in accessing resources and organizational repertoires of the informal economy. Since the informal economy usually breeds predatory and noncompliant practices (Feige 1998, 21–33), it is unsurprising that opportunist SEOs conducted opportunistic practices in a more systematic manner.

Maneuvering Ambiguity with Opportunistic Practices

This section examines how opportunist SEOs maneuvered in two-dimensional ambiguity and turned disadvantages into advantages. Nonstate SEOs, especially opportunist SEOs, were plagued with multiple disadvantages compared to state-affiliated SEOs. These disadvantages concern not only resources but also legitimacy.[19] Moreover, marginal entrepreneurs had difficulties in entering the market.

Facing these challenges and disadvantages, opportunist SEOs maneuvered in the ambiguity with opportunistic practices. There are four types of opportunistic practices only opportunist SEOs adopted: (a) entering the market by bending the rules on founders' profiles; (b) controlling the market with force and violence; (c) using fraudulent or misleading information to recruit students; (d) defying state regulators' ban and establishing branch schools in other cities. There was no opportunistic practice state and intellectual SEOs adopted while opportunist SEOs did not. In addition, opportunist SEOs went farthest in opportunistic practices shared by state and intellectual SEOs. For example, all types of SEOs used pirated or unauthorized test materials, but opportunist SEOs were the pioneers in copying and distributing these

materials. Furthermore, chapter 3 and 4 show that opportunism was not limited to noncompliance with formal regulations: compared with the other two
models, opportunist SEOs were also more noncompliant with cooperation
norms and teaching norms. Evidently, opportunist SEOs conducted opportunistic practices more systematically than did the other two models. These
practices helped opportunist SEOs overcome disadvantages in resources and
legitimacy.

ENTERING THE MARKET BY BENDING RULES

A common opportunistic practice opportunist SEOs employed was circumventing state regulations on founder profiles. No opportunist SEO had a
qualified founder. In order to obtain access to the market, opportunist SEO
entrepreneurs borrowed the names and identifications of qualified educators,
asked qualified educators to act as temporary presidents, or subcontracted
a division under an established SEO. These opportunistic practices, though
defying the education bureau's regulations, were not uncommon in China
in the 1980s and early 1990s. Within and outside of the Education Industry,
private entrepreneurs adopted these practices to get around state regulations
on founders' profiles and registration types.

All opportunist SEO entrepreneurs in this study entered the market by
using one or more of these opportunistic practices. Founders of Supernova
and Pioneers kicked off their businesses by subcontracting divisions under
licensed intellectual SEOs. I have mentioned how Su Leidong, Supernova's
founder, used to be a lecturer of English at Capital University but had to leave
the university in 1991. Afterward, he wanted to open an SEO that specialized
in TOEFL classes. Since he was not qualified as a founder, he cooperated with
founders of Nova Academy and established a TOEFL division under Nova
in 1991. Su and the Nova founders had an agreement in which Su paid 15 to
25 percent of his total revenue to Nova as a "management fee." As for Ma
Tiannan, the Pioneers founder, he subcontracted two divisions under two
different intellectual SEOs before founding his own SEO (Informants No. 17,
No. 18, No. 61).

These opportunistic practices were also commonly used in other submarkets of the Education Industry. Opportunist SEO founders in the Chinese
Graduate Exam submarket also adopted these practices to enter the market.
The founder of Blue Ocean, the leading opportunist SEO in this submarket,
was a staff member at an elite state university and, therefore, not qualified as
an SEO founder. One of the founding members of Blue Ocean recalls how the
founder used another's identification to obtain the license:

It took our founder eight months to register the school. Initially the founder talked to a retired professor. The founder said that he needed to register a school for the Chinese Graduate Exam. [He said that] he had all the other requirements, but the education bureau also required the legal representative to be a retired professor with associate level or above and with Beijing's *hukou* [household registration permit].[20] The retired professor agreed happily at first. Then when we were about to register and our founder asked for the identifications of the retired professor, the retired professor said his children opposed it. They told the professor that being a legal representative would be huge responsibility. So our founder had to find someone else. The founder used to rent classrooms from another university and he knew one of their administrators. Our founder heard one guy there had a relative who was qualified. So our founder used his name and identification to register.

(Informant No. 8)

When a qualified person's identification is used, this qualified person is, in theory, the legal representative of the SEO. This qualified person is expected to shoulder responsibility should any major incident arises. This is why the retired professor and his family members changed their minds and refused to lend their identification. Some people who allowed their identification to be used often did not participate in operating the SEO at all. All they needed to do was to show up when the education bureau came for an inspection. In most cases, these inspections were simple and the focus was on documents. It was also straightforward, according to multiple informants, to change the names of the legal representative or the president after the license was secured (Informants No. 8, No. 37). In fact, a number of SEOs whose actual founders were educators were able to replace the names of the "fake founders" with real ones.

A challenge for those who opted for the subcontracting approach was how to seek independence—break away from the host institution and register an independent SEO without a qualified profile. Though very rare, a few marginal entrepreneurs were able to succeed in registering their SEOs. Supernova, for example, was successfully registered partly because Su Leidong first spent ample time at the education bureau, cultivating rapport and bonding with officials, before asking officials to bend the rules.

Let us recall that Su paid Nova Academy 15 to 25 percent of his total revenue as a "management fee." Although Su's division was thriving, the management fee substantially narrowed his profit margin. It also became increasingly infeasible for him to take over Nova Academy because its six founders had conflict and one of the founders' children was eyeing the leadership roles at Nova (Informants No. 16, No. 26). Su left Nova, but he did not meet state regulators' requirements for an SEO founder. Still, he walked into the education bureau in

1993 and successfully registered Supernova. According to Su, what he did was spend enough time with officials and show them his respect—going to their office every one or two weeks and smoking cigarettes and chatting casually without ever mentioning the issue of registration (Supernova Archive No. 5, 83). These practices were used to increase familiarity and enhance *ganqing*,[21] and they were widely used by Chinese private entrepreneurs (Wank 2001).

The fact that private entrepreneurs did not resort to bribing to obtain their licenses is related to two characteristics of the Education Industry. One of the characteristics is that "this industry [in those years] was too exhausting and dirty, and there was not much room for rent-seeking" (Informant No. 5). The other characteristic is that a long-term reciprocal relationship with SEO entrepreneurs had practical significance for local government officials because these officials might use help from SEOs in the future. A former teacher and senior manager at Supernova and several other SEOs who had dealt with government officials in multiple cities said, "Officials know that at some point they would develop a relationship with you. Their kids might need to study abroad one day. They are smart enough to consider you as their long-term resource" (Informant No. 17).

Having said that, some entrepreneurs and senior managers in the industry recounted incidents where local government agencies, especially those outside of Beijing, collected money by imposing fines. A former Supernova senior manager who founded a branch school in Hubei province recalled that multiple government agencies used various reasons to impose fines. Once when government agencies threatened to suspend the school's license, the senior manager had to drink large quantities of alcohol with government officials and intermediaries at least ten times in order to show respect to the officials and make the trouble disappear (Informant No. 32).

With regard to the rare case of Supernova's registration, there was another favorable condition in addition to Su Leidong's *ganqing*-building strategies: Supernova's reputation among students, measured by the number of students in Su's division, led officials to make an exception for him. A veteran official at the education bureau fleshed out the details,

> Our district was the first in Beijing to require associate professor level as background for an SEO founder. You know, we have always been the leader in education, and later other districts adopted similar policies. At that time, our requirements for capital and venue were easy. I remember that at the beginning we only required RMB 50,000 as capital for individual founders. It was also pretty cheap to rent classrooms [from nearby schools]. . . . Anyway, for Su Leidong's case, we made an exception for him. He had no problem meeting the capital and venue requirements. Students liked his classes. Once he

opened a new class, that class would soon be filled up. . . . He only started renting a classroom when a class is filled up. So the cost was really low.

(Informant No. 15)

From this account, it is clear that government officials used the number of students as an indicator of an SEO's reputation. This encouraged marginal entrepreneurs who had been subcontracting divisions to strengthen their marketing and recruiting efforts, so that they could ride on their reputation and establish their independent SEOs.

CONTROLLING THE MARKET WITH FORCE

Opportunist SEOs were more likely to use coercion and violence to secure advertisement and teaching resources than did the other two models. State and intellectual SEOs were well connected to state universities. These SEOs usually stuck with the ways in which state universities recruited students. Intellectual SEOs, for example, usually enjoyed privilege in recruiting students from state universities with which SEO founders were affiliated. As one of the founders of Nova Academy recalled, they initially did not need to put out any advertisement. The only marketing strategy they needed was "putting a small table at the front gate" of their former employer (Informant No. 11). When Nova Academy launched a new program, the Haidian Education Bureau even helped this intellectual SEO put out an advertisement on the *Beijing Daily*, one of the most influential local newspapers.

Opportunist SEOs could not hope for such a favor. Some of their founders resorted to violence to secure coveted advertisement space. Three out of the four opportunist SEOs I studied in Beijing's TOEFL/GRE submarket engaged local gangs to fight for more and better spaces on poster boards on nearby university campuses (Informants No. 5, No. 61, No. 66). Su Leidong calls such incidents "advertisement war." He describes how someone hired by a competitor stabbed a Supernova marketer:

What does advertisement war mean? People I hired put my ads on poster boards. But within 15 minutes after my people left, our posters had been all covered by our competitors' posters. We had no choice but to cover their posters. Then within 15 minutes they would come over and cover ours. So it came back and forth like that and no one could dominate. So eventually it became a violent conflict. The result of the conflict was that people from the other side were more aggressive than ours. They brought knives and stabbed the guy who was doing posting for me. After that, I sent my guy to hospital and also reported this incident to the police. After a week, I heard nothing from the police. Later I went to the police station again and policemen said, "We were busy with other high crimes and murder cases. Your case is like a brawl and that is a minor case. We don't have time to work on yours. Just go back and wait."

(Supernova Archive No. 5, 58–59)

According to several veteran teachers who taught in the Education Industry in the 1990s, Supernova marketers engaged in less violent actions but they were also aggressive (Informants No. 65, No. 66). Su also involved "street boys"—young people who did not necessarily belong to any crime organization but were usually unemployed and spent much time idling on the street. Although the intent of hiring the street boys was to use violence against competitors, violent confrontations between SEOs, such as the stabbing incident, were rare because so many opportunist SEOs worked with street boys that a situation of mutual deterrence arose: SEOs used street boys to deter competitors and usually deterrence was enough to stop bloodshed. This strategy continued to be effective in the 2000s. One of the founding members of Supernova described how such strategies were used in a branch school outside of Beijing:

> We have a tough guy in our Wuhan branch school. He is now the assistant to the branch school president. At that time [in the early 2000s], he brought with him seven or eight "little brothers" who were good at kung fu. Basically they just stood there [after posting our advertisements]. If someone dares to take out the posters, they would threaten him/her. Because people saw that there were seven or eight sturdy guys there, no one dared to tear down Supernova's advertisements. . . . In some cities you really need to do this because people in those cities can be tough and sometimes bullying. Unless you show them an overwhelming stance at the beginning. . . . If you don't overwhelm them, there might be a life-threatening incident. If you overwhelm them and suppress their momentum, they actually won't touch you.

(Informant No. 4)

Besides controlling advertisement space with force and deterrence, some opportunist SEOs coerced teachers into cooperation. Among opportunist SEOs, founders of Cornerstone and Seven Swords were entangled in most of the violent actions (Informants No. 46, No. 61, No. 66). Outside of the TOEFL/GRE submarket, Sea Dragon—a leading brand in the Chinese Graduate Exam—was the best example of using violence to control teachers and advertisement space. Its founder, Long Weiping, established Sea Dragon in the province of Henan in 1994. Since Long was a marginal entrepreneur who had never worked in the state education system, he fell short in securing high-quality teaching resources. To overcome this disadvantage, he forced teachers to work for him by stopping them at their doors and/or sending gang members to their homes (Chai 2006; Informants No. 4, No. 8).

Long also realized the importance of controlling advertisement space with force. He organized a squad of seasoned gang members and street boys to monopolize every possible advertisement space. Any competitor who dared to put up posters in nearby colleges would be met with punches. With such aggressive control of advertisement, Sea Dragon quickly grew to be a leading brand in the Chinese Graduate Exam submarket in northern China.

Long's aggression was such that he went so far as to punish and assault uncooperative teachers and competitors. Long's gang members broke the leg of a teacher who refused to work with him. To stop the growing momentum of a competing SEO, Long gave the order to pour sulfuric acid on the face of a star teacher employed by this competitor. Long's brutality did not catch police attention until his squad beat to death a teacher of a local competitor. By the time he was arrested, Long had used force to control the Chinese Graduate Exam submarket for almost a decade (ibid.).

Long's actions were extreme, but he was far from the only or last entrepreneur in the Education Industry to use coercion. Even after 2000 in Guangzhou, one of the largest cities in southern China, a branch school president of Supernova encountered a situation that made him shiver: after he submitted the application for registering the branch school, he received an envelope that contained "nothing but a bullet" (Informant No. 37). At that time, Su Leidong had already survived two armed robberies and hired a bodyguard. He sent his bodyguard to Guangzhou to protect the branch school president for a month. Later, it became evident that a local opportunist SEO was trying to deter Supernova with the bullet.

RECRUITING STUDENTS WITH FRAUDULENT INFORMATION

As previously mentioned, a major legitimacy issue for opportunist SEOs is consumers' concerns about nonstate SEO founders "running away with money." At a time when private entrepreneurs were just emerging and in an industry where consumers had to pay for all services before receiving any, students and their parents widely considered private entrepreneurs in this industry as money grabbers and trusted state institutions more than nonstate ones. Due to student concerns, many opportunist SEOs had difficulty recruiting the first group of students. Su Leidong describes in detail how much he suffered from consumers' concerns:

I rented a small office room in a [state] elementary school in [the nearby region of] Zhongguancun but they did not allow me to recruit students and collect money within that room. I was only allowed to do these on an elementary student's desk and chair outside the office room. Recruiting students in that way was difficult because prospective students would think, what if this guy ran away with my money at night if I hand my money to him now? . . . Finally there came three students on one morning, and I spent half an hour to persuade them to stay, and they registered, paid tuition and left. But before their money turned warm in my pocket, two of the three returned and took their money back.

(Supernova Archive No. 5, 52–53)

As this quotation shows, recruiting the first group of students was the hardest because students had not had any experience in class. Recruiting students with educational quality could not work. Some opportunist SEOs used fraudulent and misleading information to recruit the first group of students. Again, I use the case of Supernova to show how opportunist SEOs used non compliant practices to recruit the first group of students:

I later found out that these students all acted alike, and they would take a look at the sign-up sheet in order to find out how many people had signed up for my courses. When they found no one or very few did, they were afraid and became hesitant. I knew the first dozen of students would be critical. So I was thinking, why not just fill out the sign-up sheet by myself first. So I filled out the form with about thirty fabricated names. After that, students were much more likely to pay tuition and stay.

(Ibid.)

Although using fabricated names to attract consumers was, according to multiple informants, a common and effective practice in the Education Industry in the early days (Informants No. 37, No. 74), such a practice conformed to neither state regulation about student enrollment nor cooperation norms.

USING TEST MATERIALS WITHOUT PERMISSION

Of course, state and intellectual SEOs also participated in opportunist practices. One such practice was using unauthorized test materials. This practice entails pirating or using test materials without the permission of test designers or administrators.[22] For example, it was no secret that TOEFL/GRE SEOs widely used authentic TOEFL/GRE test materials from the past without authorization from the Educational Testing Service (ETS), the designer for TOEFL and GRE. Having said that, it is worth noting that the ETS did not publish any authentic test materials through legitimate channels in China in the 1980s and early 1990s (Lu 2002, 87–97).

Although all three models were involved in this practice, opportunist SEOs spearheaded the efforts. Opportunist SEOs pioneered obtaining, reproducing, and distributing old authentic test materials when students and SEOs realized that authentic test materials were indispensable for preparing for these tests. Nonauthentic test materials, such as those published by the Princeton Review and Barron's, were allegedly no match for authentic materials and were considered too expensive for Chinese students. A popular line among students was that "authentic test materials were genuinely non-fake, while non-authentic test materials were genuinely un-genuine" (Informant No. 65). In fact, some students attended SEOs because these SEOs were where authentic test materials were available (Informant No. 23). Providing authentic test materials became a standard practice among all TOEFL/GRE SEOs.

Since authentic test materials were not available through legitimate channels, many state and intellectual SEOs used Xeroxed versions of Barron's books for a while (Informant No. 65). Seven Swords and other opportunist SEOs led the effort in introducing authentic test materials through three unusual approaches: (a) sending people to test centers as test takers and bringing out test materials secretly; (b) buying test materials from administrators who worked at test centers; (c) buying test materials from test takers who were willing to bring out test materials and sell to SEOs.

A former teacher and senior manager of Supernova and several other SEOs recounted how he, then still a college student and not yet an employee in the industry, used a combination of these aforementioned approaches to obtain test materials and make money:

> I had many authentic test materials at that time, you know, those TOEFL pamphlets. Central College was a test center and it had its own SEO. I knew a teacher there and his name is Huang. Our relationship was good so I could just buy these materials from him. . . . I also obtained test materials from an SEO and sold them elsewhere. You know, I photocopied them and then sold them in front of the classrooms of other SEOs. I remember a GRE test in April 1994 and I made RMB 1,500 in one day for selling those GRE test questions. You know, I was still a college student, and I needed to make money. That was a big incentive! Do you know how much money RMB 1,500 was at that time? To treat a bunch of friends for dinner only cost RMB 30. College tuition for one year was only RMB 400. Think about that. I became a rich guy all of a sudden. Lots of girls admired me so much that their saliva was almost dripping out.
>
> (Informant No. 17)

In comparison, intellectual and state SEO entrepreneurs usually avoided directly participating in obtaining test materials. Even so, these SEOs could not afford not to use these materials when everyone else was.

To be sure, obtaining the test materials without permission violated rules of the ETS and its Chinese partners in the state education system. Using unauthorized test materials, however, was not considered a serious issue in China in the 1980s and early 1990s. Although early intellectual property laws were passed in the 1980s, the institutional and cultural foundations for enforcing these laws were immature at that time (H. Wu 2018). With regard to education and test preparation, there was a deeply rooted Chinese culture for teaching and learning to the test. In this culture, seeking education for a specific test and decoding a test are legitimate and even appreciated (Lu 2002, 97–101). This is not to say that the Chinese culture encourages students to obtain and/or reproduce test materials without permission. The point here is that such action was not considered an egregious wrongdoing in its historical context.

State Regulations against Noncompliance Turned into Opportunists' Advantages

In the face of such opportunism, especially given the rampant deviation from state regulations and the quantity of fraudulent practices targeting consumers, state regulators did not turn a blind eye. In the early 1990s, the state made serious efforts to restore order. The education bureaus tightened regulations on founder profiles and registration processes. For example, education bureaus all over China reiterated that only founders with local residence were allowed to obtain licenses. In addition, the Administration of Industry and Commerce and street-level local governments imposed stricter regulations on a wide range of issues, such as where and how to advertise classes. Despite tightened regulations, opportunist SEOs continued to climb and maintain leadership positions. These SEOs were able to fend off regulations by navigating the ways in which the Education Industry was regulated.

Two-dimensional ambiguity provided tax advantages for opportunist SEOs. The taxation of for-profit enterprises was within the jurisdiction of tax bureaus, whereas state education institutions, all considered as socialist public enterprises and under the supervision of education bureaus, did not have to deal with tax bureaus. Since what SEOs were was unclear under the ambiguity and the related state fragmentation, no one knew whether tax bureaus or education bureaus should determine tax-related issues for SEOs.

This situation provided immense room for SEOs to maneuver and interpret state regulations in their favor. Opportunist SEOs were able to evade or reduce taxation more effectively than were other models. Since state education regulators classified the Education Industry as part of an education rather than a commercial sector, SEOs did not have to pay any tax in the 1980s. In the early to mid-1990s, when private enterprises in other industries were paying sales tax at 30 to 35 percent (Zhang Jun 2005), SEOs were paying only about 3 to 3.5 percent.[23] Very often, because of the Chinese state's weak capacity to levy taxes at that time, even the 3 to 3.5 percent tax was not collected.

One of the new regulations since the early 1990s was to collect tax more effectively. When tax bureaus started enforcing the tax regulations more strictly in the Education Industry, they inevitably entered into conflict with education bureaus due to unclear jurisdictional boundaries under two-dimensional ambiguity. One of the founding members of Blue Ocean commented on this situation:

> The tax bureau said you were engaged in market activities and you had to pay taxes. So we went to the education bureau and asked them what we could do. The education bureau said, "It is like this: we studied the laws, and they fight against each other. If the tax bureau comes to you, you can try to avoid paying if you can. You don't have to pay if you can. You do not have to pay any tax according to our laws. But you need to pay taxes according to their laws." So I figured out that we could go to the tax bureau and keep pestering them. We tried to not pay the tax, if possible. If we indeed needed to pay, we wanted to bargain for less.
>
> (Informant No. 8)

As the last sentence of this long quotation shows, the possibility to realize the tax benefits hinged on bargaining with government officials. However, not every founder was familiar or comfortable with such practices. Among the four opportunist SEOs I studied, three founders either nagged tax bureau officials and negotiated for a lower tax by themselves or sent their financial managers—usually their family members—to tax bureaus to negotiate.[24] In comparison, founders of the two intellectual SEOs were afraid to negotiate with officials. Of course, negotiating and bargaining were very common in China's black market and is arguably characteristic of any black market in the world (Geertz [1978] 2011). But negotiating a tax rate was considered a serious deviant practice by professors and administrators from Chinese state universities (Informants No. 10, No. 11, No. 6). In other words, the capacity to use negotiation under ambiguity provided opportunist SEOs substantive comparative advantages.

Another advantage for opportunist SEOs was that under two-dimensional ambiguity, regulations and sanctions against opportunism fell most heavily on the more compliant organizations. As mentioned earlier, the relationship with the state and the informal economy was different among the three models. The influences from the informal economy were clearest on opportunist SEOs, whereas the state education system most strongly shaped state and intellectual SEOs. Although all three models were similarly ambiguous, state and intellectual SEOs adhered relatively more closely to being nonprivate and not-for-profit than did opportunist SEOs. State and intellectual SEOs were also more likely to establish close contacts with local education bureaus and used practices familiar to state regulators.

Accordingly, education bureaus were more aware of the practices of state and intellectual SEOs. Compared to opportunistic practices of opportunist SEOs, minor deviations of the other two models attracted more attention from state regulators. State regulators also enforced regulations on state and intellectual SEOs stringently through effective channels. For example, state regulators' familiarity with the state and intellectual SEOs enabled them to widely advertise state restrictions, such as the ban on cross-regional expansion, on the campuses of these two models (Informant No. 11). State SEOs suffered the heaviest blow from the unintended consequences of strengthened regulations. In the Chinese Graduate Exam submarket, heightened state regulations eventually drove state SEOs out. Education bureaus in the 1990s and 2000s were determined to fight opportunistic practices within this submarket. Due to their awareness of state SEO practices, state regulators concluded that the biggest problem in this submarket was that state SEOs were involved in leaking the test and interview information of their host universities to students. In 2004, the Ministry of Education demanded state SEOs in the Chinese Graduate Exam be separate from their host universities or quit the market. It was during this time that highly predatory opportunist SEOs, such as Sea Dragon, regained their competitiveness against state SEOs (Chai 2006). Escalated state regulations unintentionally contributed to the success of opportunists and the prevalence of their opportunistic practices across the market.

Conclusion

This chapter investigates how opportunist SEOs benefited from two-dimensional ambiguity and rose to be market leaders. After introducing the context and the succession of top leaders in Beijing's TOEFL/GRE submarket, I show how all SEOs resorted to the state education system and the informal economy for resources and organizational repertoires. Having said that, the ways in which the three organizational models drew on the state education system and the informal economy were different. Specifically, opportunist SEOs were more closely connected with the informal economy and they played the leading role in introducing resources from the informal economy to the Education Industry.

Compared to the other two models, opportunist SEOs were less compliant with state laws and other formal regulations. They conducted opportunistic practices systematically. Adopting these opportunistic practices enabled opportunist SEOs to overcome disadvantages in market entry, resources, and legitimacy. Under two-dimensional ambiguity, regulations against opportunism were also turned into benefits for opportunist SEOs. As opportunist SEOs maneuvered in the ambiguity and boosted their competitiveness, state SEOs lost their leadership. The rise of nonstate SEOs and the withering of state SEOs facilitated the retreat of state influence in this industry. As opportunist SEOs climbed to the top, their opportunistic practices, such as cross-region expansion, became widely accepted in the Education Industry.[25]

3

Be More Aggressive Than Your Employees

Dumping classes [by teachers] is like what happens when you run a restaurant.... Suppose we have just opened a restaurant and hired a chef. But we don't know how to make the signature dishes of this chef, and the brilliant cooking art of this chef has made our restaurant popular. At this time, this chef will observe and ponder. Soon he will find out that this restaurant depends on him for survival. Then he will ask the owner if he could get some shares of the restaurant, or he might ask for a raise. If the owner says no, this chef will leave for sure. This restaurant will surely face the consequence of closure.

(SUPERNOVA ARCHIVE NO. 5, 80)

Have you ever wondered about the relationship between the taste of a restaurant's menu items and its survival? With a few friends operating Chinese restaurants on the West Coast of the United States, where Asian cuisine (and culture in general) are booming, I have heard some anecdotes about this relationship that fit the quotation starting this chapter: these Chinese restaurants, usually small in size and dependent on a few signature dishes made by a certain chef, often face the dilemma when hiring chefs. If the hired chef cannot produce tasty foods, the restaurant will go under. But if the hired chef is so capable that the taste of his or her dishes fully captures the hearts of customers, the restaurant may go out of business even sooner. In the face of rapidly growing business, the chef will often bargain for higher pay and might even break the agreed upon terms and conditions with the owner. SEO entrepreneurs in China in the 1980s and 1990s encountered this same dilemma.

This chapter turns its attention to the internal power dynamics between teachers and entrepreneurs, highlighting their opportunistic practices that are noncompliant with cooperation norms.[1] Opportunistic practices discussed in this chapter refer to actions that take advantage of other social actors, such as making false promises and reneging on agreements. This chapter focuses on the TOEFL/GRE submarket in Beijing from the 1980s to the early 1990s, the same market and historical period as the previous chapter. I start with the relatively strong bargaining power of individual teachers in early years, especially those who held senior titles at state universities and young teachers who were popular among SEO students.

The ambiguity of the Education Industry, strong bargaining power of early teachers, and the entrance of more young teachers into the Education Industry were the underlying conditions for teacher opportunism. Opportunistic practices by teachers deviated from the trust-based cooperation norms. These practices posed a grave existential threat to intellectual and opportunist SEOs.[2]

My findings reveal that opportunist SEO entrepreneurs fended off teachers' opportunism more successfully than did intellectual SEO founders. Opportunist SEO entrepreneurs adopted both coercive and noncoercive practices to fight against teacher opportunism. During this process, opportunist SEOs sustained their positions as market leaders while intellectual SEOs lost their edge. Opportunist SEOs became the only remaining prototype of private enterprises in the Education Industry. The last part of this chapter zeros in on how some leading opportunist SEOs developed new approaches for teacher management that had the effect of preventing teacher opportunism. As these approaches matured, both teachers' opportunism and their bargaining power declined.

Early Teachers and Their Bargaining Power

Thanks to the distinct social and institutional contexts of the Education Industry in the 1980s and early 1990s, the employment relationship between SEOs and their teachers was volatile. During this early period, Beijing's TOEFL/GRE market was thriving in the absence of sophisticated marketing strategies. As table 1.1 shows, the number of Chinese students studying abroad was increasingly rapidly, so the demand for TOEFL/GRE classes was skyrocketing. Therefore, despite the intensified competition, the major challenge for SEOs was not recruiting students. From the standpoint of organizational survival, the threat came from within—how to recruit and retain teachers. This is especially true because teachers were the key attraction for students in this era when only rudimentary marketing strategies, such as posters and flyers, were used for course promotion.

China's institutional environment for employment relationships was undergoing a fundamental transition during this period. Across industries, the former socialist lifelong employment and "iron bowl" under the *danwei* system were in decline, but the new contract-based employment was not yet widely implemented.[3] An employment contract only became a necessary component, at least in theory, for establishing an employment relationship in 1994 when the Chinese state codified the first Labor Law. Enforcing what this law required took a much longer time. Unsurprisingly, employing teachers without employment contracts was a common practice in the Education Industry during this period (Informants No. 10, No. 11, No. 65). Even for teachers who started with contract-based employment in the early 2000s, they most often signed service contracts.[4] Using service contracts allowed SEOs to provide teachers only with hourly wage, skipping both monthly base salary and other employment benefits.

In the absence of contract-based employment, the relationship between SEO employers and employees was highly unstable. Conditions of employment were often agreed verbally and were subject to constant negotiations. Terminating the employment relationship before an agreed upon end date was virtually effortless. To exacerbate the volatility, the Education Industry was non-capital-intensive, and the noncompete clause was unheard of during this period. In other words, the initial capital for founding a new SEO and the legal and social costs for using the new SEO to compete with former employers were so small that they could be ignored. Therefore, there was little for teachers to worry about when launching direct competition against a former employer. In this situation, teachers could easily stage exit-and-entrepreneurship—the process through which a teacher quits an SEO and immediately opens a competing SEO close by.

Under this volatile institutional environment for employment relationship, teachers' key role in boosting enrollment and their capacity to stage exit-and-entrepreneurship elevated their bargaining power. Indeed, both SEO entrepreneurs and their employees engaged in bargaining, and it was equally common for either party to move first and terminate the employment relationship prematurely. It is also difficult to measure individuals' bargaining power despite the common knowledge of the weakness of Chinese professional associations.

From a comparative perspective, however, early SEO teachers had relatively strong bargaining power. Compared to employees in many other industries, SEO teachers were more likely to work part time and were less dependent on employers. Compared with post-2000 SEO teachers, teachers in earlier years also boasted stronger bargaining power. This is manifest in the fact that the teachers enjoyed greater autonomy in determining their pedagogies and work schedules than did later generations (Informants No. 5, No. 8,

Lu 2002). There was little an SEO entrepreneur would or could do when an early teacher made up his or her mind to teach a class in a particular way. In comparison, SEO teachers during the post-2000 era faced ever-expanding restrictions from employers on what and how to teach. The SEO control on teacher schedules also tightened after 2000. For example, although Supernova and Doo & Cool teachers loathed the ideas that teachers should attend in-person meetings and prepare classes together in offices, these ideas were all put into place in the 2000s (Informants No. 58).

Another underlying condition for teachers' strong bargaining power has to do with the fact that the majority of early SEO teachers were state university faculty members who worked part time at SEOs (Informants No. 4, No. 8, No. 10, No. 11, No. 61). These part-time teachers considered their SEO jobs as moonlighting opportunities to make some extra money. Although for these teachers, income from SEOs classes far exceeded state university salaries, their social status and welfare benefits came primarily from their university jobs. Their dependence on SEO employers, therefore, was relatively low. Teachers' low dependence discouraged them from taking seriously the decisions for joining or departing an SEO. Two current state university faculty members who once worked as part-time teachers at SEOs mentioned that they did not spend much time thinking through the decision to work at SEOs because it was like offering some casual help at local businesses and making some extra money (Informants No. 6, No. 85).

Furthermore, most early teachers were senior faculty members or experienced junior ones at state universities. Their dependence on SEOs was even lower compared with other junior faculty members and graduate students, which further bolstered the bargaining power of early teachers. As mentioned previously, state SEO administrators considered the teaching opportunity at their SEOs as a reward for state university faculty members. Following the seniority logic that was prevalent in state universities, state SEO administrators gave priority to senior faculty members.

In addition, state regulators demanded nonstate SEO founders and teachers be educators. State and intellectual SEOs followed the requirements of state regulators. Thus, these SEOs preferred to employ and retain senior faculty members. Two cofounders at Nova Academy, for example, said that Nova and other intellectual SEOs always hired renowned professors from top state universities even if hiring these teachers cost more money (Informants No. 10, No. 11). As one of the cofounders said:

> Since one of our founders was a retired professor of Russian language, we used
> his personal connections to invite senior professors at nearby universities to

teach at our school. We had to pay high salaries for them to come. We also had to keep secret for them, you know. At that time universities did not allow them to teach outside. To help these senior professor come to our classes, we also had to rent cars and had to pay RMB 50 per day to drivers. We even had to pay money to the gatekeepers [of these teachers' universities] in order to allow our cars to go through. But these were the best professors, so it was worth it.

(Informant No. 11)

Opportunist SEOs, especially those whose founders had worked in the state education system, initially also depended on senior faculty members as teachers. Take the first-generation teachers at Supernova for example. Active only for a short period in 1991, they were a group of experienced and middle-aged (forty to fifty years old) faculty members from the English Department of Capital University. They were Su Leidong's colleagues, but older and more senior than Su (Informants No. 4, No. 28; Supernova Archive No. 5). In sum, all three types of SEOs were subject to the strong bargaining power of early teachers, especially those who are senior faculty members.

The seniority and strong bargaining power of early teachers were also visible in other submarkets, such as the Chinese Graduate Exam submarket. Given the paramount importance of Chinese Graduate Exam test score in the admission of students to state universities, Chinese Graduate Exam SEOs and their students preferred teachers who were associated with the state education system. Early teachers at Chinese Graduate Exam SEOs were mostly senior or retired professors of state universities, and these teachers called the shots on how to teach. As one of the founding members of Blue Ocean recalled,

We started with three old lady professors from three departments of Northern University. Later, we had retired professors from three elite universities to teach for us. . . . When I asked them if they could teach in a different way, they said, "Is it me doing the teaching or you doing the teaching? Simply because you pay me does not mean I have to teach your way. I teach my way." We respected that. We respected our teachers a lot.

(Informant No. 8)

The seniority and rich experience of early teachers meant that they had quite a bit of say with regard to what and how to teach. SEO entrepreneurs found it unnecessary or difficult to intervene in teaching (Informants No. 8, No. 65). In the face of such difficulties, as well as senior teachers' strong bargaining power and weak commitment to SEO jobs, SEO entrepreneurs started to recruit junior faculty members and graduate students as new teachers. Questing, a leading intellectual SEO, was known as one of the earliest to hire graduate students of English from elite colleges as teachers (Informants

TABLE 3.1. Profiles of Supernova's Second-Generation Teachers

Teacher No.	Gender	Age	Full-Time Jobs/Education	Courses Taught at Supernova
Teacher No. 1	Male	29	PhD Student, National College of Foreign Affairs (Department of English)	TOEFL Grammar
Teacher No. 2	Male	27	Staff Member, Capital University (Foreign Affairs Department)	TOEFL Vocabulary
Teacher No. 3	Female	26	Lecturer, Capital University (English Department)	TOEFL Listening
Teacher No. 4	Male	26	Masters Student, Central Academy of Sciences (Institute of Automation)	GRE courses

Source: Supernova Archive No. 2

No. 61, No. 65). Among opportunist SEOs, Seven Swords rose to be a market leader in the late 1980s with a teaching team of young graduate students.

Supernova altered its hiring standards and employed more young teachers. Its second-generation teachers, who were most active between 1991 and 1995, encompassed two groups from state universities: junior faculty members and graduate students. Table 3.1, which is created from a part of Supernova's Official Registration Form (Supernova Archive No. 2), features the gender, age, and full-time jobs of the four second-generation teachers. As shown, all four teachers were in their twenties in 1991, with an average age of twenty-seven. Two of them were graduate students, one was a lecturer, and the other was a staff member at a state university. The profiles of these four teachers were significantly different from those of the first generation. Although these second-generation teachers were also from the state education system, they were much younger and boasted more junior status than those of the first generation.

Opportunistic Practices and Their Discontents

TEACHERS' OPPORTUNISTIC PRACTICES

As has happened to Supernova, SEOs since the early 1990s have been increasingly filled with junior faculty members or graduate students as teachers. Although the majority of them still worked part time at SEOs, some of them developed long-term commitment to SEO jobs and spent more time preparing for classes. Their young ages, adequate class preparation, and eloquence helped them build fame among students. They became star teachers. Having star teachers was critical to an SEO's success in the 1990s because the marketing of SEOs was based on teacher names and the word of mouth among students (Lu 2002; Informants No. 5, No. 17). Multiple SEOs built their brand names on the shoulders of star teachers. A former teacher and senior manager at Supernova and several other SEOs recalled the central role of star teachers:

> Students at that time searched advertisement posters only for teacher names, not organization names. . . . That was a time of individual heroes. Students only talked about "so-and-so was going to give a class so let's join that class." They didn't care which organization you were from. In those years, you had to follow good teachers as if these teachers were superstars. Students followed the names of teachers, not the brands. It was those teachers who held up brand names and made those brands famous.
>
> (Informant No. 17)

Another former Supernova star teacher and shareholder corroborated this point:

> How did these SEOs build their names? Basically it was due to the contribution of extraordinary teachers. The best teachers in those early days were unique. They were mavericks. It was all because of the charisma of these teachers. That was a time when teacher names were above brand names. Students came to our classes first because they were looking for a particular teacher. The influence of the brand name came secondary.
>
> (Informant No. 5)

Associated with the increased influence of young star teachers were their greater material expectations for SEO jobs. Compared to their predecessors, these young teachers were more economically motivated: many young teachers were attracted to the Education Industry not to earn some extra money but to make a fortune. They were not shy of using whatever means possible to guarantee greater monetary payoffs. For example, multiple young teachers used fake names, made-up stories, and other tricks to obtain interview opportunities at Supernova (Lu 2002). These practices were opportunistic in the sense that they twisted information and deviated from the trust-based cooperation norms.

Of course, entrepreneurs also resorted to opportunistic practices, and it was not uncommon for them to be the first in breaking agreements when interacting with teachers. In this booming industry and at a time when the contract-based employment relationship was underdeveloped, both parties resorted to opportunistic practices frequently. Asking which party initiated opportunistic practices is like asking the chicken-or-egg question. Since this chapter examines only the survival of organizations, here I only examine teachers' opportunistic practices and entrepreneurs' responses. Teachers' well-known opportunistic practices include skipping classes, pulling students away, hold-ups, and dumping classes.

Skipping classes—not showing up to an agreed class or switching to a higher-paying SEO in the middle of a course—clearly broke the trust-based cooperation norms between entrepreneurs and teachers. In Beijing's TOEFL/GRE submarket, skipping classes emerged in the early 1990s as more and more junior faculty members and graduate students joined the teaching force of intellectual and opportunist SEOs. Having opted for the higher pay in the Education Industry over stability and benefits at state universities, some of these young teachers no longer cared much about their reputation within the state education system. A state university faculty member and a staff member who worked at SEOs mentioned that it was not uncommon for young teachers in the 1990s to skip classes (Informants No. 6, No. 8). For example, a young faculty member used to only teach weekday evening classes as a part-time teacher at an SEO, but then he and the SEO founder agreed for him to also teach weekend classes; however, when students were waiting for the teacher on a Saturday morning, he was standing on the podium of another SEO without telling the entrepreneur of the previous SEO simply because the other SEO offered higher wages (Informant No. 6).

Skipping classes occurred in many submarkets, not just the TOEFL/GRE submarket. In the Chinese Graduate Exam submarket, it was even more prevalent since working for multiple SEOs was a standard practice in this submarket (Informants No. 8, No. 21). Although students looked up to senior professors as authoritative figures, junior faculty members from state universities started to build their reputations by teaching in an untraditional way, such as predicting test questions. In order to maximize their monetary reward, some of these junior professors constantly compared pay from different SEOs and skipped classes that paid less. One of the founding members of Blue Ocean described how such a young star teacher skipped classes:

> Teacher Cheng taught in multiple SEOs. He would teach for whoever pays him more money. . . . Cheng did not keep his words to us. He did not keep his words to anyone. In those years, he was so influential among students that hundreds of students would follow him if he summoned them. . . . That time Cheng had agreed to teach a class that had 1600 students. The class started at 8:30 a.m., but students waited till 1:00 p.m. to see Cheng. He only taught for half an hour and then left [for another SEO]. Sometimes I felt that I also wanted to beat him up.[5]
>
> (Informant No. 8)

This star teacher—Cheng—was a junior faculty member in the department where the Blue Ocean founder worked as a staff member. In other words, some young and popular teachers cared about neither their promises with employers nor their reputations in state universities.

SEOs suffer from even heavier blows when departing teachers "pull students away." This is the equivalent of taking advantage of employers by stealing their customers. For a teacher with an ambition to establish his or her own SEO, pulling students away was worth considering because such action would save much effort. The weak institutional environment, such as the absence of the noncompete clause, made teachers hesitate even less when pulling students away.

Some teachers began pulling students away even before they took actions to quit their jobs. In such cases, a teacher secretly transferred students enrolled at his or her employer to another school under his or her control. Alternatively, a teacher who was partnering with a host SEO through subcontracting recruited students to his or her secret school without sharing the enrollment data and relevant revenue with the host SEO.

Supernova, for example, was the victim of multiple schemes of pulling students away in the 1990s and 2000s. There were multiple cases where teachers pulled students away from Supernova and recruited them into their own secret SEOs (Informants No. 29, No. 41, No. 48). In another case that occurred in Shanghai in 2000, a few teachers who were not affiliated with Supernova used Supernova's brand name to recruit students. Su Leidong was furious not only because such practices took advantage of Supernova's name but also because Shanghai was a city of strategic importance for Supernova's future growth. Su sent a debit card to those teachers, asking them to deposit all the tuition they collected into the card account (Informants No. 61, No. 65). Eventually these teachers refused. Su had to accelerate his plan to establish a branch school in Shanghai in order to preclude students from being recruited to counterfeit Supernova schools. Although this case was not between an employer and its employees, what these teachers were doing was no different from stealing students from Supernova.

Although he was a victim of having students pulled away, Su possibly engaged in similar practices before he founded Supernova. As mentioned in the previous chapter, Su was unqualified as a founder, so he had to subcontract a division under Nova Academy. According to the subcontracting agreement, Su had to pay 15 to 25 percent of the division's total revenue to Nova as a "management fee." Paying such a fee narrowed his earning margin. According to a veteran teacher for and an entrepreneur of several SEOs (Informant No. 61), Su decided to move some existing students to an unregistered class under his control so that he would not have to pay the management fee for these students. It is worth noting that when I was cross-checking this incident, the responses from other two informants were mixed.[6] It is difficult to confirm whether or how such an incident occurred three decades ago, so I suggest using caution when reading about this incident. Having said that, I include the veteran teacher's description because he provided many details about this incident, as I elaborate in the next section.

While pulling students away often bled employers slowly, teachers' hold-ups and class dumping dealt their bosses a swift and fatal blow. In a hold-up, a teacher uses his or her bargaining power, in the form of threatening to leave, to request higher wages.[7] Dumping classes, standing up students without notice, takes the threat to the next level. Both practices involved breaking away from agreed conditions. Compared to skipping classes when a teacher usually just fails to show up once or twice, dumping classes means cutting all remaining classes even though teaching these remaining classes is required in the employment agreement. While skipping classes does not necessarily upend the employment arrangement, a teacher's dumping of classes often results in his or her abrupt termination of employment.

As one can imagine, hold-ups and class dumping by teachers can quickly turn a prosperous SEO into a mess. Su describes how a teacher's hold-up and dumping of classes created a crisis for Supernova:

He [the teacher] kept asking for higher pay, and at the end, he said he would dump classes if I would not raise his pay. I was being generous, but you would always meet someone like this. His demand for monetary interest goes far beyond what you can offer. I have encountered this. He was halfway through the course, and he said, "Teacher Su, I hope you could raise my pay." And I said, "Your pay is already pretty high." He said he had a simple request, "There are a total of forty-four classes for this course. I taught fourteen classes so I would need the money for those fourteen classes." I asked him what he meant by the money for those fourteen classes. He told me it meant 25 percent of the total revenue of the whole course. I asked him who would be responsible for all the cost for recruitment, office expenditures, marketing and classroom rentals. He said, "I don't care."

But the pay raise he proposed was too much for me. Had I accepted that, it would be like distributing all my revenue to teachers. I would end up having nothing. Then my original goal for establishing this school would not be reached. Also if I had raised pay for one teacher, other teachers would have seen it too. So his demand was not being met no matter what. The result was that this teacher dumped [the remaining] classes and left.

He did not go to the class that very night. Only then did I realize the consequence of him dumping classes: there was no one else who could replace

him. I went to appease students but students wouldn't budge. Students started
complaining and making big scenes. They protested really hard. Eventually I
had to refund all the money for this entire class. Not a single penny left. Except
for the Quantitative Reasoning class the quitting teacher was teaching, all the
other classes resumed. That's how students settled.

(Supernova Archive No. 5, 79)

Such opportunistic practices by teachers were destructive. A number of
once popular intellectual SEOs, such as Questing and Nova Academy, lost
steam after their star teachers staged one or more of these opportunistic
practices.

Even if a teacher only participates in exit-and-entrepreneurship, arguably
not necessarily an opportunistic practice, such an act can jeopardize his or
her employer's business. For example, Ma Tiannan had worked for, and quit,
multiple SEOs before founding Pioneers. According to a veteran teacher who
had taught in multiple SEOs, Ma taught for Questing, Mercury, and Seven
Swords—two intellectual SEOs and one opportunist SEO—before he embarked on entrepreneurial endeavors (Informant No. 65). All these SEOs depended on Ma, their star teacher. After Ma left, Questing and Mercury could
not hold on to their leading positions.

EMPLOYERS' RESPONSES

SEO entrepreneurs adopted a variety of strategies to cope with teachers' opportunistic practices. For entrepreneurs who conducted teaching, a straight-
forward and common strategy was to put more teaching loads in the hands of
themselves and their family members. The more courses entrepreneurs and
their family members could teach, the less menacing teachers' opportunistic
practices became. Su Leidong, for example, managed to teach all classes except Quantitative Reasoning of the GRE. In his account below, he recalls how
his capacity to cover most classes prevented teacher opportunism and how
his failure to cover Quantitative Reasoning paved the way for a disaster:

> Generally, I was able to teach every course at Supernova. But there was one
> course I could not teach at all. That was a quantitative class, called Quantita-
> tive Reasoning. It was [for] the quantitative reasoning [section] of the GRE.
> For me, it was my weak spot. When organizing this class, therefore, I needed a
> capable horse. So I had to hire a teacher who specialized in this class. . . . Then
> when he looked around, he found that I was able to pitch in every course any-
> time except for his course. So he started playing tricks with me, demanding
> pay raise again and again. Eventually, he said he would dump classes if there
> were no pay raise . . .

If there is no strong team at the beginning and no abundant financial resource to fall back on, I have to be the chef myself. . . . Actually I was the chef
in Supernova at that time. But there was one popular dish I did not know how
to cook. That led to the situation. . . . If I cannot be the chef, I can hire more
chefs. It is less likely that all these chefs will fire the boss simultaneously. My
restaurant will be safer. Of course, hiring multiple chefs will increase my cost,
but it is still better than the danger of closing the restaurant. So I basically
hired and trained four people in that area [of GRE Reasoning]. After that, no
teacher in that area ever fired me again.

(Supernova Archive No. 5, 78–80)

Evidently, Su put his aforementioned "chef theory" into practice—making
himself the chef helped fend off opportunism of others. He also hired more
chefs to reduce the dependence on any particular one.

Mobilizing family members to teach was also effective in reducing dependence for teachers as a group. For example, Ma Tiannan, the founder of
Pioneers, not only taught a wide variety of courses himself, but he also involved his father for a large amount of teaching. A former teacher and senior
manager at Supernova and several other SEOs once attended Pioneers as a
student. As he recalled,

Pioneers started about the same time as Cornerstone and Su's division under
Nova Academy. The founder, Ma Tiannan, was born in the 1960s. His father,
Old Ma, was also a teacher there. Pioneers was basically a family business operated by Ma, his father Old Ma, his sister and his father's ex-wife. Ma and his
father cotaught many classes. I was a student at Pioneers then. I did not know
the old guy giving lessons to us was [Ma's] father.

There was one time when Pioneers people were handing teaching materials to us, and they told us there would be a change of teacher for the upcoming
class. Some students were happy and told Pioneers people "better never let the
old guy come back again. He does such a poor job in teaching." I was complaining [about his father], too. I was talking to a little girl. The little girl was
responsible for student registration. I didn't know at that time she was Ma's
sister! I told her the old teacher was knowledgeable but he was too slow. Lots
of students were sleeping. . . . Of course his father was knowledgeable. . . . He
wrote a book on translation theory.

(Informant No. 17)

Apparently, Ma asked his father to conduct teaching even though his father was not popular among students. The fact that Ma and his father could
cover a large proportion of classes made Pioneers relatively resilient in the
face of teacher opportunism.

Despite the benefits of putting teaching in the hands of entrepreneurs and their family members, such a strategy was a luxury. Not many SEO entrepreneurs were able to undertake teaching themselves. Entrepreneurs of the two intellectual SEOs included in this book, Questing and Nova Academy, did not teach any TOEFL/GRE classes. With regard to the four opportunist SEOs I studied, only the entrepreneurs leading Supernova and Pioneer were teachers. Similarly, entrepreneurs of leading SEOs in the Chinese Graduate Exam, such as Blue Ocean and Blue Wings, did not conduct teaching themselves.

Nor was it easy to put teaching in the hands of family members. Indeed, every single intellectual and opportunist SEO established before 2000 and described in this book started as a family business. But in most cases, family members of entrepreneurs were only responsible for nonteaching functions, such as finance and logistics. For example, although both Nova Academy and Questing involved family members in operation, none of these family members participated in teaching. The same is true for Supernova and other opportunist SEOs. Among Ma's multiple family members working at Pioneers, only his father participated in teaching.

Another strategy adopted by entrepreneurs was going tooth-for-tooth with opportunistic teachers: fending off opportunism with opportunism. Opportunist SEOs were able to come up with more opportunistic and aggressive approaches than did the other two models. A handful of opportunist SEO entrepreneurs, especially those who had not had any work experience in the state education system, used coercion on their teachers with or without the presence of the teacher opportunism.[8] I mentioned Sea Dragon, an opportunist SEO in the Chinese Graduate Exam submarket, in the previous chapter. Long Weiping, the founder of Sea Dragon, forced teachers to cooperate with him by stopping them at their doors and beating uncooperative teachers.

Of course, coercion by entrepreneurs often ended up speeding teachers' exit-and-entrepreneurship. For example, Seven Swords was number one in terms of enrollment around the year 1990. But its entrepreneur often scolded teachers and sometimes resorted to violence, which eventually led to the departure of Ma Tiannan and Gong Ming, its two star teachers (Informant No. 65). Soon after these two star teachers left and students followed them, Seven Swords lost its competitiveness.

Despite the existence of the coercive approach, it was an extreme measure used by only a handful of entrepreneurs. In both TOEFL/GRE and the Chinese Graduate Exam submarkets, only highly marginal entrepreneurs who had never worked in the state education system resorted to force. For other entrepreneurs, the more effective and appropriate response to teacher opportunism was noncoercive. These noncoercive practices entailed snitching, preemptive moves, buying out, divide and conquer, and other practices that were not based on trust or cooperation norms. The key, again, was to use opportunism to fend off opportunism.

Su's handling of teachers' betrayal was a classic example. As mentioned previously, Su was alleged to have pulled students away to an unregistered SEO of his while he was still working under Nova Academy. According to a veteran teacher for and an entrepreneur of several SEOs, Su's actions were followed by opportunistic practices of two teachers working for Su. They considered this situation an opportunity to secretly take over Su's division. Eventually, Su was able to quell their uprising by resorting to snitching and buying out. This veteran teacher and entrepreneur fleshed out more details,

> He [Su] started pulling students away to another school of his. Two teachers working in Su's division were not happy about this. Later they realized that this could be their opportunity. These two teachers went to see a competitor's founder one evening. The idea was that they would work together, keep running the division and stop Su from pulling students. . . . I heard they talked for a long time that night. They wanted to take over the division from Su or ask the competitor's boss to lead the division. . . . But what happened next, according to one of the two teachers, was that Su went to talk to him before dawn. And this teacher changed his mind [and chose to side with Su again]. Su made some good promises to these two teachers. I think this is why they changed their minds. . . . Later when we talked about this incident, some people who participated in the revolution against Su called that switching-side teacher "Yuan Shikai."[9] . . . It would have been interesting if Su had been "let go" from Nova Academy. In that case, you know, that competitor and the two star teachers would keep the brand Nova Academy. It will be a different story.
> (Informant No. 61)

As the quotation shows, the two teachers worked in secrecy with a competing brand's founder so that they could welcome the founder as a new leader and oust Su from the leadership position of the division. Su's reliance on snitching, his preemptive move and buying out of rebel teachers prevented him from losing the control of the division. Again, I kept this account because its details lend some credence to its validity; however, my cross-checking produced mixed findings.[10]

While Su was pulling students away, leaders of Nova Academy did not take sufficiently aggressive actions to contain his opportunistic move. In comparison, Su was able to stop rebel teachers' opportunism with counteropportunism. The different responses were associated with different fates: Nova Academy was unable to retain Su and lost its place in Beijing's TOEFL/GRE market after Su left; Su was not only able to keep his two teachers but also able to launch Supernova as an independent brand.

This case also shows the stark contrast between intellectual and opportunist SEO entrepreneurs as two groups. Although some intellectual SEOs responded to teacher opportunism with opportunistic practices, on average opportunist SEOs resorted to opportunistic practices more often and used these practices more effectively than did intellectual SEOs. Accordingly, opportunist SEOs were more resilient in the face of teacher opportunism. Among the four opportunist SEOs I studied in Beijing's TOEFL/GRE submarket, only Seven Swords succumbed after its star teachers staged exit-and-entrepreneurship. In contrast, both intellectual SEOs in this study—Questing and Nova Academy—lost the edge after their star teachers employed opportunistic practices or exit-and-entrepreneurship.

Taming Teachers and the Prevention of Their Opportunism

As state and intellectual SEOs had lost their momentum by the early 1990s, the competition within the group of opportunist SEOs increasingly occupied the center stage in Beijing's TOEFL/GRE submarket. The next chapter unpacks the role of pedagogy in separating winners and losers among opportunist SEOs. Here I extend the discussion on the power dynamics between teachers and their SEOs as well as the implications of the power dynamics for the competition among opportunist SEOs.

Going tooth-for-tooth was not the only approach for fighting against teacher opportunism. Another approach that systematically dampened teacher opportunism lay in taming teachers and reducing their bargaining power. In fact, many practices of this approach, such as adopting market-based teacher evaluation, were not devised purposively as responses to teacher opportunism. Rather, these practices were initially enacted for other purposes. Implementing these practices came with unintended consequences: teachers became more replaceable than had previously been the case. Teachers' opportunism became more tenable as their capacity to use bargaining power was restricted. Among the few entrepreneurs who were exploring the taming approach were Pioneers and Supernova founders. Between the two, Supernova entrepreneurs went further.

MARKET-BASED TEACHER EVALUATION

Across the Education Industry, teachers had rarely thought about asking students to evaluate their teaching by the early 1990s (Informants No. 23, No. 61, No. 65). In other Chinese for-profit sectors, the idea of customer rights was only just beginning to sprout.[11] Conceptualizing students as customers was unheard of. No SEO active in the 1980s conducted student evaluation of teachers (Informants No. 10, No. 11, No. 65). The absence of student evaluations of teachers does not mean the lack of course evaluation. During the 1980s and early 1990s, most SEO entrepreneurs and teachers assessed their class quality by measuring students' educational gains—how students improved on test scores or English. Former students of intellectual SEOs in Beijing and Shanghai recalled that teachers regularly checked the homework of students and assigned quizzes to ensure awareness of students' educational progress (Informants No, 23, No. 88). In sum, course assessment initially unfolded as teachers evaluating students.

Course assessment took a 180-degree turn following the rise of opportunist SEOs. These SEOs gradually shifted to a market-based teacher evaluation system and thus tended to look at student impressions about teacher performance. In the early 1990s, Pioneers and Supernova were spearheading the movement toward student evaluation on teacher performance. Ma Tiannan at Pioneers was among the first to ask all students to provide written comments for teachers, and later asked students to provide numerical evaluation. Despite his pioneering spirits, Ma's reform was incomplete in the sense that he did not tie teacher evaluations with pay or critical personnel decisions, such as hiring or firing. According to the former student at Pioneers and another informant familiar with Pioneers and Supernova, Ma's father received low scores on student evaluations, but the evaluation did not mean anything since it did not reduce any benefits of Ma's father (Informants No. 17, No. 18).

In comparison, Supernova went further to upgrade the evaluation system and tied the evaluation to critical personnel decisions regarding teachers. Su initially allowed students to boo a teacher with whom they were not happy, and he gave students the permission to shift to other classes at the same level (Informant No. 5; Supernova Archive No. 5). Later, Su implemented a new evaluation system. Under this system, students evaluated teachers with a numerical system on a scale from one to five. Often in the penultimate class, administrative staff distributed questionnaires to students and asked students to provide an evaluation for all their teachers. A former star teacher and senior manager at Supernova commented on how this evaluation system, though simple in format, trumped many advanced evaluation systems later developed by state universities,

At the beginning, the evaluation was pretty simple. Students only gave us "grading" on a scale of five to one. It was like excellent, or good, or fail. Nowadays Chinese universities also ask students to evaluate teachers; students are asked lots of detailed questions, like "how is the academic level" and "how

does the professor present the class." Now looking back, we might have lost
the gist of it if Supernova had adopted a complex evaluation system like that.
At that time, what mattered was whether students were happy. What mattered
was whether they thought they had a cool experience in our classes.

(Informant No. 7)

More importantly, evaluation was tightly connected with teacher income
at Supernova. Since working for an SEO was based on hourly wages without
any base salary, the income of a teacher was made up of three parts: (a) per-
class hourly wage (with each class usually 2.5 hours), (b) number of classes
assigned to teach, and (c) a bonus. All three parts were based on Su's decisions and his negotiations with teachers, instead of any formal or transparent formula. Su used student evaluation as the basis for a teacher's per-class
hourly wage, number of assigned classes, and bonuses, although he also took
into account teacher's credentials and seniority.

As Supernova and its teachers became increasingly popular in the mid-
1990s, other SEOs in TOEFL/GRE and the Chinese Graduate Exam followed
suit and adopted similar market-based evaluation systems. The diffusion of
this evaluation system altered the relationship between SEOs and teachers:
teachers were transformed from authoritative figures to service providers.
According to two former Supernova teachers, what mattered most under
the new student evaluation system was making students happy (Informants
No. 5, No. 31).[12] An investigative report on Supernova provides a clue to the
market-based evaluation:

> It is not easy to become a Supernova teacher. Among those Supernova teach-
> ers who were kicked out by students from their teaching posts, there were pro-
> fessors from Capital University and Masters and PhD degree holders. There is
> only one standard here—whether students are satisfied and whether teaching
> is effective, regardless of whether you are a professor or whether you are a
> Masters or PhD degree holder. In a university's class, it does not matter if a
> professor teaches well. If a teacher presents his/her class well, students will be
> listening; otherwise, students can just leave. Not here at Supernova. Students
> have paid!
>
> (Lu 2002, 47)

Apparently, this market-based evaluation reduced the bargaining power
of teachers who were still faculty members of state universities. This is because their bargaining power used to be associated with their credentials, seniority, and low level of dependence on SEOs, but these factors mattered less
when market-based evaluation was used as the primary indicator for their

performance. Having said that, market-based evaluation empowered teachers in a new way. It gave students the power to manufacture star teachers. The bargaining power of star teachers was elevated. As the chef metaphor suggests, now student evaluation—a form of market force—can manufacture a star chef and jeopardize the survival of the restaurant.

To prevent opportunism by star teachers, Su rarely put teacher names in advertisements as many competitors did. A former teacher and former branch school president at Supernova commented,

> Supernova rarely put teachers' names on those posters or advertisement. Many other SEOs did that. Su was concerned about whether our teachers would become too arrogant and would leave to establish their own SEOs. Another thing was that there might be emergencies. If you put someone's name on the flyers, what happens if this teacher is sick? What are you going to tell students if the teacher they have is different from the flyers?
>
> (Informant No. 22)

SPECIALIZED TEACHING AND THE COTEACHING MODEL

Supernova took taming to a new level by upgrading the general teaching model to specialized teaching, and further still to a coteaching model. General teaching refers to the model under which a teacher is responsible for covering multiple and even all subjects of a test.[13] As I expand on in the next chapter, this model fits the idea that preparing for the TOEFL/GRE was about improving well-rounded language competency.

A veteran teacher who previously taught in multiple SEOs discussed how Questing, one of the earliest nonstate and intellectual SEOs, adopted the general model:

> Questing was initially giving lessons in English [as a second language], and I remember they used a comprehensive English textbook published by a professor from the Central College of Foreign Languages. But later students started to ask for TOEFL classes. You know, student demand triggered the boom of the industry. That was 1986 or 1987. Questing's boss heard some good things about Ma Tiannan. [At that time] Ma was [still] a graduate student at the Central College of Foreign Languages. . . .
>
> So Questing's boss just gave the entire TOEFL course to Ma and told him, "You will teach everything, from listening [and] grammar to reading and writing." At that time, there was not much specialization.
>
> (Informant No. 65)

In the 1980s and early 1990s, the taken-for-granted model for teaching English was having one teacher cover listening, grammar, reading, and writing. The vast majority of SEOs in Beijing started with this generalized model (Informants No. 11, No. 61). Even by the late 1990s, when Supernova had wiped out other local competitors and made the general model outdated in Beijing, leading SEOs in Shanghai were still asking one teacher to cover all TOEFL subjects (Informant No. 23).

Supernova took the lead in the transition into a specialized teaching. Under this new model, a teacher specialized in teaching one subject or a few related subjects. For example, some teachers only taught TOEFL listening classes, while others were only responsible for TOEFL writing. The initial consideration for adopting this specialized approach was reducing boredom. According to one of the founding members of Supernova, "at that time we had forty classes for one TOEFL course. So if students had the same teacher [and this teacher teaches all forty classes], this teacher would become a boring guy no matter how funny he is" (Informant No. 4).

When Supernova began implementing the specialized model, it did not carry out the model systematically. It was not uncommon for one teacher to cover multiple subjects but for another to specialize in one subject. There was also variation across different tests. Compared to TOEFL, GRE remained in the general model for a longer time. As a former star teacher at Supernova recalled, "There was no systematic specialization. In GRE classes, for a while we only had the division between the verbal section and the quantitative section" (Informant No. 5). Table 3.1, shown earlier, also supports this claim: the three TOEFL teachers worked under the specialized model while the GRE teacher worked under the general model.

Shortly after, Supernova further upgraded specialized teaching to a coteaching model. Under this model, any course had to be taught by multiple teachers, with each teacher specializing in one particular subject. For example, a typical Supernova TOEFL course had four teachers, one for TOEFL listening, one for TOEFL grammar, one for TOEFL reading, and one for TOEFL writing. At the end of the course, the performance of each teacher was perfectly comparable because the same group of students was evaluating all teachers.

Su upgraded specialized teaching to coteaching to check and balance the bargaining power of teachers. As one of the founding members of Supernova recalled:

Another issue [for the old teaching model] was that it was not comparable [when one teacher taught a whole course]. This teacher would think he was doing a pretty good job. Students would have no one with whom to compare to the teacher, and they would not know whether this teacher was good or not. But if you ask four teachers to go into the same classroom, students will immediately find out who does not teach well and this guy will be under a lot of pressure. It is actually a competitive system in a benign way. It is about making teachers check, balance, and compete with each other. And if we have a teacher specialize in one section, that teacher is more likely to excel in this section.

(Informant No. 4)

Although this coteaching model seems to come with obvious advantages, few competitors imitated what Supernova did. A Supernova senior manager sent me his analytical essays on the K-12 submarket in 2015, and he explained in one of the essays why the coteaching model was so difficult to adopt:

Other SEOs usually avoided this coteaching model because it was difficult to handle. Teachers differed from each other substantially, so students would complain [about the different styles]; teachers also competed with each other, so there were attacks and even smear campaigns against each other in front of students, which led to intensification of internal conflict. The Supernova founder resisted pressure and pushed for this model, whose benefits far exceeded the expectation of the designer. This coteaching model breaks an English course into multiple parts. Each teacher is only responsible for one part and will polish his/her teaching under the incentive of student evaluations, which will push teachers to go beyond their limit in teaching.

(Supernova Archive No. 20)

As this quotation suggests, the effects of Su's reform, especially the effects of coupling the coteaching model with market-based evaluations, went beyond his expectation. This coupling transformed teaching into a Burawoyian game:[14] teachers became intrigued about competing with each other for higher evaluations. As a former top leader at Supernova and a current entrepreneur of another SEO said, the competition among teachers unfolded along at least three lines: competition between teachers of the same class, competition among teachers working on the same subject, and potential competition among teachers working on related subjects, such as among teachers of TOEFL listening and IELTS listening (Informant No. 13).

The coteaching model also had a long-term effect: it crippled teachers' capacity for exit-and-entrepreneurship. Since each teacher only taught a small portion of TOEFL/GRE classes under the coteaching model, it was much less likely than before for him or her to quit and establish an SEO by himself or herself for two reasons. First, any individual teacher under the coteaching model lacked the comprehensive knowledge of a test to singlehandedly carry out his or her entrepreneurship. In comparison, teachers under the previous general model were able to cover all subjects, thus an individual teacher could act like a well-rounded chef to establish and support his or her "restaurant." Second, coordination and cooperation were a daunting task under the coteaching model because of the intensified competition among teachers. Thus, concerted exit-and-entrepreneurship by a group of teachers at the same time became difficult, if not impossible. The Supernova senior manager I cited previously provides further details about the crippling effect of the coteaching model:

> On its face, this model is only beneficial to the improvement of teacher capacity. From another perspective, a teacher can only teach one section of the test and lacks the capacity to teach the entire course. Teachers like this, even if possessed of high teaching capacity, do not dare to leave Supernova with the expectation of easily starting an entrepreneurship. Put it in another way, even if a teacher like this leaves Supernova, he can take neither students nor reputation with him. For an example, it is impossible for students to give up lessons on grammar, reading, and writing because a vocabulary teacher leaves. And four elite teachers who coteach a class usually have some opinions [against each other], so the probability of them leaving together is smaller than the probability of four vice presidents of a company leaving at the same time.
>
> Here some readers might ask, "Are these teachers stupid? Why don't they teach a wide variety of courses?" These teachers are not stupid at all, but there is a trap here. A person's time and energy are limited. If you teach a wide variety of courses, each one of your subjects is most likely to lag behind those who only teach one subject. You won't be able to match the level of the leading teacher, so you are afraid to leave. If you only teach a single subject, you are still afraid to leave because you cannot cover the whole course by yourself.
>
> (Supernova Archive No. 20)

Conclusion

This chapter examines the internal power dynamics between SEO teachers and their employers as well as the implications of such power dynamics on the rise of opportunist SEOs. I highlight opportunistic practices that violate cooperation norms between the two parties. I show that the institutional environment during China's early stages of market transition and the ways in which early SEOs were organized at that time gave rise to rampant opportunistic practices by teachers, such as dumping classes and pulling students away. Compared to intellectual SEOs, which often succumbed to teacher opportunism, opportunist SEOs were more likely to survive teacher opportunism due to entrepreneurs' opportunistic defenses. By the early 1990s, opportunist

SEOs had not only outcompeted state SEOs but also pushed intellectual SEOs to the periphery of the market. Faculty members and educators associated with the state education system no longer formed the major entrepreneurial force afterward. As the vibrant model of nonstate organizations, opportunist SEOs became the only prototype of private enterprises in this industry.

The last part of this chapter features a few new developments in teacher management by leading opportunist SEO entrepreneurs. I emphasize how reforms on teacher evaluation and specialization dwarfed teachers by weakening their bargaining power. These new efforts did not necessarily violate cooperation norms, but they surely increased the replaceability of teachers. I also show that some SEOs went farther than others in utilizing these new developments. For example, Supernova's market-based teacher evaluation and coteaching model, though initially not designed against opportunism, had the effect of curbing teacher opportunism. These new developments in teacher management set the stage for the topic of the next chapter—opportunism in terms of breaking from pedagogical norms.

4

Not Much English Taught at Our English School

A foreign language is a weapon in the struggle of life. The TOEFL test, for many Chinese students, is a fight against their destiny. . . . In April 1989, before I went abroad, I signed up for a "TOEFL Intensive Course" at a foreign language SEO called Guanghua. . . . What attracted me in the advertisement of this SEO was that "courses are taught by overseas returnees with US master's degrees and US citizens."

QIAN NING (1996, 42–44)

The second sin of Supernova is that it does not take English as English. What is English [according to Supernova teachers]? It is the key to the US, a bunch of symbols that can help you climb the social ladder—Supernova thinks that is what English is; they have turned English into vocabulary, and vocabulary into jokes.

LU YUEGANG (2002, 112) citing a Supernova student

Karl Marx once proclaimed, "A foreign language is a weapon in the struggle of life."[1] He may have foreseen the growing importance of English when he said that. But he could not have predicted how far Chinese youth would take English-learning during their struggles for overseas studies. Together, Chinese students and teachers have developed myriad ways of conquering English and English-based standardized tests, such as the TOEFL. The two quotations that serve as epigraphs to this chapter offer a stark contrast between the popular pedagogy of the TOEFL in the 1980s and that of the late 1990s. Since the early 1990s, crafting a novel and distinct pedagogy has become a key in the competition within the group of opportunist SEOs.[2]

The TOEFL in the 1980s was, as Qian's (1996) aforementioned quotation suggests and as test designers intended, largely a test of English as a foreign language. If we were to sign up for a TOEFL preparation course in Beijing in this period of time, our course would most likely be structured for enhancing our well-rounded language competency and proficiency. Our teachers would probably be state university faculty members of English who checked our progress with quizzes and homework. Courses taught by native English speakers were also popular among students.

The second quotation presents a contrasting picture of a TOEFL course in the late 1990s and early 2000s—it is no longer only about English. If we were to attend a TOEFL class then, we would most likely travel to Beijing and sit in a large Supernova classroom with hundreds of fellow students. In Supernova classes, we can expect two distinct elements: test-cracking skills, and jokes and motivational stories systematically prepared by Supernova teachers. Some students, such as the one Lu (2002) cited in the epigraph to the chapter, considered incorporating these elements a "sin." But many Supernova students welcomed this approach and idolized Supernova teachers as superstars. With the help of this distinct teaching approach, Supernova had wiped out most of its local competitors, controlling over 80 percent of the TOEFL/GRE market share in Beijing and over 50 percent for all of China by 2000 (Lin 2020).

Until 2010, Supernova's approach to teaching—large class size, noninteractive lectures with heavy emphasis on test-cracking skills, jokes and motivational stories, and rigid class schedules—was touted as its winning formula and continued to thrive as the most popular approach in the TOEFL/GRE submarket. This approach is in stark contrast with the selling points of US and Canadian SEOs: small class, interactive pedagogy, and flexible schedule.

This chapter focuses on the evolution of the prominent teaching model in the TOEFL/GRE submarket as well as its implications for the competition dynamics, privatization, and marketization of the Education Industry. By the early 1990s, a relatively clear teaching norm[3] had taken shape: teaching and learning the TOEFL and GRE were about enhancing English language proficiency.[4] From then on, some opportunist SEOs engaged in opportunistic practices of breaking away from these existing teaching norms.

I begin with an inquiry into the competition among opportunist SEOs and their divergent trajectories in engaging in opportunistic practices. Of particular interest is how some SEOs primarily involved breaking regulations and cooperation norms, while other SEOs shifted the focus of their opportunistic practices to deviating from existing teaching norms. I show that the degree to which opportunist SEO entrepreneurs were embedded in the state education system was an indicator of the divergence among these SEOs: although compared to entrepreneurs of state and intellectual SEOs, opportunist SEO founders were in general only tangentially connected to the state education system, those moderately marginal entrepreneurs who had worked in the state education system prior to their entrepreneurship were more deeply embedded in the system than others. With access to both the state education system and the informal economy, these moderately marginal entrepreneurs revolutionized the teaching norms of the Education Industry. Although marginal entrepreneurs in general had the upper hand in their competition with state and intellectual SEO entrepreneurs in the 1980s and early 1990s, in the competition afterwards among marginal entrepreneurs the winners were those less marginal and more deeply embedded in the state education system.

I illustrate how some moderately marginal entrepreneurs not only broke away from existing teaching norms but also developed new ones. Although both Pioneers and Supernova transformed TOEFL/GRE training from English classes to test-cracking skills, Supernova went one step further and instilled in students a new norm—good TOEFL/GRE teachers and classes ought to be motivational, patriotic, and entertaining.

Supernova built the mass teaching model by blending the new norm with a new group of young teachers, large class size, high pay for teachers, and other organizational repertoires. The mass teaching model was crystalized after these elements became interdependent and reached a relatively stable configuration.[5] The mass teaching model was integral to Supernova's rise to dominance in China's TOEFL/GRE market. At the end of this chapter, I present Roaring English—an opportunist SEO and market leader in the spoken English submarket—as an additional case. I elucidate how Roaring English developed its own version of the mass teaching model and how its success largely fits the pattern illustrated by the Supernova case.

From Teaching English to Coaching Test-Cracking Skills

Not all opportunist SEOs were able to break free of the existing norms of teaching. The extent to which an entrepreneur was embedded in the state education system is an indicator of whether he or she is a highly marginal or moderately marginal entrepreneur as well as how far his or her SEO could deviate from existing norms. Overall, moderately marginal entrepreneurs who had worked in the state education system were more likely to move beyond disrupting laws and regulations, and shift their focus to revolutionizing teaching norms.

Table 4.1 compares the degree of embeddedness in the state education system among the four opportunist SEO entrepreneurs. The degree of embeddedness for Seven Swords and Cornerstone entrepreneurs is low because neither entrepreneur had worked in the state education system prior to their foray into entrepreneurship. Pioneers' entrepreneur had a high degree of embeddedness: Ma Tiannan had been a student and junior faculty member in

TABLE 4.1. The Degree to Which Entrepreneurs Are Embedded in the State Education System

	Degree of Embeddedness in the State Education System	Went to College?	Conducted Teaching?
Seven Swords	Low	No	No
Cornerstone	Low	No	No
Pioneers	High	Yes	Yes
Supernova	Medium	Yes	Yes

Sources: Multiple informants

a state university prior to becoming an entrepreneur, and he continued to teach full time at this university after he founded Pioneers. In comparison, Su Leidong of Supernova had a moderate degree of embeddedness. He had also been a student and a junior faculty member at a top-three state university, but he had quit the university teaching position before he founded Supernova. In accordance with their low level of embeddedness, the entrepreneurs of Seven Swords and Cornerstone had never gone to college and did not teach in their SEOs. In contrast, the entrepreneurs behind Pioneers and Supernova had gone to college and were the major teaching force at their respective SEOs.

The disparate levels of entrepreneurial embeddedness led their SEOs to divergent trajectories. Most notably, differentiated embeddedness was associated with varying levels of access to teaching resources, such as teachers and facilities. Indeed, Seven Swords and Cornerstone also started with faculty members from state universities, but they lacked access to high-quality teaching resources, especially reliable resources from elite state universities. These two SEOs lost their edge soon after one or two star teachers left.

In contrast, Supernova's first-generation teachers came exclusively from Capital University's English Department (Informants No. 4, No. 28; Supernova Archive No. 5). Although these teachers did not stay long, their presence left students with the impression that Supernova's teachers received solid training and were trustworthy. In addition to teachers, in the early 1990s Su used his former colleague connections to access Capital University's language lab for TOEFL listening classes (Informants No. 9, No. 73). While many students in other SEOs were complaining about the poor sound quality of old-fashioned cassette players in front of large classrooms, for a while some Supernova students were able to sit in the lab and put on modern headsets.

Different levels of embeddedness of these entrepreneurs in the state education system also led to their diverse approaches to teachers and teaching. As mentioned in the previous chapter, Pioneers and Supernova entrepreneurs were more capable of fending off teachers' opportunistic practices than the other two founders because the former group undertook teaching themselves. Since the founders of Seven Swords and Cornerstone did not teach themselves, they had to depend on others as teachers. Some teachers were emboldened by this situation. They felt that they could do anything they wanted. For example, teachers at Seven Swords recruited students for themselves by "using the school title in posters they printed by themselves" (Informant No. 17). Founders of Seven Swords and Cornerstone had to use hardline approaches to grapple with teacher opportunism. The Seven Swords founder scolded and hit teachers to keep them in line (Informant No. 65). To be sure, the founders of Pioneers and Supernova also used opportunism against opportunistic teachers. Nonetheless, these two founders did not limit their opportunistic practices to breaking rules or defying cooperation norms. They upgraded their teacher management arrangements.

When TOEFL/GRE courses were first offered in the 1980s, it was accepted among teachers that teaching TOEFL/GRE was the equivalent of improving students' English proficiency. TOEFL/GRE teachers, most of whom were English faculty members and teachers, emphasized a well-rounded program of listening, reading, and writing as language foundations. For them, students could only achieve high scores if they improved their English proficiency. Accordingly, these teachers frowned on the idea that preparing for the TOEFL/ GRE requires only decoding test question patterns.

Pioneers and Supernova founders took the lead in reorienting teaching attention from building English language proficiency to drilling test-cracking skills. These two entrepreneurs pushed the change by personally exploring new teaching styles. Ma Tiannan of Pioneers not only emphasized the vitality of improving English proficiency but also dived into Barron's test preparation books and authentic test materials, summarizing the test question patterns (Informant No. 65). He also asked his teachers to "cover more authentic past test questions in class so that students would be happy" (Informant No. 17).

Su Leidong of Supernova also found it imperative to concentrate on test-cracking skills when teaching TOEFL. As described in the previous chapter, Su and the first-generation Supernova teachers could not see eye to eye with each other. One of the reasons for their disagreement was that Su blamed these teachers for emphasizing English over test-cracking skills (Supernova Archive No. 5). Su criticized the way they taught the TOEFL and compared their approach to his own:

> These "academic school" teachers taught TOEFL Reading classes the same way they taught English at universities. They just pedantically analyzed one sentence after another, and they analyzed grammar and vocabulary. As a re-

sult, they often couldn't finish one long paragraph of reading in a single class, while I could finish seven to eight paragraphs. When they taught listening, they could only cover about ten dialogues, but I covered more than a hundred dialogues. Then students started to give me feedback. Their first complaint was that they did not get enough information from these "academic school" teachers. The second complaint was that these teachers' classes were entirely academic and pedantic. Their teaching was not specifically designed for test-preparation, and these teachers had not even taken the TOEFL test themselves. The third complaint was that these teachers could not teach in a passionate and lively manner. They did not teach with charming language or a sense of humor or anything pertaining to the characteristics of our time.

(Ibid., 64–65)

Su himself explored various ways to unpack and deliver test-cracking skills in class. For example, he collected all of the available authentic past GRE test materials and conducted a statistical analysis on the frequency of the vocabulary used. This analysis was the foundation of his best seller on GRE vocabulary. In this book and in his classes, he applied mnemonics, including some that were self-designed, so that Chinese students could memorize a corpus of GRE words in a short period of time. The way he taught how to memorize the meaning of *charisma*, as documented in one of the audio recordings of his lectures, is a classic example: "We can remember the meaning of 'charisma' by breaking it down: think about 'cha' as China, think about 'ris' as rise, and 'ma' as (Chairman) Mao. Mao rises in China. Mao is a political leader with *meili*.[6] Now it is fairly easy for us to remember that 'charisma' means *meili*" (Supernova Archive No. 7).

In addition to applying mnemonics, he demanded his teachers develop their own test-cracking tricks by decoding authentic past test materials. Since no ETS official guide was published in China in the 1980s and 1990s, teachers and Su had to compare notes to reach the best guess about the correct answer. Then teachers analyzed the frequency and patterns of test questions and answers. As shown in the second quotation at the beginning of this chapter, some teachers promoted "magic skills" based on their analyses. A book published by a star Supernova teacher, based on his class recordings, summarizes some of these "magic skills" as follows:

Test makers at ETS will never distort the reality [of the US society]. Their so-called principle of test making determines this. For example, there are lots of TOEFL listening questions that are about concerts. Whenever they talk about concerts, the topics are always the same: only good comments, not a single bad word! All those questions and answers are saying how nice last night's concert was. What a wonderful time we had. . . . So there is no need for us to develop excellent listening comprehension capacity. As long as we can figure out that the question is about a concert, and one of the answer choices says, "The concert is excellent," that is the correct answer. . . .

There are also many TOEFL listening questions about food and related situations. Whenever they talk about apple pie, the answer is definitely "delicious." You never make mistakes if you choose an answer that implies "delicious." When they talk about pizza, the answer is always awful. If you don't believe it, you can check all the authentic TOEFL test materials.

(L. Wu 1998, 7–8)

Su not only asked his teachers to focus on test-cracking skills but also preferred them to be lively, passionate, and humorous in class. This is why the student quoted at the beginning of this chapter complained that Supernova classes turned English into jokes. The same student goes further to comment on how Supernova not only made TOEFL less about English but also made tests less about tests:

> The fourth sin of Supernova is that it does not consider tests to be tests. If you open Supernova class notes, you will see many astonishing skills for cracking tests. Quite a few teachers claim that you can get most of the listening comprehension questions right even if you don't listen. . . . The way Supernova teaches us to crack English tests is like asking elementary school students to pass an IQ test: check the answer "delicious" when you hear or see "ice cream" in the question.
>
> (Lu 2002, 112)

Arguably, coaching students with such test-cracking skills is opportunistic to the extent that such coaching deviated from existing teaching norms and the intended goal of the test. More importantly, most of these test-cracking skills aim at finding a short cut—figuring out correct answers without systematically enhancing language proficiency.

While both Su and Ma took the lead in adopting such opportunistic practices, Su went one step further. Su and his teachers not only shifted their focus from English to test-cracking skills but also further developed new teaching norms that featured noneducational elements, such as motivational stories, nationalist comments, and entertaining performances. The next section shows that Su and his teachers developed this new norm to such a systematic level that few SEOs in other countries have achieved.[7]

That Su went further than Ma in revolutionizing the teaching norm mirrors their differentiated embeddedness in the state education system: Su had already quit his job at Capital University prior to his foray into entrepreneurship, whereas Ma kept his position as a full-time faculty member at the

Central College of Foreign Languages while operating Pioneers. After cross-checking multiple interviewees, I confirmed that Su was one of the earliest state university faculty members in Haidian District to dedicate himself to the Education Industry business as a full-time entrepreneur (Informants No. 8, No. 9, No. 61, No. 65). When leaving the university, Su had fewer entanglements from the English education establishment than other part-time entrepreneurs. He "had no choice but to walk toward the end of the tunnel" (Informant No. 65).[8] In comparison, Ma has been intertwined with the orthodox English-teaching community.

Mass Teaching as a New Teaching Model

An entrepreneur's social embeddedness is an indicator for how far his or her SEO will deviate from existing teaching norms. However, this indicator does not determine whether a new norm will be established. Nor does this indicator provide a clue to how a new teaching model will take shape.

This section demonstrates how Supernova crafted and crystalized mass teaching as the new and dominant model for teaching the TOEFL and GRE. I start with performative pedagogy, the core of mass teaching. Then I illustrate how multiple components of mass teaching reinforced each other and eventually became interdependent.

PERFORMATIVE PEDAGOGY AS THE CORE

As the content core of mass teaching, performative pedagogy prioritizes elements that are not directly related to educational materials. These noneducational and performative elements, known as *duanzi, chedan, chuishui*, or *xianpian* in Chinese, highlight motivational stories, nationalist comments, and entertaining performances such as jokes, singing, and dancing.[9] After this pedagogy was implemented systematically at Supernova in the mid-1990s,[10] Supernova teachers spent a substantial proportion of their class time on performative elements. According to two Supernova teachers' observation and estimate, teachers at Beijing Supernova School used an average of 20 to 50 percent of their class time on performative elements, and some of their classes were so hilarious that laughter among students could be heard almost every ten minutes (Supernova Archive No. 31).

Motivational stories frame a student's study-abroad process as exceeding his/her limit and completing his/her life. Teachers who resort to motivational stories discuss studying abroad as an end in life, not a means. A former Supernova student recollected what impressed him at Supernova:

In the eyes of Supernova teachers, the US is a place we should and must go. In every ceremony and class, Supernova teachers passionately called upon us to conquer the US. It seems to them that our Chinese students are born for the US. . . . According to Supernova, studying abroad is not a means, but an end. If you can study abroad, you are a winner; otherwise you are a loser. In this massive wave of studying abroad, we should not belittle the role of Supernova. I do not know if we have thought about what we would do after we go abroad. Probably we are studying abroad simply for the sake of studying abroad.

Lu (2002, 112)

Since overseas study is a must in life, one's life is incomplete if one does not study abroad, according to a Supernova's internal publication for students (Supernova Archive No. 4). Only those who aspire to go abroad will enjoy a promising life.

Supernova teachers also depicted the process for preparing for the TOEFL and GRE as an invaluable life experience. To Chinese students, preparing for these standardized tests requires an immense time commitment memorizing vocabulary and taking mock tests over and over. On the one hand, the Supernova founder and teachers framed these processes as boring, exhausting, and frustrating. On the other hand, these processes were, according to Supernova teachers, opportunities for transformation. Such framing is evident in Supernova's motto: "Pursue excellence and challenge limits. Hew from the mountain of despair a stone of hope. Our lives will eventually shine" (Supernova Archive No. 30). According to Su, a person can only transcend himself or herself if he or she can keep fighting for a simple goal, such as mastering GRE vocabulary. In an internal publication for students, he elaborates on this logic as follows:

In our lives, the most touching days are those when we fight for a simple goal wholeheartedly. We should be proud of those tiny and trivial goals. If we put together all those tiny and trivial goals, we will get a magnificent achievement.

(Supernova Archive No. 39, 20)

Other Supernova teachers expanded on this logic. In front of students and a reporter, a well-known GRE teacher at Supernova recalled how he had prepared for the GRE when he was in college:

When I was in college, I often prepared for the GRE in the library until 1:00 a.m. In order to get back to my dorm faster and get enough sleep, I had to take a short cut and climb over a fence. My fellow students and I climbed over it so often that it finally collapsed. The university then had it restored. That broken and restored fence became my most beautiful college memory. It is evidence that I chased my dream every single day like a proud hero.

(Supernova Archive No. 15, 5)

Nationalist comments are the second major discourse category under performative pedagogy. These comments frame studying overseas as learning from the West first and returning to build China later.[11] When using nationalist comments, teachers claimed in class that the reason Chinese students were wasting countless hours on boring tests such as the TOEFL and GRE was because of China's underdevelopment and English's language supremacy (Supernova Archives No. 11, No. 38). Also, teachers would often ask students to imagine what would happen if China were to grow stronger. With jokes and colorful language, teachers would guide students to conclude that a stronger China would spare future generations from the miserable experience of preparing for the TOEFL/GRE. As a star teacher at Supernova proclaimed in class,

> We are preparing for TOEFL today with the purpose of making China really competent so our future generations will never have to prepare for TOEFL. When they [our future generations] become teens as we are now, they can act like American teens, traveling around the world with backpacks, enjoying sunshine, beaches and other beauty in their lives. So they do not have to waste their valuable youth on the boring TOEFL and GRE like their fathers' generation did. Finally, let me give this class my last wish and hope: get out [of China] soon and come back soon.
>
> (Supernova Archive No. 25, 6)

By the same token, teachers would ask students to imagine a new world order under China's leadership. That would be a time when foreigners needed to learn Chinese, to pass "Chinese TOEFL," and even study Chinese calligraphy in order to be admitted to Chinese colleges, as several students described about their learning experience in their essays for Supernova's internal publications and forum (Supernova Archives No. 8, No. 11, No. 43).

Furthermore, performative pedagogy consists of various forms of entertainment performed by teachers in class, such as jokes, banter, singing, and dancing. What made this joking and banter special was that many of them were mocking Su Leidong, and mocking one's boss was unusual in a society that takes authority seriously (Lu 2002). This joking and banter made the Supernova community look democratic and made Su look like a gentleman with tolerance. In addition, some jokes and banter about Su created an image of a hillbilly entrepreneur from a rural area while reminding students how rich and generous he was.

For example, a series of jokes and banter talked about how Su had given wages to teachers in bags of cash. By exaggerating the size of Su's bags and his mysterious ways of stockpiling cash at home, teachers presented a private entrepreneur who was so successful, rustic, and adorable that students expected to meet him. Since Su also cultivated the ritual of personally greeting students in the middle of some summer and winter classes, students' curiosity and expectation about him guaranteed that these greetings always kicked off with storming applause and cheers of students.

To add more suspense and elements of entertainment to stories about Su, teachers even included sex and the role of female teachers. Here is a story a teacher shared in a recorded class:

> Su likes money, but he is a peasant so he does not like putting money into the bank. So what does he do? He hides tons of money in a bucket underneath his bed. When it is time to give wages to teachers, he calls them into his bedroom. In the shocked eyes of those teachers, he starts lifting the bed and pulling bags of money out of the bucket. At the beginning, all we had were male teachers. But later, we had a female teacher. Su told that teacher to come to his house after work, and she complied. Upon arriving, Su told her to come to his bedroom. That girl was terrified and wondered what Su would do to her. When entering the bedroom, the girl was petrified because Su had already started lifting the blanket on the bed. What happened next was even more astonishing to the girl. Su lifted the bed and pulled money out of a bucket!
>
> (Supernova Archive No. 26)

By 1996–97, the performative pedagogy had become the norm of teaching at Supernova. At a time when entertainment choices in China were limited, the aforementioned performative elements appealed to students. The reputation of Supernova teachers as being motivational, patriotic, and funny spread across the country like wildfire. Students came to Supernova with a specific expectation to look for these types of teachers as well as their jokes and performances. Finally, Supernova codified this norm by claiming that its teachers had special characteristics and spirits. A video Supernova prepared for its twelfth anniversary party elaborated on these characteristics and spirits as follows:

> There are three characteristics of Supernova's teachers: they are knowledgeable, righteous, and patriotic. Teachers at Supernova not only need to convey knowledge to, and answer questions from, students. They also need to instill in students patriotism and self-motivation. They need to use their sublime personal quality to influence students. [They should do so] by sharing their self-reflections and experiences, by advocating our national integrity and patriotism, by evoking the confidence of students in being Chinese, by spurring students' learning interests, and by guiding students out of perplexity and running toward success along the right track. These are the essential components of the Supernova Spirits.
>
> (Supernova Archive No. 3)

THE EVOLUTION OF THE PERFORMATIVE PEDAGOGY

How did the performative pedagogy come into existence? Performative pedagogy was not a product of deliberate design but rather the result of long-term trial and error. This process started with, and was an extension of, Su's own teaching.

Su's own teaching style consists of motivational stories and entertaining elements that are based on his own life stories.[12] Before his entrepreneurship, Su's life was not impressive, especially in the eyes of his fellow university students. He was admitted to Capital University after two failed College Entrance Examination experiences. He was looked down on in the university because of his rural background and strong rural accent. After graduating from college, he became a faculty member at Capital University, but it was said that he had this opportunity because many top fellow students opted to study abroad. He was also struggling initially as a junior faculty member. To better compete with his fellow teachers at Capital University and teach his students to never give up, Su incorporated painful experiences and embarrassing moments of his life into his teaching. He also decided to introduce elements that were considered inappropriate in mainstream pedagogy at that time, such as popular English songs and Greek mythology (Supernova Archive No. 5, Informant No. 4).

Regardless of the educational effectiveness of these elements, students started to welcome Su's approach, and he started to build his popularity among students. A longtime faculty member of Capital University's English Department, also a former part-time teacher at Supernova, provided a clue about how popular Su was among students and new teachers. According to her, Su was already a role model for Capital University's new faculty members when she just joined Capital. The English Department's director also asked new faculty members to shadow Su's classes in order to learn some teaching techniques (Informant No. 39).

At Supernova, Su developed his personal teaching style into a pedagogy other teachers could adopt. He accomplished this first by hiring and training a new generation of teachers. I call these the third-generation teachers. Most active between the mid-1990s and early 2000s, they were the major promoters and bedrock of performative pedagogy.

Table 4.2 compares four representatives of the third-generation teachers with those from the second generation. I selected these four third-generation teachers as representatives because they were the most popular among students and became the only teachers selected by Su to be the earliest shareholders.

TABLE 4.2. The Second and the Third Generations of Teachers at Supernova

Generation	Teacher's No.	Education Background	Major	Full Time or Part Time	Course Taught at Supernova
Second Generation	No. 1	BA elite university[a] MA elite university	English	part time	TOEFL Listening
	No. 2	BA elite university	English	part time	TOEFL Vocabulary
	No. 3	PhD elite university	English	part time	TOEFL Grammar
	No. 4	MS elite university	Engineering	part time	GRE Logic and Quantitative
Third Generation	No. 1	BS nonelite university	Engineering	part time to full time	GRE Logic and Quantitative
	No. 2	MS elite university BS nonelite university	Biology	part time to full time	GRE Vocabulary
	No. 3	MS elite university BS nonelite university	English	part time to full time	TOEFL/IELTS
	No. 4	BA elite university	German	part time to full time	GRE Reading

[a] Elite universities are defined as top-ten universities according to overall ranking.
Sources: Supernova Archive No. 2; Lu 2002; multiple informants.

As shown, the profiles of the third generation differ markedly from those of the second generation. First, only one of the third-generation teachers majored in English. In comparison, three out of four second-generation teachers had been trained in English-related majors. And the differences between the two generations lay not only in their majors. All second-generation teachers had attended top-ten elite universities. Among the third-generation teachers, three out of the four finished graduate programs at top-ten elite universities but did not earn their undergraduate degrees at top-ten elite universities, and one never received any education from a top-ten elite university.[13] Furthermore, while all second-generation teachers remained full-time faculty members and administrators in state universities and worked at Supernova part time, third-generation teachers were the earliest group of Supernova teachers to transition from part-time teachers to full-time teachers and managers.

These differences between the two generations led to their disparate levels of motivation for working at Supernova. For second-generation teachers, teaching at Supernova was merely their part-time job for extra income. But for the third-generation teachers, they were motivated to make money at Supernova and were willing to take dramatic actions. In order to win interview opportunities, one of the third-generation teachers stopped Su's car in the middle of the road and another called Su's cell phone under the disguise of an old friend of Su's (Lu 2002). The high level of motivation of the third-generation teachers translated to their commitment to the job. To shine as star teachers at Supernova, they were willing to spend dozens of hours preparing for a single lesson (Informant No. 46).

The change in social backgrounds of the second-generation and third-generation teachers was not a mere coincidence but began because Su Leidong altered his hiring standards. By the mid-1990s, Su had realized that popular teachers did not have to have majored in English. In fact, some of the best second-generation teachers, though they had superb academic qualifications, could not capture the hearts of students because their poor presentation skills made their classes like "pouring dumplings out of the mouth of a kettle" (Informant No. 4).[14] Therefore, Su shifted the emphasis to nonacademic qualifications, such as public speaking ability.

Under this new standard, the newly hired third-generation teachers were a group of people who often spoke in an exaggerated and showy fashion in public and who dared to talk about anything (Informants No. 1, No. 5). Not having majored in English, these teachers were also prone to talk about topics broader than those typically covered by English teachers. A faculty member at an elite state university recalled an unforgettable experience when he was still a college student and was attending Supernova in the summer. He described how Teacher Deng, one of the four representative third-generation teachers, blew him away:

> This Teacher Deng was quite a character. He taught GRE Vocabulary. If he showed superb capacity in English vocabulary, that was natural. But his class was filled with all the detailed and insightful analysis of Jin Yong's *wuxia* novels.[15] I considered myself sort of an expert in this field, you know. But that a teacher of GRE Vocabulary could know Jin Yong so well really blew me away.
> (Informant No. 21)

The third-generation teachers directly participated in developing the performative pedagogy. Although Su's personal style drove the change, the process through which this pedagogy matured was collective and experimental. Third-generation teachers developed patterns of performative discourses through trial and error: because students react positively to an improvised discourse, teachers realized the effect of a discourse and kept modifying the

discourse in subsequent classes. A former Supernova star teacher and shareholder recounted the process:

> At the very beginning, those non-educational elements (*xianpian*) were some-
> what improvised. . . . But if you say something in a class and you find it wel-
> comed by students, you will continue talking about it in the next class. If you
> say something and students have no response, you will stop talking about it.
> So after numerous rounds of trial and error, every sentence you say becomes
> of interest to students.
>
> (Informant No. 5)

Since crafting a performative element is a trial-and-error process, it usually requires a long time for a piece of such pedagogy to become entertaining
or motivational. The fact that Supernova teachers often repeatedly taught a
large number of similar courses helped these teachers modify a piece. More
importantly, this trial-and-error process means that veteran teachers and
teachers with high student evaluations, who have more classes to teach, have
more opportunities to practice. As for new teachers and those whose evaluations are stumbling, developing performative pedagogy is a formidable task
because these teachers are often assigned fewer classes. In other words, this
trial-and-error process favors well-established teachers. The star teacher I
just quoted commented on this situation:

> In such a situation, new teachers found it difficult to survive because they did
> not have enough classes to make a living and for practice. At that time, Su
> did not care whether he could train new teachers. He was more concerned
> about making students happy. His priority was to "nail students down (*gaod-
> ing xuesheng*)," to make them stay and put their money into his pocket first.
>
> (Informant No. 5)

To systematically and rapidly reproduce performative pedagogy among
new teachers, Su recorded his own and veteran teachers' classes. Many new
teachers learned about how to present performative elements by simply listening to cassettes and imitating what they heard.[16] Tape recorders sped up
Supernova's training of new teachers. This is especially true when new teachers needed to prepare performative elements for a newly assigned class in a
short period of time.

As the formula for crafting performative elements became increasingly
clear to all Supernova teachers, they learned how to design their own performative elements. Teachers invented and shared formulas for performative
elements. One of the formulas is combining motivational and entertaining
elements. Below are two stories that were variants of the same story and that
were created with this formula.

Example 1: A girl got on a bus to attend a Supernova class. On this crowded bus, a boy's T-shirt caught the girl's attention. There was a line on the T-shirt— "GRE AT WALL." The girl could not understand it and murmured, "Why was GRE at the wall?" When she got to the class and asked another student about this, the other student laughed and told her to put the letters together. It was "GREAT WALL."

(Lu 2002, 109)

Example 2: A boy was about to take the GRE. He put great effort into it and recited Su's Red Bible even while he was walking. One day, this boy saw a girl who was wearing a T-shirt that had English letters on it. He came closer and found that the letters were "GRE AT WALL." The boy was thinking, "What does 'GRE AT WALL' mean? Why is GRE at a wall?" The boy followed the girl to her apartment. The girl saw him and asked, "Why are you following me?" The boy told her about the strange words on her back, and the girl said, "My T-shirt says GREAT WALL."

(Lu 2002, 110)

Combining motivational and entertaining elements, these stories attempt to dramatize the behaviors of GRE-addicted students and use such behaviors to motivate other students.

THE CRYSTALLIZATION OF MASS TEACHING

Mass teaching as a model includes more than performative pedagogy. It entails a stable configuration of seven components: (a) performative pedagogy; (b) large class size, with average student/teacher ratio exceeding 100 to 1;[17] (c) low tuition; (d) high wages for teachers; (e) non-English-major teachers; (f) a market-based evaluation system; and (g) the coteaching model. At the outset, Su Leidong and teachers did not adopt a component with a deliberate goal of matching it with another, although it was natural to use large class size and low tuition given the socioeconomic context in the 1990s. Over time, these elements gradually coupled with each other.

It was common for TOEFL/GRE SEOs in Beijing in the early 1990s to cram over 100 students into one classroom (Informants No. 17, No. 4, No. 65). This is because student demand was high and most students were concentrated in Haidian District. In other words, the large class size was initially a result of the demand rather than a deliberate design by SEOs. In light of the socioeconomic development and the large class model, all SEOs started with low tuition. Su cut the tuition even lower to cannibalize his competitors. In a local market where all competitors fought for the same group of students for survival, "having one more student in my class means one less in competitors' classrooms" (Informant No. 17).

Moreover, Su provided his teachers with high wages (Informants No. 4, No. 17). The coexistence of the low tuition and high wages was possible thanks to the large class sizes and hence high profit margin. At the beginning, Su also undertook much of the teaching and marketing himself to reduce cost. For a typical TOEFL class consisting of forty sessions, Su typically taught twenty sessions without pay, so that the tuition revenue could cover the wages of the other teachers (Informant No. 4). Su also conducted his own marketing, such as putting up posters and distributing flyers. These practices allowed Su to offer his teachers higher pay than his competitors could.

In the mid-1990s, Supernova teachers' wages reached a level that was double those of teachers at other SEOs. Star TOEFL/GRE teachers at Supernova earned over RMB 1,000 per session during this era when the average monthly income for Chinese was below RMB 1,000.[18] Although there was considerable variation among teachers and over time, the consensus was that Supernova teachers' incomes were as high as Chinese entrepreneurs and even exceeded those of the average Harvard University professor during the late 1990s and early 2000s (Informant No. 36; Lu 2002, 162). Su's low price drew students from his competitors, and in the meantime, his high wages turned competing SEOs into teacher training schools for Supernova.

Over time, the seven components of mass teaching were so intermeshed that they became interdependent. For example, the coteaching model and the performative pedagogy reinforced each other. Asking students to evaluate multiple teachers for the same class presupposes putting the evaluation more on comparable standards, such as humor, and less on educational and academic capacity. In addition, the coteaching model pressured teachers of the same class to learn from each other's performative pedagogy as well as use pedagogy to roast each other in order to earn higher evaluations in this highly competitive evaluation system.

Similarly, there is compatibility between market-based teacher evaluation and performative pedagogy. The market-based evaluation system put the power of evaluation in the hands of students. Since students were experts of neither English nor tests, their standards deemphasized academics and prioritized whether a teacher was motivational, funny, or patriotic. Having said that, spending too much time on jokes and other noneducational content can hurt a teacher's evaluation. The key, according to a veteran teacher, was balancing educational content and noneducational as well as "using whatever means to make students like you" (Informant No. 31). Some teachers went so far as to use misleading information to win admiration from students. For example, there were teachers who exaggerated their capacity to recite English-Chinese dictionaries, and there were others who bragged about their astronomical wages or education experience in front of students (Informants No. 31, No. 38). A famous teacher even made up stories about how he took care of his disabled girlfriend in order to make students feel touched in classes (Luo Yonghao 2010, 40–42).

Furthermore, large class sizes added to the necessity and potency of the performative pedagogy.[19] To begin with, large classes made it extremely difficult, if not impossible, to monitor the educational gains of students through checking homework or organizing quizzes. Compared to monitoring student educational gains, using student impressions as the foundation for teacher evaluation was logistically more feasible for these large classes. In addition, large crowds rendered stories more poignant and jokes more hilarious than had they been when performed for a small group. As a veteran teacher recalled, telling a joke in front of five hundred students feels like "students' laughter would lift the roof and storm you in waves"(Informant No. 31).

Since student experience was the foundation of evaluation, Supernova teachers and managers also rode on unfavorable circumstances to evoke favorable experience of students. During summers when there were blackouts or high temperatures, for example, Supernova staff lit candles or put huge ice cubes in classrooms to continue teaching (Informants No. 9, No. 13, No. 22). Learning with candles or ice cubes gave students the impression that they were overcoming obstacles to pursue their dream. In this atmosphere, teaching and learning were turned into a sacred experience (Lu 2002, 245).

By the late 1990s, a systematic mass teaching model had taken shape. Under this model, a large class with hundreds of students no longer appeared by accident. Rather, a particular kind of pedagogy, a peculiar group of teachers and related evaluation system systematically produced large classes. Large classes were so taken for granted that even the student-teacher ratio for some of Supernova's spoken English classes was as high as, and sometimes higher than, 100 to 1 (Supernova Archive No. 5). Classrooms across Supernova branch schools in the 2000s were structured to house hundreds of students. Students in the back rows had to rely on TV-like monitors that were attached to ceilings and dispersed across classrooms' rear and corners in order to see teachers and their blackboard writing clearly. As all elements became interdependent with each other, mass teaching crystallized.

Mass Teaching and Supernova's Dominance

By the late 1990s, Supernova has become a monopolistic player in Beijing's TOEFL/GRE submarket and a dominant brand across China. Figure 4.1

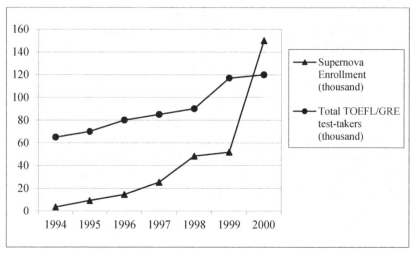

FIGURE 4.1. Annual Enrollment in Supernova Compared with Total TOEFL and GRE Test Takers in China

Note: The only available data for the number of GRE test takers in China during this period is in 2000 when 10,161 candidates took the test (correspondence with ETS). The number of TOEFL test takers in China in the same year was 110,364 (D. Qian 2010), tenfold higher than that of GRE test takers. The number of GRE test takers increased rapidly during 1999–2000 because ETS launched the computer-based GRE in China in 1999. Therefore, it is safe to infer that the number of GRE test takers is no more than one-tenth of that of TOEFL test takers between 1994 and 1999. I obtain the total number of each year by adding the number of TOEFL test takers and the inferred number of GRE test takers in that year.
Sources: Lu (2002) and D. Qian (2010).

provides a clue to Supernova's dominance. As we can see, in the 1990s Supernova's annual enrollment increased at a faster pace than the total number of TOEFL and GRE test takers in China. In 1999, when Supernova classes were concentrated in TOEFL/GRE, its annual enrollment had already eclipsed half of the total number of Chinese TOEFL/GRE test takers. Most notably, Supernova's annual enrollment in 2000 even surpassed the total number of Chinese test takers for that year even though Supernova only added two new branches.[20]

Mass teaching was crucial to Supernova's dominance. A group of young and eloquent teachers, when coupled with the iconoclast pedagogy, captivated the hearts of young students. After taking classes at Supernova, students shared their class experiences and teachers' quotes with their friends and classmates. Students enthusiastically told their peers that Supernova teachers and classes were "motivational," "inspirational," "lively," "funny," and even "soul-touching" (Supernova Archive No. 16; Lu 2002).

Mass teaching turned Supernova into a cult. Attending Supernova classes became a fad among Chinese students. Supernova conquered a nationwide market without conducting any nationwide marketing campaign. Because of the word-of-mouth effect, students came from all over China to attend its classes in Beijing. Students had to wait in long lines to sign up for Supernova classes several months before the classes started. The more crowded Supernova classes were and the harder to sign up for its classes, the more students wanted to take them.

Another major contribution of mass teaching and performative pedagogy for Supernova's success is that they mobilized potential consumers who had yet to consider studying abroad or taking TOEFL/GRE classes. To understand this, it should be noted that many students attended TOEFL/GRE classes even though they did not have a clear agenda to study abroad. According to two veteran Supernova teachers, the informal surveys they conducted in classes found that during 1996 and 1997, 30 to 50 percent of their students had attended GRE classes before deciding to study abroad (Informants No. 7, No. 22). Figure 4.1 lends credence to this claim as we find more students in Supernova's TOEFL/GRE classes than at TOEFL/GRE test centers. Note that I am not suggesting that such a large portion of students never *thought of* studying abroad before they attended Supernova. Rather, what the evidence illustrates is that many students had not *thought through* or made up their minds to pursue higher education overseas before they attended Supernova. Some Supernova students specifically recalled that they did not think through the idea of studying overseas before taking classes at Supernova, according to several essays these students shared on Supernova's website and internal publications (Supernova Archives No. 4, No. 10, No. 22).

At first glance, attending a TOEFL/GRE test-preparation school before deciding to study abroad sounds counterintuitive. However, recall that students were attracted to Supernova as a result of the word-of-mouth effect. Accordingly, student rationales for attending Supernova were not necessarily to learn anything specific. Rather, many students rushed into Supernova classes to admire a particular teacher, feel the motivational atmosphere, quench their curiosities about why Supernova was so popular, or simply because they had nothing to do over the summer (Lu 2002, 112). Students followed their peers to Supernova because they feared that they would be isolated if "everyone else was going" (ibid.).

Once students attend Supernova, they are systematically exposed to well-prepared motivational stories and nationalist jokes that call on them to embark on TOEFL/GRE tests and overseas studies. A dozen students recalled in their essays for the Supernova website that they had become more determined to study abroad after they had attended Supernova classes (Supernova Archives No. 6, No. 10). In short, the mass teaching and the performative pedagogy not only helped Supernova beat its competitors in the market but also created new demands that expanded the market.

Of course, it is possible that mass teaching and performative pedagogy were conducive to the success of Supernova simply because they boosted test scores. Indeed, many Chinese students who scored high on the TOEFL and GRE had attended Supernova classes before their tests (Lu 2002). There is also no gainsaying that providing students with test-cracking skills, motivation, and a community of test takers could have helped students in a variety of ways.

With that said, there is no systematic evidence that students performed better because of Supernova classes. Throughout the 1990s, no pretest or post-test was administered at Supernova, nor were any statistical tests performed to control for other factors. Statistical analyses conducted later on other Chinese SEOs suggest that the average effects of SEO classes are not significant when student family background, locations, and other factors are controlled (e.g., Zhang Yu 2013; Zhang and Xie 2016). Moreover, at least one reason why Supernova produced so many high-achievers is its location: as mentioned, Supernova originated from a district in which over thirty Chinese universities were concentrated and its original headquarters was even right next door to several of China's top universities. A former teacher and senior manager at Supernova and several other SEOs commented on the significance of these top universities and their students:

> In our GRE and TOEFL classes [in the 1990s], the majority of the students came from [top universities such as] Capital University and Central Academy of Sciences. At that time, about 70-80 percent of students came from these universities. . . . So Su Leidong felt that his students were elitists. Their high scores were not the result of the pedagogy at Supernova. It was simply that we got the best students. We got the elite students. We all knew that. I would say that these students' English was as good as those who had majored in English.
> (Informant No. 17)

The Case of Roaring English

The TOEFL/GRE was not the only submarket where teachers started with language instruction but ended up telling motivational stories and nationalist comments in class. The spoken English submarket also witnessed this deviation from teaching norms. Roaring English, a leading brand in this submarket, forged its distinct mass teaching model and achieved nationwide success.

Roaring English emerged as an opportunist SEO in the southern megacity of Guangzhou in 1994. Its founder, Duan Ping, had been a marginal entrepreneur. Unqualified to be an SEO founder, he circumvented state regulations and registered a cultural and consulting firm. Similar to Su and Ma, Duan had access to the vast state system because his full-time job was anchoring an English program at Guangdong Broadcasting Group, a state-owned media agency.

Duan conducted teaching and played the critical role of breaking from existing norms of teaching spoken English. In the mid-1990s, the local norm of teaching spoken English emphasized the capacity to build dialogues more than pronunciation. Scholastic Times, an intellectual SEO led by an English-major professor who had returned from the United States, was an advocate and defender of the existing norm in Guangzhou (Informants No. 1, No. 72).

Roaring English disrupted the existing norm by promoting the importance of pronunciation and, more importantly, combining pronunciation practice with hand gestures. In Roaring English classes, Duan led hundreds of students to practice English pronunciation by using hand gestures to reinforce their mouth and tongue positions.

Duan further molded his own version of performative pedagogy by adding motivational and nationalist slogans. Roaring English's motivational and nationalist slogans were delivered in a highly emotional and sometimes racist way (Y. Zhang 2002). In between pronunciation drills, Duan often asked students to shout motivational and nationalistic slogans with him. Consider the following recordings of Duan's speeches:

> Let me ask you a question: what on earth is our purpose of learning English? All of you speak after me: to conquer the three biggest markets—the US, Japan and Europe. Making money around the world! Speak louder: making money around the world. . . . Now open your mouth wide and speak after me: I enjoy losing face! Follow my gestures! I enjoy losing face! Have you learned this sentence: I want to be a successful person. Now shout it out after me: I want to be somebody! Something!
>
> (Roaring English Archive No. 1)

> Never let your country down! Never let your country down! Never let your country down. . . . I am the most capable! I am the one who can endure hardship! I will succeed! I enjoy losing face!
>
> (Roaring English Archive No. 2)

Duan also combined his pedagogy with other elements to build his own version of the mass teaching model. Duan's version of mass teaching was similar to Su's in that they both relied on large class sizes, non-English-major teachers and performative pedagogy. That said, there were marked differences between the two. Duan's mass teaching was based on his solo teaching: all students recruited to Roaring English were supposed to learn spoken

English directly from Duan. Other teachers, often with the title of teaching assistants, had to teach English exactly the same way Duan did. They were not supposed to use their own methods or refine Duan's pedagogy. Even their gestures had to be the same as Duan's. In comparison, Su Leidong encouraged teachers to develop their own signature stories, slogans, and jokes. Relying heavily on Duan's recipe, Roaring English teachers were even more replaceable than Supernova teachers.

It took a long trial-and-error process for Duan to combine his mass teaching and media experience into a stable configuration. According to two former managers at Roaring English, Duan initially generated all his revenue from SEO classes (Informants No. 49, No. 55). To further capture the hearts of young students, in 1998 Duan used native speakers of English to initiate the "English training camps" model. Duan held his first "training camp" in a tourist town in southern China, where students had to pay a high tuition for seven days of English immersion. To recruit a large number of native speakers as teachers and reduce the dependence on these teachers, Duan contacted a group of Baha'i adherents from the United States (Informant No. 55). These teachers willingly came to China to teach English free of charge.

Duan also explored a new model using his experience and resources from the state media system. He compiled English-teaching materials on cassettes and in books that featured his motivational stories, nationalist slogans, and hand gestures for pronunciation practice. He realized that he could generate revenue by selling these cassettes and books and began to use large classes as a marketing strategy: students came to public squares to practice English with him for free and then he introduced them to his latest books on sale. This model was a perfect match with his solo teaching: he only needed to appear in a city once, and students could still learn from him by buying his books and cassettes.

Roaring English crystallized its mass teaching by combining free classes and media content, which earned it a national reputation. In a 2004 survey conducted by Social Survey Institute of China, Roaring English was voted the number-one most well-known SEO for spoken English in China. Its success redemonstrates how an opportunist SEO broke with existing teaching norms and achieved success with a new norm.

Conclusion

This chapter investigates the third dimension of opportunistic practices— breaking from teaching norms. Although TOEFL/GRE preparation was a new market, there was a relatively established teaching approach because professors from state universities had been the early teaching force, and they had transposed the norm of teaching English to the TOEFL/GRE market. The 1990s saw fierce competition among opportunist SEOs. While all opportunist SEOs attempted to upgrade their teaching, only those whose entrepreneurs were moderately marginal and had solid connections with the state education system made headway. Moreover, I document how Supernova pushed teaching norms into encompassing test-cracking skills and performative pedagogy.

This chapter provides insight into how opportunist SEOs' victory continued to shape the Education Industry's privatization and marketization in the 1990s. The two previous chapters have illuminated how opportunist SEOs as a group outcompeted the other two models and facilitated the retreat of the state. This chapter goes further to show how novel market-oriented practices, such as market-based evaluation, matured and became an essential part of a new teaching model.

Findings of this chapter also suggest that only SEOs whose marginal entrepreneurs had access to the state education system enjoyed sustained leadership. These market leaders, such as Supernova and Roaring English, made their pedagogy the new norms in their respective submarkets. New norms sustained these opportunist SEOs' leadership. Their lasting leadership not only maintained the momentum and directions of the ongoing bottom-up privatization and marketization but also propelled the privatization and marketization forward with new teaching models.

PART II

How Opportunism Persists amid Changes

Kidnapping Kids for Their Own Good

> Organizations formed at one time typically have a different social structure from those
> formed at another time. . . . The organizations formed at any given time must obtain the
> resources essential to their purpose by the devices developed at the time. Since these
> devises differ, the structures of organization differ.
>
> ARTHUR STINCHCOMBE (1965, 154–64)

> SEO classes for "Math Olympiad" and for high-performing students have invaded our
> K–12 schools. They [SEO classes] have brazenly kidnapped our students, especially
> high-performing students. They have misled and harmed a whole generation of young
> kids. They are more damaging than pornography, gambling and drugs.
>
> Everyone knows that "Math Olympiad" training is no longer a cultivation of genu-
> ine interest or hobby, but a highly commercialized school selection process that re-
> volves around middle school admission. Many parents I know act like ants in a hot pot
> every day, so anxious about what to do.
>
> YANG DONGPING (2009)

The evolution of the Education Industry is a tale of two eras: before and after the early 2000s. Most of this industry's attendants were college students
before the turn of the century. Afterward, K–12 students increasingly formed
the major student group. Additionally, there has been a growing participation
in SEO classes by high-performing students.[1] This is the new image of the
Education Industry that Yang Dongping, one of the most vocal educational
researchers in China, was depicting in the long epigraph for this chapter.
These trends, together with the fact that the weekends and vacations of K–12
students had been increasingly filled with SEO classes, led to Yang's outcry
that students were "kidnapped" into SEO classes.

By introducing the K–12 submarket and the implication of its expansion for the Education Industry's competition dynamics, this transition chapter shifts the focus from the emergence of opportunism to its change and continuity. In doing so, this chapter connects the first and second parts of the book. I first describe policy and institutional environment changes on this industry's supply side since the early 2000s, especially the regulatory shift toward greater tolerance for for-profit education and lingering ambiguity-inducing policies. In this environment, leading opportunist SEOs that survived the 1990s, such as Supernova, Roaring English, and Blue Ocean, maintained their leadership and defended the teaching norms they promoted. At the same time, educators left the center stage of entrepreneurship. Managers and business individuals from the for-profit sector entered the Education Industry and established new SEOs, such as Duvell.

Policy and institutional environment changes on the demand side unleashed new opportunistic practices and engendered the formation of a vast K–12 submarket. New state education policy that espoused relaxed education philosophy, together with quasi-egalitarian and nearby residency–based admission policies, spurred new demand for K–12 SEO classes. The spike in demand for these classes catalyzed the emergence and maturity of new opportunistic practices, such as organizing seat-occupying classes. New policies and changed institutional environment imprinted newly established SEOs with teaching models and organizational repertoires that were fit for the characteristics of K–12 students, and many of these new SEOs rode on emerging opportunistic practices to become new market leaders.[2] These new opportunist SEOs also promoted the necessity of K–12 classes. By creating new demand, new opportunists expedited the formation of the K–12 sector as the Education Industry's largest submarket.

The New Era and Opportunists' Sustained Leadership

THE CHANGING ENVIRONMENT AND THE
EDUCATION INDUSTRY'S SUPPLY SIDE

Let me begin by discussing changes in the policy and institutional environment, especially the changes that affected the supply side—how SEOs were registered and operated. In the late 1990s, state regulators ramped up pressure to restrict private ownership and for-profit operation of SEOs. In 1997, the Peoples' Congress passed the Regulations on Non-State Education. The sixth clause of the regulations confirmed the not-for-profit nature of nonstate education, and the forty-third clause further declared that when a nonstate SEO dissolves, the SEO's remaining assets "should be left to the supervising government agency for arrangement after paying off overdue salaries and debts" (Ministry of Education of the People's Republic of China 1997).

After the regulations were implemented in 1997, entrepreneurs of the Education Industry expressed deep concerns. Some entrepreneurs even interpreted the regulations as the state's move to take over private businesses. For example, a reporter documented Supernova's founder's disgruntlement as follows:

> Although he [Su Leidong] has been the president of Supernova School, once the school stops operating, all of this school's properties will be confiscated by the supervising education bureau and redistributed. At best, he could get back the same amount of money he invested at the time of founding. . . .
>
> Right after the regulations were implemented in 1997, they [Su and his associates] started pondering [these issues]. They kept operating from 1997 to 2000 while kept pondering . . . Exactly because of this [policy environment], Supernova has never owned any property since the time of founding. All its offices and classrooms were rented. All its teachers were on temporary contracts. Supernova made a fortune, but it also spent a large sum of money. Their teachers were paid high salaries and each of their classrooms was equipped with an air conditioner. Not a single university or college in Beijing could do that.
>
> (Y. Wang 2003)

It is evident that the 1997 regulations frustrated private entrepreneurs and discouraged entrepreneurs from further investing into their SEOs.

Despite these restrictions on nonstate education, the late 1990s and early 2000s witnessed a somewhat paradoxical policy trend—growing tolerance for education marketization that started with the expansion of China's higher education system. From the late 1970s to 1998, the enrollment of China's higher education system expanded at a steady pace. But the system was rocked in 1999 when top state leaders decided to significantly increase the number of higher education students. The rationale for increasing enrollment included boosting the sluggish domestic consumption after the Asian financial crisis, fighting the rising unemployment, furthering the state's legitimacy, and meeting Chinese citizens' long-held meritocratic values (e.g., Tsang 2000, 21; Bai 2006). In the wake of this policy change, the annual growth rate in higher education enrollment exceeded 40 percent in 1999 and 2000 and remained over 20 percent until 2004.[3] This policy change extended the neoliberal ethos that advocated for the efficiency as well as the role of education in economic growth. This ethos was reflected in the "Industrialization of Education" campaign that was endorsed by top state leaders.

The policy trend in favor of education marketization reached its peak in the early 2000s.[4] In 2002, the People's Congress passed the Non-State Education

Promotion Act. For the first time, the act suggested that nonstate SEO founders and investors were entitled to "reasonable rewards" (Tao and Wang 2010,
117). Passing this act cleared some obstacles for the rise of formally private,
for-profit, and corporately operated SEOs. In theory, SEOs were still forbidden to transfer school tuition into corporate revenue. But after the passing of
the act, state regulators began to turn a blind eye to the corporate operation
of SEOs. Once state regulators acquiesced, SEO entrepreneurs explored various ways of injecting tuition into their corporate entities. One of the ways was
called affiliated transactions.[5] One of the founding members of Supernova
described the changes after the act passed:

> No, there was no way you could transfer the tuition from a school into corpo-
> rate revenue. It is impossible, even today. What you could do though is use an
> affiliated transaction. Back then [before the passing of the act in 2002] it was
> absolutely impossible to do such a transaction. There were the [1997] regula-
> tions. After a nonstate education institution stopped operating, the remaining
> property did not belong to any individual. The government had the right to
> take care of the liquidation. So our corporation was just an empty shell. Our
> school was put underneath the corporate entity . . .
>   Later, we gradually changed the structure into a school held by a corpora-
> tion. You know, after the passing of the act, we could ask the corporation to
> delegate educational research and management to schools, so that there was
> an affiliated transaction [between school and corporation]. . . . So the law of
> 2002 was very important. There was legal ground here. Affiliated transaction
> is no longer illegal. . . . Today, these transactions can be done more easily be-
> cause we can simply consolidate accounting statements.
>   (Informant No. 4)

Despite the state's growing tolerance for corporate and for-profit operations, a considerable level of ambiguity still hovered over the Education Industry. Most notably, this promarket act insisted that nonstate education was
"public enterprise" and a "component of the socialist education enterprise"
(Tao and Wang 2010, 31). Nor did state regulators clarify the standards and
details of the so-called reasonable rewards for founders and investors. Many
private entrepreneurs, though welcoming the change, found the act unclear
or inadequate. According to one of the founding members of Blue Ocean:

> Laws in China have always been fighting against each other. The first article
> of the Non-State Education Promotion Act says that Chinese nonstate educa-
> tion organizations cannot use profit making as a goal. This is why Supernova
> and all other high-performing SEOs cannot list themselves on Chinese stock
> markets. This is the legal barrier and policy bottleneck, OK. If you want to go

IPO, you have to be a commercial organization, making revenue and profit. Government officials are pretty strict about this.

Now we have the Non-State Education Promotion Act. But we also have the Education Act of 1995. These laws have always been fighting against each other. One of the articles in the Non-State Education Promotion Act says that founders and leaders of a nonstate education organization can receive "reasonable rewards." The wording here, *reasonable rewards*, is like playing Tai Chi.[6] How much can be called "reasonable"? How much is "unreasonable"? Also, another article of the act says that any profits generated by a nonstate education organization cannot be used for distribution [among shareholders or founders]. They can only be used to ameliorate educational equipment and infrastructure or to expand the scale of education. These demands are at odds with each other.

(Informant No. 8)

Lingering ambiguity opened new channels for registering new SEOs. In the wake of the act, some scholars proposed the idea of classifying SEOs into for-profit and not-for-profit categories (S. Wang 2011). For for-profit SEOs registered at the Administration of Industry and Commerce, specific regulation guidelines were left to the State Department of China. However, the State Department did not issue any guidelines until 2012.[7] In other words, it was unclear which SEOs could be registered as for-profit. New entrepreneurs utilized the ambiguity and entered the market. A large number of newly founded SEOs turned away from education bureaus' strict requirements and registered themselves as corporations at the Administration of Industry and Commerce (Zhong 2012). These corporations described their businesses as educational consulting.

Doo & Cool Education Inc.—the largest and most competitive K–12 player from the mid-2000s until the late 2010s—is a case in point.[8] Li Yan and his schoolmate founded Doo & Cool in 2003 when they were still graduate students at Capital University. Before becoming an entrepreneur, Li had worked as a part-time K–12 teacher at a local SEO. He had not had any work experience in the state education system. Not qualifying as a founder according to education bureaus' regulations, Li could not establish his own SEO. A "member of the first generation to embrace the internet" (Informant No. 67), Li registered an internet company—Math Olympiad Web—in 2003. That happened to be the year of the severe acute respiratory syndrome outbreak. The epidemic forced schools to close, and parents' and students' eyes turned to the internet. Page views for Math Olympiad Web skyrocketed. To manage the website, Li registered Math Olympiad Culture Corporation. He used this corporation to organize SEO classes as educational consulting programs. In other words, Li

represents a new generation of marginal entrepreneurs who established opportunist SEOs by circumventing regulations set by the education bureau.

As entrepreneurs increasingly registered their SEOs as corporate entities
at the Administration of Industry and Commerce, education bureaus were
obliged to alter their founder profile requirements. While the requirements
in the 1980s and 1990s were strict on founders' social backgrounds, new policies shifted the focus to founders' economic backgrounds (Informants No. 4,
No. 15). Starting in 2007, for example, the Beijing Education Bureau stipulated
that an SEO founder did not need to be a member of the state education system and only needed a bachelor's degree and relevant educational experience
for at least five years. With regard to their economic backgrounds, new SEO
founders needed to provide RMB 500,000 worth of registration capital and
prepare a reliable venue of at least five hundred square meters (ibid.).

Since education bureaus shifted the focus of registration requirements to
founders' economic backgrounds, financial capacity of entrepreneurs became
what mattered most in the registration process. In other words, one's lack
of financial capital increasingly became his or her major barrier for market
entry. In the meantime, supplemental education continued to prove to be
a financially rewarding business. More and more financially well-off non-
educators entered this industry to seek economic return. These financially
well-off people included those who had worked in for-profit industries prior
to founding new SEOs. For example, the three founders of Duvell, a major
competitor of Doo & Cool in the K–12 submarket, had previously worked
as managers in a large information technology corporation. Similarly, the
founders of United IELTS and Lingua Fun had worked in foreign Fortune
500 corporations before their entrepreneurship. From the early 2000s on, faculty members and educators associated with the state education system no
longer formed the major entrepreneurial force in the Education Industry. For
all the ten SEOs in this book that were founded after 2000, only one founder
had had full-time work experience in the state education system. Founders
with less than bachelor's degrees were also nowhere to be found. This is in
stark contrast with how the situation was before 2000 when founders were
primarily made up of educators of the state education system and the socially
marginal individuals without college education.

Environmental changes affecting the industry's supply side were beyond
Chinese government policies. Another area of change in the 2000s had to do
with China's ever-deepening engagement with the world economy. China
joined the World Trade Organization (WTO) in 2001. According to the
WTO treaty, China needed to open its Education Industry and higher education markets to foreign organizations, although China could maintain its

exclusive control over the formal and degree-granting K–12 education. Following China's entrance into the WTO, leading foreign SEO brands rushed to the goldmine of the Chinese market. Some foreign brands that had already established branches in China by the early 2000s accelerated their expansion. For example, Nasdaka English and English Excellence—two foreign brands that targeted spoken English—launched all-out campaigns in China. They promoted the so-called Western model—operating small, interactive, time-flexible, service-intensive, and high-tuition classes.

Furthermore, China's engagement with the world economy triggered demand for new overseas tests, such as IELTS and the Scholastic Aptitude Test (SAT). The number of IELTS takers increased from 20,000 in 2000 to 350,000 in 2010, almost twice the number of TOEFL takers that year (Lin 2020). Even though Chinese students had to travel to Hong Kong or overseas to take the SAT, the number of test takers increased from 1,000 in 2006 to 30,000 in 2010, a thirty-fold expansion over four years (ibid.).

EXISTING LEADERS AND THE DIFFUSION OF
NEW TEACHING NORMS

Top market leaders of the Education Industry that survived the fierce competition in the 1990s, all opportunist SEOs, continued as market leaders after the early 2000s. In the TOEFL/GRE submarket, Supernova maintained its domination across China. Blue Ocean also kept its leader status in the Chinese Graduate Exam submarket, although its influence across the Education Industry lagged behind Supernova. As one of the founding members of Blue Ocean admitted, "Supernova was No. 1 in the sky while Blue Ocean was No. 2 on the earth" (Informant No. 8). In the spoken English submarket, Roaring English started to feel the pressure from new competitors but was still able to hold its influence in rural areas.

As market leaders, these opportunists became less interested in disrupting the teaching norms they had established. As they promoted their norms, and as their competitors imitated them, their norms diffused across the Education Industry. Supernova's actions were exemplary. Throughout the 2000s, Supernova not only stuck with mass teaching for its TOEFL/GRE classes but also applied this teaching model to spoken English and other classes that were supposedly interactive. During 2008–9 when the momentum for the small-class model was building, revenue from large classes still accounted for about 70 percent of Supernova's total revenue (Informant No. 60; Supernova Archives No. 45).

Since mass teaching was crucial to Supernova's success, its competitors—mostly local brands in cities outside of Beijing—sought to follow suit and adopt mass teaching. It is tempting to assume that mass teaching was easy to copy. For example, adopting market-based evaluation seemed to be a straight-forward move. However, few SEOs were able to implement mass teaching in its entirety. It proved difficult, if not impossible, to lock in all relevant elements of mass teaching in a short period of time. A current senior manager and former branch school president at Supernova described the frustration of a competitor:

> When we were founding a new branch school, we designed the school layout to have many large classrooms. So basically we were copying Beijing's mass teaching model. We trained about thirty or forty new teachers. You know, we recruited the best teachers from local SEOs, and we asked them to listen to our tapes and keep practicing. On the first day of our grand opening, four thousand students showed up. Within two months of opening, about thirty competing SEOs were out of business. On that first day, the founder of a major competitor came to take a look at our classes, and a student's parent recognized him. Our front desk informed me, so I went to greet him. This President Li [of the competing SEO] told me, "There is no way I can copy your model. It looks amazing. But I cannot afford such expensive teachers because I do not have so many students. Since I cannot afford great teachers, I cannot recruit so many students!"
>
> (Informant No. 36)

Apparently, President Li gave up mass teaching not because it was un-attractive. Rather, he had found it difficult to lock in some seemingly contradictory organizational repertoires. Despite the difficulty in fully imitating mass teaching, performative pedagogy—the core of mass teaching—diffused across China as the taken-for-granted approach for teaching the TOEFL/GRE. Those who operated TOEFL/GRE classes on a different model faced increased pressure. For example, Pioneers had to retreat from the TOEFL/GRE altogether because, according to the founder, the whole TOEFL/GRE market was polluted by the "entertaining and vulgar approaches" represented by mass teaching (field notes, 5/09/2015).

Old and New Opportunistic Practices in the K–12 Submarket

THE CHANGING ENVIRONMENT AND THE EDUCATION INDUSTRY'S DEMAND SIDE

China's education reforms and overall shift in policy agendas since the early 2000s affected not only SEOs but also their students—the demand side of the Education Industry. Although education policies governing SEOs became increasingly tolerant toward nonstate SEOs and their market-oriented practices, the new top party leadership steered overall policy agendas to emphasize equity and social justice (e.g., Gallagher 2005; Naughton 2007, 108). In light of this shift in overall agendas, some education policies also started to lean toward egalitarianism.

Such a policy combination—neoliberal policies combined with egalitarian agendas—led to unexpected outcomes. Let me illustrate this point by showing how education reforms in Beijing and nationwide contributed to heightened anxiety of K–12 student parents, soaring demand for K–12 SEO classes and the rapid formation of a vast K–12 submarket in Beijing. From the 1980s to the mid-1990s, Beijing's middle school admission policies were similar to those of other major Chinese cities and were evidently performance-based: elite state K–12 middle schools selected high-performing students primarily based on an examination for elementary school graduates (Zhang, Huang, and Li 2014). But in the late 1990s and early 2000s, Beijing's education bureau radically changed course. To promote equity for both students and schools and allow each middle school roughly equal chance to admit well-performing students, the education bureau abolished the use of the selective examination as the basis for middle school admissions (ibid.). All Beijing middle schools switched to the nearby residency–based admission policy (21st Century Education Research Institute 2012). Under the new policy, student admission was based on the combined consideration of residence proximity and computer-based random assignment.

Ironically, this equity-oriented reform sowed anxiety among both parents and educators. At that time, when the commercial housing market had just started to pick up steam, the anxiety did not reside primarily in the frustration of skyrocketing housing prices near elite middle schools. Rather, this anxiety was rooted in people's perception of the dislocation between the policy intent and the reality. Two realities mattered most here. First, middle school and high school education still revolved around the selective College Entrance Examination. The root of Chinese education after the reform was no less competitive or meritocratic than before.

Second, although the nearby residency–based admission policy aimed at equity, it only addressed the surface inequality in selecting students. The inequality on a deeper level—the allocation of resources across different schools and especially between regular and key schools—was kept alive. Regular and key schools had vastly different success rates in helping their students land in universities, and students' parents were well aware of the difference. As a result, parents were worried that their chances to be selected by key middle schools could be reduced under the new policy, and key middle schools were anxious that the new policy could hurt their chance in enrolling high scorers. Both parents and school leaders were racking their brains to find ways to get around the new admission policy.

Other education reforms that were implemented at the national level also added fuel to the fire of parent anxiety. One of these reforms aimed at alleviating students' schoolwork burden, which was similar to Japan's movement toward relaxed education.[9] Chinese educators have since the 1950s diagnosed heavy workload, long school hours, and the practice of teaching to the test as the major malaise of the Chinese education system (Hu and Yin 2015). Middle school students in the 1960s had to spend sixty to eighty hours a week at schools (ibid.). Then, some Chinese educators promoted the idea of replacing examination-oriented education with quality-oriented education.[10] In the 1980s and 1990s, K–12 students still had to go to school for six days and usually stayed there until 5:00 p.m. Students had to spend a large portion of their time in formal schools. There was no time for supplemental education. Even when some students were lagging behind and their parents saw the necessity of supplemental classes, they would first turn to their own schoolteachers for informal tutoring.

In the 2000s, state education policy makers were determined to reduce school hours. Despite such effort, an early study found that elementary school students in Beijing spent an average of nine hours a day in schools, with the vast majority of students arriving at 7:30 a.m. and leaving at 4:30 p.m. (Guo and Yang 2008). In 2009, China's Ministry of Education went further to demand local education bureaus make effective changes to realize shorter school hours, and all local education bureaus issued strict guidelines to comply. As a result, typical school hours in the late 2000s and 2010s were shortened to six hours and students had to leave school at around 3:30 p.m. This reform caused headaches for families whose parents had to work in the afternoon, which, along with increased downtime for students, stimulated demand for SEO classes.

It is worth noting that none of the aforementioned reforms was primarily driven by neoliberal agendas. In fact, many of these new policies aimed at reducing student workload and containing market behaviors within the formal education sector. Ironically, some of these reforms had the effect of encouraging students to attend SEOs. Nothing illustrates this better than the new policies banning in-school tutoring by schoolteachers. Diagnosing tutoring by schoolteachers within their schools as a symptom for deviating from the socialist education's not-for-profit nature and as a cause for students' heavy burdens, top state regulators at the Ministry of Education and their local agencies issued numerous restrictions on tutoring within schools, including after-school tutoring. By March 2015, sixteen out of China's thirty-one provinces and province-level regions had issued unconditional ban on schoolteachers' involvement in any form of "tutoring with reward" (Zhang and Yao 2017). The Ministry of Education also issued a series of mandates that detailed punishment for teachers if they participated in tutoring (ibid.).

Although state regulators sometimes did not enforce these bans seriously, such bans discouraged schoolteachers from conducting tutoring within their own schools. K–12 schoolteachers who had been used to making extra money from in-school tutoring had to look for part-time work at SEOs. As school days became shorter and as in-school tutoring became increasingly unavailable, urban middle-class families had to seek out-of-school supply for supplemental education. Previous studies have found that families who opt for K–12 SEO classes are disproportionately urban middle class or above.[11] It is also worth noting that there was a phenomenal growth of urban middle-class and wealthy families in the 2000s and 2010s. According to the World Bank standard middle-income definition, China's middle-income group increased from 0 to 44 percent of the total population from 1989 to 2015.[12] The population of wealthy families expanded as well.[13] Facing shortened school days and determined to translate their purchase power into class status, China's emerging middle-class and wealthy families sought solace in SEO classes.

OLD AND NEW OPPORTUNISTIC PRACTICES

In the wake of the soaring demand for K–12 SEO classes, existing market leaders sought first-mover advantage. They applied their familiar teaching practices to K–12 SEO classes. For example, Supernova moved fast to offer classes to high school students and introduced mass teaching into these classes. To increase class size and make full use of its test-cracking experience, Supernova targeted high school seniors who were about to take China's College Entrance Examination. A senior manager at Supernova explained the rationale of many Supernova branch school presidents:

> I have asked a few friends at Supernova: "If you were appointed as a branch school president and you emphasized K–12 products, which class would you start with?" Without exception, they all told me that they would start with College Entrance Examination preparation classes [for high school seniors]. This is because there is exceptionally strong and firm demand for such classes. As long as we have excellent teachers, we can immediately recruit a large number of students. In the meantime, our students' College Entrance Examination results will become our advertisements based on student word of mouth, beefing up our influence. . . . If we start with the College Entrance Examination

and other high school classes, we can grow our student numbers and revenue rapidly, but in reality it is fairly difficult to pass our reputation to high school juniors and below.

(Supernova Archive No. 20)

As the end of this quotation indicates, Supernova could no longer depend on word-of-mouth marketing to promote its mass teaching among K–12 students. It was difficult to spread the reputation of Supernova classes from high school seniors to juniors and below. Moreover, selling the idea of mass teaching to high school juniors and younger students was challenging. Parents of these students were more involved in the decision-making process than parents of college students. Parents of K–12 students were also less interested in the performative pedagogy of teachers than the educational progress of students.

Despite the change in consumer taste, Supernova initially did not want to replace mass teaching. Supernova teachers were used to the mass teaching and insisted on using it. Anyone who attempted to explore alternative methods was met with discouragement and doubt. Some Supernova teachers who had previously taught in formal K–12 schools experimented with a small class model that emphasized score improvement and student retention—retaining old students and moving students in lower grades to higher-level classes. However, Supernova supervisors and colleagues did not welcome such an experiment when it was first conducted in the mid-2000s. A former branch school president recalled how his K–12 department director, a former teacher at a formal K–12 school, implemented a new model but was met with questions and doubts:

Previously, teachers had taught the same stuff to students across seasons. Teachers were all teaching how to crack the College Entrance Examination. Everyone only knew how to deliver the teaching for eight hours. A lady in my school initiated the new four-season-retention model. We found that her classes were all small. You know, previously, we had all thought the bigger the better, but this lady told us that a class with more than forty people would negatively impact quality. At that time, we knew nothing about educational quality. We only needed to have star teachers who could deliver brilliant classes to large audiences. She told me, "We wouldn't be able to remember the names of the students in a class of over forty people." So I asked her, "Why do we have to remember their names?" And she said, "So how are we supposed to answer questions from their parents about how their kids are doing when we are having parent-teacher meetings?" I could not answer her questions. These are problems we never had before.

(Informant No. 48)

The new K–12 submarket also bred new opportunistic practices. Let me use Beijing's seat-occupying classes to illustrate how a new opportunistic practice flourished. As mentioned previously, parents had grievances and complaints about the new nearby residency–based admission policy in Beijing. Key middle schools were also discontent with this new policy. According to a state middle school teacher in Beijing, teachers in key middle schools disliked students who came through the nearby residency–based admission process because these students tended to lag in academic performance (Informant No. 70).

New opportunistic practices were invented to derail the nearby residency–based admission policy. The most infamous opportunistic practice was initiating and promoting seat-occupying classes. There are two basic types of seat-occupying classes: those that were directly operated by key middle schools, and others that were jointly operated by key middle schools and nonstate SEOs (Zhang, Huang, and Li 2014).

Regardless of their types, the function of these seat-occupying classes is the same: circumventing the nearby residency–based admission policy and acting as the agency of key middle schools to recruit well-performing students (ibid.). In these classes, students would receive multiple rounds of challenging tests, such as tests in the name of Math Olympiad, and top performers would be recommended to relevant key middle schools. In other words, students who could perform well in these classes could earn seats in these key middle schools. Since these seat-occupying classes defied the nearby residency–based admission policy, educators who were involved tried to keep these classes under the radar or disguised them as regular SEOs.

Both the scale of seat-occupying classes and their impact on the middle school admission were immense. According to a survey on seat-occupying classes in Haidian District in 2010, there were 106 seat-occupying classes that served for, and were housed by, seven key middle schools of this district (21st Century Education Research Institute 2012). Another study estimates that, although only 15 percent middle school students were admitted through seat-occupying classes, almost all elementary school students and their parents once attended seat-occupying classes (Zhang, Huang, and Li 2014). As middle schools and parents rushed to these seat-occupying classes and used these classes to maneuver around nearby residency–based admission, the percentage of students admitted through the nearby residency–based process declined from 80 percent to less than 50 percent in 2010 (21st Century Education Research Institute 2012).

Unsurprisingly, the popularity of seat-occupying classes exacerbated the anxiety of students and their parents. First, the chance of being admitted to key middle schools through seat-occupying classes is small. In 2010, only about 10 percent of those who attended seat-occupying classes were selected by the seven key middle schools. Second, the expenses for seat-occupying classes added a financial burden to participating families. For those who attended seat-occupying classes from the third grade to the sixth grade, their total expenses often exceeded RMB 100,000, a nonnegligible amount for Chinese urban middle-class families in the 2000s (21st Century Education Research Institute 2012). Third, participating in these seat-occupying classes cut short students' leisure time and added a larger schoolwork burden. Yang Dongping, the vocal educational researcher cited previously, vehemently criticized the negative impact of seat-occupying classes on student lives:

> There are numerous children who have neither winter/summer break nor weekends, exhausting themselves in all kinds of SEOs. At dawn, these children keep their eyes closed while their parents help them put on their clothes. These kids often make up for their sleep a bit in the car, put some random breakfast in their mouths and continue to study until late night. In order to get into key middle schools, each kid has to sign up for multiple SEOs organized by these middle schools. Some of these SEOs are called seat-occupying classes. Just like their names, these SEOs' classes are disgusting.[14] They are rotten!
>
> (Yang 2009)

Given these negative effects, it is no wonder over 90 percent of parents interviewed in a survey considered seat-occupying classes as the "archenemy" of a fair admission process (21st Century Education Research Institute 2012). Besides seat-occupying classes directly causing anxiety by themselves, the rise of these classes also spurred demand for other SEO classes in relevant areas, such as Math Olympiad. As Yang's comment suggests, participating in seat-occupying classes is often associated with attending "all kinds of SEOs."

Private entrepreneurs established new SEOs and devised new approaches to ride the popularity of seat-occupying classes. One of the new approaches was the "school-within-a-school" model. Under this model, private entrepreneurs rented classrooms within formal K–12 schools and offered test-preparation classes to students in these host K–12 schools. For example, Hercules Education, a Beijing-based SEO, used its connections with the state education system to set up a dozen schools-within-schools in key middle schools. Hercules also organized tests for, and offered classes to, elementary school students who were interested in enrolling in seat-occupying classes at key middle schools (Informant No. 67). In other words, Hercules depicted itself as an upstream supplier that could screen and coach students for seat-occupying classes and key middle schools.

Hercules was far from the only SEO that built classes around the popularity of seat-occupying classes. Another example is Doo & Cool. Doo & Cool initially specialized in Math Olympiad classes for K–12 students and did not offer seat-occupying classes directly. A Doo & Cool senior manager particularly stressed the differences between the SEO's classes and seat-occupying classes:

> Our classes are different from seat-occupying classes. Very often state K–12 schools create their own seat-occupying classes. These K–12 schools use seat-occupying classes to recruit students. Think about that, these seat-occupying classes have obtained all the performance records of a number of prospective students. So their host K–12 schools can just whip the cream. But we are different. We are independent from those formal schools.
>
> (Informant No. 58)

Despite the distinction, riding on the popularity of seat-occupying classes was integral to Doo & Cool's rapid expansion. Since most seat-occupying classes considered math the most important subject for screening incoming students, frenzied parents sought high-quality math SEO classes. Doo & Cool seized this opportunity to promote Math Olympiad. Using its online portal Math Olympiad Web, Doo & Cool leaders instilled in parents the idea that training in Math Olympiad classes was the first step for enrolling their children in seat-occupying classes (Informant No. 95). The Doo & Cool senior manager just quoted confirmed the link between the SEO's Math Olympiad classes and seat-occupying classes:

> Most students I know signed up for two classes. They first came to our classes and then tried to sign up for seat-occupying classes. They came to us to learn about Math Olympiad, and they went to seat-occupying classes to show their performance in math and secure a place at their dream school.
>
> (Informant No. 58)

Consequently, demand for Math Olympiad classes soared as seat-occupying classes became popular. By building a name as the leader in Math Olympiad, Doo & Cool established a symbiotic relationship with seat-occupying classes and itself as a major supplier for the latter. Doo & Cool did not directly challenge state admission policies. But by riding on the popularity of seat-occupying classes as opportunistic practices, Doo & Cool made such practices more visible and accessible. In this sense, Doo & Cool was also an opportunist SEO that indirectly deviated from state regulations.

There were other new forms of opportunistic practices. Since K–12 SEO classes were tied to the formal K–12 education sector, state schoolteachers were involved in creating new forms of opportunistic practices. For example, some state schoolteachers cut educational content from their classes in state schools. These teachers told students that these contents were only to be taught in SEO classes, and these teachers were affiliated with those SEOs (Informant No. 70). In so doing, these schoolteachers brought in revenue to SEOs and earned high wages. Apparently, these practices violated state regulations and professional codes for teachers. The fact that Beijing's education bureaus publicly condemned such practices multiple times confirmed their prevalence (21st Century Education Research Institute 2012).

THE RISE OF K–12 MARKET LEADERS AND THE EXPANSION OF THE K–12 SUBMARKET

Early opportunistic practices in the K–12 submarket, such as organizing seat-occupying classes, were noncompliant with state regulations. Subsequent opportunistic practices shifted to breaking from mass teaching and reassessing the characteristics of K–12 students. New market leaders and opportunist SEOs, such as Doo & Cool and Duvell, redefined this submarket's teaching standards.

Unlike Supernova, which applied the mass teaching model to the K–12 submarket, Doo & Cool and Duvell developed teaching models that fit the characteristics of K–12 students. One of these characteristics was that K–12 students needed standardized teaching materials. With a rigid national curriculum dictated by the Ministry of Education, students and teachers in China's formal K–12 education sector have always had clear expectations about what ought to be taught in each grade. Therefore, K–12 SEO classes had to meet these expectations. There was no way K–12 SEO classes could be organized like Supernova's TOEFL/GRE classes, where "a student with a score of 600 and another with a score of 200 had no problem attending the same class" (Supernova Archive No. 5). In a K–12 SEO class, a fifth grade teacher was not supposed to cover the educational content of a sixth grade teacher (Informant No. 67).

SEO classes for K–12 students are also distinct because these classes encompassed multiple subjects. Some subjects, such as math, physics, and chemistry, demanded more standardized answers than did English. As a Doo & Cool senior manager mentioned, "Doing math, physics, and chemistry is different from doing English. It is about working out specific questions and the right answers. We might teach in more colorful ways if we taught English. We cannot do that when we teach math. So the difference is in our genes" (Informant No. 58).

Doo & Cool and Duvell tailored their K–12 classes according to the characteristics of K–12 students. Both brands used small classes, and their small classes were offered along with intensive nonteaching services, such as initial testing, placement, and student progress monitoring. Doo & Cool focused on small classes with fewer than thirty students. Duvell took the small-class trend to a new level by promoting its one-on-one model.

The emphasis on nonteaching services distinguished Doo & Cool and Duvell from previous market leaders that had originated in other submarket markets. For example, TOEFL/GRE students were mostly college students who did not need as much nonteaching services as did K–12 students, and the TOEFL/GRE submarket budded during a period when the idea of service was rudimentary in China. As one of the founding members of Supernova said, "TOEFL/GRE students in the 1980s and early 1990s did not need homework checks, tests, or counseling. They had clear objectives and were highly self-motivated" (Informant No. 4). Under mass teaching, students only cared about teachers and their teaching. In fact, poor nonteaching service became a signature of Supernova classes.

Doo & Cool and other K–12 market leaders also preferred small classes and intensive services because K–12 students tended to be local and more immobile than TOEFL/GRE students. This was not only because K–12 schools were dispersed but also because K–12 students could not freely travel to attend classes. Parents of K–12 students are usually concerned about their children traveling to faraway classes. Attracting K–12 students from other cities into the headquarters' large classes was difficult. Therefore, capturing the vast K–12 submarket required opening learning centers close to students.

Since Doo & Cool and other K–12 market leaders could not capitalize on class size, their growth depended on student retention. Doo & Cool was among the first to primarily promote lower-grade classes and student retention. A Supernova senior manager noted how special Doo & Cool's strategy was:

> If you search Doo & Cool classes, you will be surprised that the majority of their branch schools do not even have College Entrance Examination classes or other high school classes. Usually when they establish a new branch school, Doo & Cool Headquarters does not allow offering classes beyond the seventh grade. They also focus on entry-level classes for middle school and even the fourth and the fifth grades at the elementary school level. Of course the demand for these lower grades are not as high as those for College Entrance Examination or upper grades. The enrollment and revenue for these lower grade classes are also limited. The revenue for a first-year Doo & Cool branch school is often at the million RMB level, thus often receiving disdain and scorn from local competitors and other large SEOs. These organizations think Doo &

Cool is neither courageous nor competent enough for senior grade classes. But this is why the Doo & Cool model excels.

A really competent company can resist the temptation of short-term growth. A successful new branch school invests all its resources and best teachers into its entry-level classes and making every effort [to keep] students for the next level and spreading the reputation among local students and parents. A year later, those sixth graders who just completed their Doo & Cool classes will carry their recognition for Doo & Cool. Unlike students in the College Entrance Examination classes, who leave the K–12 system, those sixth graders will continue their seventh grade classes. In this way, Doo & Cool will meet the demand and offer classes for seventh graders and use the relatively experienced teachers to stay with those students.

(Supernova Archive No. 20)

With their student retention models and symbiotic relationship with seat-occupying classes, Doo & Cool and other emerging leaders in the K–12 submarket promoted the idea of SEO classes for all K–12 students. Doo & Cool also encouraged the participation of high-performing students, which altered the previously common perception among Chinese about SEO classes for underperformers. In other words, Doo & Cool was one of the major agents for shifting the function of SEO classes from merely "remedial" to both "remedial" and "enrichment" (Baker et al. 2001). Given the surging demand for Doo & Cool, it became difficult to sign up for its K–12 SEO classes. Attending Doo & Cool classes was the new fashion among K–12 parents in Beijing.

The success of new market leaders and their small classes pressured existing leaders to phase out mass teaching in the K–12 submarket. Supernova, for example, not only switched to small classes but also followed suit to develop non-English courses, such as STEM courses. As Su recalled:

A few years ago we started a comprehensive transition [in product strategy]. The first transition concerned the changing age of students. Previously, 80 percent of Supernova students were college students, but now we are moving toward [attracting] students from high schools, middle schools, and elementary schools. So the age cohort of our students is getting smaller. As students get younger, a closely related change is the shift in [our] teaching model. For example, grown-ups like us sit in a large class and might not have any problem at all, as long as teachers give great lectures. Many people might even prefer such large classes because these classes are relatively cheap. But when it comes to high school, middle school, and elementary school students, their decision about whether to attend large classes is not up to these students themselves. Parents will say that their kids are not disciplined enough. So we need to move fast to change our classes to small ones. Previously there were three hundred people in one class, but now we need to transform our classes into classes of thirty. Only then will parents want to send their kids here. That is a transition.

The second transition is the shift in subjects. Since parents are asking, "Mr. Su, my kid is taking English classes with you, and do you think my kids can take classes in other subjects with you too? Do you have classes for other subjects?" If there hadn't been any, they would have gone to other SEOs, and they might not have come to my English classes afterward either. So eventually I had to make further adjustment and offer classes on multiple subjects.

(Supernova Archive No. 5, 158)

As new and old market leaders plowed into the K–12 field, the participation rate for K–12 SEO classes climbed. For example, the participation rate among K–12 students in centrally administered municipalities and provincial capital cities increased from 55 percent in 2004 to 67.7 percent in 2014.[15] In major met- ropolitan areas such as Beijing and Shanghai, the participation rate was even higher. According to a survey conducted in Beijing, 87 percent of third to sixth graders have attended K–12 SEO classes, and the rate among fourth and fifth graders was as high as 92 percent (21st Century Education Research Institute 2012). As more K–12 students joined SEO classes, their peers were obliged to follow in order not to be left behind. This is why Yang Dongping claimed that students and their parents had been "kidnapped" into SEO classes.

Conclusion

This transitional chapter outlines the changed landscape of the Education Industry after the early 2000s. I trace how the drastic shift in the policy and institutional environment affected the industry's supply side. New education policies and China's entrance into the WTO smoothed SEOs' transition into for-profit corporations in the early 2000s, although a substantial level of ambiguity lingered. Some existing leading opportunist SEOs were able to sustain their market leadership and, at the same time, new entrepreneurs entered the Education Industry and founded new opportunist SEOs.

State education policies also shaped the demand side of the Education Industry. Ironically, state regulators' good will to alleviate student workload and reduce educational inequality unintentionally contributed to the demand spike for K–12 SEO classes. The surge in demand also spawned an array of new opportunistic practices, such as organizing seat-occupying classes. Riding on these new practices, emerging opportunist SEOs, such as Doo & Cool, not only consolidated their market leadership but also made attending SEO classes a new necessity among K–12 students.

As the K–12 and other nationwide submarkets took shape, the competition dynamics of the Education Industry changed. Market leaders quickly morphed into national chains, and the competition among them was no longer confined to any single local submarket. In addition, leaders of each submarket no longer only competed with other SEOs within their submarket. Instead, they also competed with leading SEOs of other submarkets. The overall landscape of this industry's upper echelon started to look like one generalist SEO—Supernova—competing with multiple specialists.[16] In K–12, Supernova was competing with Doo & Cool and Duvell. Supernova also expanded in the submarkets of spoken English, the Chinese Graduate Exam, and the IELTS, positioning itself as a major contender for market leadership with Roaring English, Blue Ocean, and United IELTS.

There Are No Professional Managers in China

Middle and top managers form an entirely new class of businessmen.
ALFRED CHANDLER (1993, 3)

I've always wanted to get rid of the control of my family [over Blue Ocean]. But there are no professional managers in China. The managers I hired totally gave me a lesson.
FOUNDER OF BLUE OCEAN (Field Notes, 5/13/2014)

When a faculty friend from a top Chinese university introduced Blue Ocean's founder Gao Wenbo to me, this friend confided, "Gao is like the Nameless Sweeper Monk in those kung fu novels. You know, the Shaolin kung fu master who wears plain clothes and sweeps the floor as nobody. You won't believe how influential and rich Gao is when you meet him. Even today, he still works full time at our university as an ordinary staff member, carrying documents to meetings for administrators and dealing with all kinds of routine matters" (field notes, 4/03/2014).

After two hours of talking with Gao in a large empty classroom in his university, I found Mr. Nameless was clearly not regretless. What struck me most was his regret for the decision to delegate power to his senior managers, as indicated in the second quotation at the beginning of this chapter. Eyes filled with disappointment, Gao stared at the ceiling and told me how much effort he had spent transitioning Blue Ocean from a family business to a corporation run by professional managers. His effort did not pay off. The managers he hired either left or betrayed him by colluding with investors to take over the SEO from him. Failure to build a managerial team limited Blue Ocean's options to expand outside Beijing: unable to send managers to build directly managed branch schools, Blue Ocean had to depend on franchisees and partners in other cities for local cooperation. As we shall see, China's weak institutional environment for such local cooperation in the 2000s subjected Blue Ocean to a new wave of opportunistic practices.

This chapter unravels the winding coevolutionary process between the rise of managers at leading SEOs and the new development of these SEOs' opportunistic practices in cross-region expansion in the 2000s and 2010s. By rise of managers, I mean the growth in number and influence of non-kinship-based managers and the crystallization of their career path. Whether and how the rise of managers materialized at leading SEOs—mostly opportunist SEOs—is one of the key indicators for how far the formalization process has advanced in the upper echelon of the Education Industry.[1]

After specifying the dimensions of the managerial revolution, this chapter unpacks three tracks of the coevolutionary process: the fast track, the slow track, and the exception track. Opportunist SEOs founded after the early 2000s, such as Doo & Cool and Duvell, were on the fast track for developing managerial teams. Not founded as family businesses, these SEOs did not have to worry about how to remove founders' powerful family members. I use the case of Doo & Cool to show how its rise of managers and cross-region expansion reinforced each other. These opportunist market leaders were established in a period of time when managerial resources and relevant organizational repertoires became readily available. The changed institutional environment selected the managerial form as the new dominant form, facilitating the success of these new SEOs.

In contrast, many opportunist SEOs and market leaders that survived the 1990s, such as Blue Ocean and Roaring English, were on the slow track for both managerial development and cross-region expansion. The vast majority of them were initially founded as family businesses and managed by the founders' family members. As many other Chinese family firms have experienced, these market leaders scrambled to build functional managerial teams partly due to their entrenched family control and the family-manager conflict.[2] Failure to build managerial teams at these leading SEOs was associated with their reliance on shaky local cooperation, which opened the gates for opportunistic practices by their local partners. As opportunistic practices impeded the national expansion of these market leaders, the development of their managerial teams was further hampered. Their lack of progress on the slow track epitomizes the predicaments of many opportunistic SEOs that struggled to adapt to the changing environment.

Among opportunist SEOs and market leaders that survived the 1990s, Supernova was on the exception track. Despite its origin as a family business, its early adoption of an informal partnership structure attenuated the founder family's control, hastened the growth of the managerial team and paved the way for a decentralized model of directly managed branch schools. This decentralized model put substantive decision-making power and a high level of autonomy in the hands of branch school presidents. In the meantime, branch school presidents' opportunistic practices, such as embezzling tuition revenue, put this giant opportunist SEO at risk. The Supernova founder responded to these opportunistic practices with opportunism. Opportunistic practices of both the entrepreneur and his employees, together with the decentralized model, shaped Supernova's course of managerial revolution.[3] Supernova's exception presents a story of successful adaptation to the changing environment.

The Managerial Revolution in the Education Industry

To the extent that Chandler (1993) considers full-time and salaried managers to be the "visible hand" of the market, all SEOs before the early 2000s were somewhat handicapped. Most SEOs relied on founders and their family members for daily administration and coordination. All leading opportunist SEOs, such as Supernova, Roaring English, and Blue Ocean, were promoting teaching models that required little internal coordination or nonteaching services. A small number of teachers were able to deliver classes to a large number of students. Accordingly, there were few full-time managers between top leaders and ordinary teachers. A clear managerial ladder or career path was unheard of.

Within ten years, the landscape of the Education Industry has been completely different. By 2010, a new class of full-time, salaried, and non-kinship-based managers had taken root in market leaders, such as Doo & Cool, Duvell, and Supernova. This was a managerial revolution on the following dimensions. First, non-kinship-based managers increasingly occupied senior positions and their decision-making power had taken hold. Founders' family members, once powerful in Supernova and other market leaders, lost their influence. Second, the number of managers and their ranks ballooned. At the level of branch school president alone, Supernova promoted more than fifty-one managers within a ten-year period and Doo & Cool promoted at least fifteen. This is only one of the senior manager ranks that connected multiple layers of top managers with multiple layers of midlevel managers.

Third, a relatively clear structure of managerial ladder and career path began to take shape. For teaching-intensive SEOs such as Doo & Cool and Supernova,[4] the primary path for managers was promoting teachers from within rather than hiring managers from outside. Both SEOs espoused the idea that "those who teach well shall be leaders (*jiao er you ze shi*)" (Informants No. 32, No. 33, No. 36, No. 58). As a Doo & Cool senior manager said, "All our branch school presidents, except one, came from the teaching front line. They have to come from the front line to know how to fight" (Informant No. 58). The path from ordinary teacher to top leadership positions had also become increasingly clear in these SEOs—climbing to heads of teaching/ teacher management departments within branch schools, then branch school presidents, corporate division chiefs and then top leadership positions, such as vice presidents.

This leads to the fourth dimension. Indeed, the formal rules and procedures for selecting and promoting managers had not been fully implemented by 2010. But the conception of corporate control,[5] with regard to which group held legitimate decision-making power, had become increasingly clear. There were two contrasting conceptions of control. For Doo & Cool and Supernova, educational managers—managers who grew out of teaching positions— became much more powerful than managers of noneducational departments, such as finance and sales. In contrast, Duvell's managerial team was primarily based on its sales team and its most powerful managerial group was sales managers. Of course, not every market leader had a successful revolution. Many market leaders that survived the 1990s, such as Blue Ocean and Roaring English, were not able to push forward their managerial revolution even if they made serious attempts to do so.

The Fast Track: Doo & Cool's Managerial Revolution and Its Centralized Model of Cross-Region Expansion

Newly founded market leaders, such as Doo & Cool and Duvell, were born in a time when managerial resources and repertoires were much more readily available than before. From the 1980s to the early 2000s, the managerial class budded and mushroomed in China's booming economic sector. The growing number of Master of Business Administration (MBA) programs and degree holders provides a clue to the scale and speed of the change. Nine top Chinese universities began to offer MBA education in 1991. In 2003, the number of Chinese universities offering MBA degrees increased to eighty-nine, and they admitted 15,788 MBA students in that year (Warner and Goodall 2010).

The early 2000s also witnessed a more blurred line between the Education Industry and the for-profit economic sector. The passing of the Non-State Education Promotion Act in 2002 made this industry more hospitable to for-profit operations. Entrepreneurs, managers, and investors from the for-profit economic sector flocked to the Education Industry, bringing in managerial resources and relevant organizational repertoires. Duvell is a classic example. This K–12 leader specialized in one-on-one tutoring and copied the sales-oriented managerial structure of technology firms. This occurred because Duvell's three entrepreneurs used to work as managers in a domestic technological firm prior to their entrepreneurship, and these entrepreneurs transposed popular managerial repertoires of the high-tech industry to the Education Industry.

The relatively smooth managerial revolution of Doo & Cool and Duvell also benefited from the fact that they thrived in the new K–12 submarket. As mentioned in the previous chapter, this submarket is inherently more service-intensive than TOEFL/GRE, thus presupposing more managerial coordination. The K–12 submarket, with its young students and deep involvement of parents, was also distinct in its shift from teacher performance to educational gains and well-rounded services. Accordingly, Doo & Cool and Duvell organized teams on student counseling and student progress monitoring.

The fact that the two market leaders were imprinted with the organizational repertoires of the 2000s further facilitated their managerial revolution. To begin with, Doo & Cool and Duvell did not start as family businesses, so they encountered little resistance or entanglement from founders' family members when empowering non-kinship-based managers. As I will show in the next section, all market leaders founded before 2000 started as family businesses. But newly founded SEOs started with a different structure. Duvell, for example, did not involve any family members of the three founders. Although girlfriends of the two earliest Doo & Cool founders participated in the entrepreneurial process, these women had left before other cofounders joined the enterprise (Informant No. 67).

Second, these new market leaders were more open-minded than their predecessors about introducing managerial resources and relevant organizational repertoires from other industries. The previous generation market leaders, such as Supernova and Blue Ocean, first hired their financial managers from founders' family members. This is not only because family members were the most trustworthy in the uncertainty of the market transition but also because early SEO entrepreneurs had been embedded in the state education system prior to founding their SEOs. These entrepreneurs lacked connections and know-how about the managerial resources of the outside world. Even when Supernova had to get rid of its kinship-based financial manager in 2000, it had no choice but to follow the recommendation of a domestic consulting firm and accepted that firm's own financial manager (Informants No. 9, No. 73).

The situation is different for newly founded market leaders. Duvell entrepreneurs, for example, never thought of themselves as educators. From the beginning, they viewed their SEO as an internet company that helped connect teachers with students. These entrepreneurs did not hesitate to borrow the service-intensive and sales-oriented managerial structure of their previous employer into Duvell. According to a former Duvell manager, 70 to 80 percent of Duvell managers started in the sales department that was responsible for connecting with parents, recommending course deals and monitoring the completion of course hours in accordance with tuition paid (Informant No. 62).

Doo & Cool was born in 2003 when the passing of the Non-State Education Promotion Act made for-profit operation more acceptable than had previously been the case. The two founders were still graduate students, but they were open to bringing in managers with transferrable managerial tool kits from other industries. Since they could not find any manager with relevant work experience within the Education Industry, it did not take long for them to hire a pizza store's manager to supervise their first learning center. As one of Doo & Cool's cofounders recalled,

> We have a Teaching Affairs Department that was in charge of operating learning centers. These departments are like those fulfillment centers of online retailers. They only take care of things like managing classrooms and welcoming students. When we had just started the business, we were a bunch of graduate students. We did not even know how to select front desk receptionists. We explored by ourselves for a while but we couldn't find anyone with experience in managing learning centers. Then we thought this part of our business [of operating learning centers] was similar to restaurants. So we hired a manager from a pizza chain store. He did a good job.
>
> (Informant No. 67)

Third, Doo & Cool and Duvell faced weaker bargaining power of teachers. When Doo & Cool and Duvell entered the market, there were a wide variety of organizational repertoires, such as standardization, that could be used to make teachers more replaceable. Doo & Cool was a pioneer in standardizing education content in the Education Industry. It required teachers to use centrally prepared textbooks and built a well-known model of "big backstage and small front stage." Under this model, teachers who were teaching and performing on the front stage were not necessarily the creators of educational content. Instead, they followed the materials and guidance that had been prepared by a team on the backstage. Teachers thus grew dependent on the organizations. Teachers were born "with pacifiers in their mouths" (Informant No. 53). The bargaining power and irreplaceability of teachers became negligible.

Accompanying the low bargaining power of teachers was the new market leaders' emphasis on collective culture. For example, Doo & Cool promoted the idea that collective efforts trumped individual heroism. Doo & Cool required teachers prepare classes together on campus. In comparison, Supernova teachers prepared their lessons individually and were only required to come to campus when there were classes to teach. Su Leidong rarely monitored Supernova teachers' class preparation processes until Doo & Cool's approach was widely diffused in the Education Industry in the 2000s. A Doo & Cool senior manager commented on the importance of collective preparation this way,

> We took collective preparation seriously. It has been a long time since our teachers were first required to come to campus to prepare for classes. They got paid RMB 50 each time they came. I am sure you know Supernova teachers never did that. They taught their own stuff. Our teachers teach the same stuff. It is like we have a big central kitchen. When our teachers first started, we also organized them to do military training, [complete] a ten-thousand-meter run, and read motivational books together.
>
> (Informant No. 58)

DOO & COOL'S CENTRALIZED MODEL FOR CROSS-REGION EXPANSION

Let me use Doo & Cool as an example to show how the managerial revolution was intertwined with the course of cross-region expansion.

Doo & Cool sent its managers to build an elaborate network of branch schools all over China. From 2003 to 2010, according to one of its financial statements, Doo & Cool built six directly managed branch schools in Beijing, Shanghai, Shenzhen, Guangzhou, Tianjin, and Wuhan, as well as 109 directly managed learning centers and 87 service centers in these cities (Doo & Cool Archive No. 1). Doo & Cool's approach was distinct in that it adopted a centralized model. This model is centralized because top leaders of branch schools all came from the corporate headquarters in Beijing. More importantly, this centralized model put most strategic decision-making power within the headquarters. One of the cofounders of Doo & Cool explained how its centralized model operated and how little autonomy the headquarters granted to branch school presidents:

> There was no control problem [for branch schools at Doo & Cool]. The human resources and finances of branch schools were all under the control of the headquarters. The headquarters hired financial managers for the branch

schools. Branch school presidents had little evaluation power over these financial managers. . . . Branch school presidents did not even have to worry
about financial performance. . . . We used educational indicators to measure
presidents, not financial performance. . . . Issues like purchasing, construction
and interior renovation are also all left to the headquarters. . . . Otherwise,
wouldn't branch schools have become independent kingdoms?

(Informant No. 67)

Based on this description, we can summarize the characteristics of Doo &
Cool's centralized model as follows:

(a) There was strong control and coordination by the headquarters. Rather than
    allowing each branch school president to build his/her own subordinate mid-
    level managerial team, Doo & Cool's headquarters was responsible for hir-
    ing, training and evaluating all midlevel managers for all branch schools.
(b) The headquarters in Beijing, rather than each branch school, was respon-
    sible for dealing with external affairs of each branch school, such as rela-
    tions with local governments and major public events.
(c) Branch school presidents were responsible for educational performance,
    not financial performance. In short, branch school presidents at Doo &
    Cool did not enjoy elaborate control over issues at their branch schools.

A veteran Doo & Cool senior manager recalled how this centralized model
was based on a strong headquarters whose power was established early on:

Our branch school presidents did not have to know many things. In every
function, such as finance and human resources, our headquarters provided
a huge amount of support to branch schools. . . . Our headquarters is very
strong. . . . We have a system, and we only need our branch school presidents
to follow the system. You know, when our headquarters predict the rate of
growth for a branch school for the next year, the result wouldn't be a lot different from the prediction no matter who the president is. . . .

This type of strong control and coordination was there at the very beginning. Some people have asked if we only started to enforce strong control
after a bunch of our teachers left and joined our competitor in 2006. That was
not the whole story. We started this model much earlier. It was in our genes.
You have to know that this [founding team] is a group of STEM students.
We would rather set up a system that can fix all the holes. We don't like to be
always arguing and negotiating with others.

(Informant No. 53)

With this centralized model, Doo & Cool was able to enforce formal procedures across all branch schools. Its top leaders did not need to use infor-

mal approaches to monitor branch school presidents. A Doo & Cool senior manager who was familiar with Supernova commented on the differences between the two SEOs, "Supernova does not like managing people with institutions and systems. They like using people to manage people. Your boss decides the hourly wage you get, right? Doo & Cool is more like managing people with a system. You get to know how much you can make just by looking at that system" (Informant No. 58).

Doo & Cool's centralized model, in turn, molded the career ladder and future trajectories of managers. We can use the rank of branch school president as an example. Under the centralized model, fourteen of the fifteen branch school presidents were sent down from its power center—the headquarters and the Beijing School, as shown in an internal document provided by a Doo & Cool manager (Doo & Cool Archive No. 3). Since the power center was in Beijing, the destination after being a branch school president was to return to the headquarters in Beijing to serve as a general manager for a major product line.

More importantly, the centralized model kept most of the strategic decision-making power of branch schools in the hands of the headquarters. Branch school presidents did not have opportunities to sharpen their managerial and decision-making skills. It was difficult, if not impossible, for branch school presidents to develop well-rounded managerial tool kits. Consequently, the turnover rate of Doo & Cool branch school presidents was low. Few of them departed to start their own entrepreneurial career.

The Slow Track: Existing Market Leaders' Family Control and Persistent Opportunism in Cross-Region Expansion

SEOs founded prior to the 2000s encountered difficulty building a managerial class. Their major obstacle was the control by founders' families. All of the local and national market leaders founded in the 1990s—Supernova, Cornerstone, Pioneers, Blue Ocean, Roaring English, and United IELTS— were opportunist SEOs and started as family businesses. All of them, except for Supernova, were still firmly in the hands of the founder's families in the early 2000s.[6] By then, none except Supernova had developed a managerial structure with clear hierarchies or career ladders for managers.

Reliance on family members of these SEOs impeded their managerial revolution. First of all, the managerial revolution entails implementing formal procedures and rules, but it was difficult to apply these impersonal principles to family members. For example, the founder of Pioneers adopted a teacher evaluation system based on student feedback. Although he used the evaluation to determine the pay level and course load of other teachers, he did not apply this principle to his father who was teaching at Pioneers (Informants No. 17, No. 18).

Secondly, since all top and strategic managerial positions were under the control of family members, non-kinship-based managers could not climb to high ranks or earn a competitive salary, not to mention exerting their power and influence over others. At Roaring English and United IELTS, for example, the founders and their relatives fulfilled most top leadership positions. Non-kinship-based managers at Roaring English faced a clear glass ceiling: the highest title a non-kinship-based manager could obtain was manager of either the Editing Department or the Speaker Team Department. Both departments held limited strategic influence. In contrast, firm-level strategic positions were only open to family members (Informant No. 49). At United IELTS, the founder and his wife shepherded every function of the SEO all the way until its IPO. They also held the vast majority of the equity shares. Non-kinship-based managers were allocated neither equity nor futures until the last minute before United IELTS went public in 2010 (Li Haoyu et al. 2015).

Although these market leaders attempted to promote the status of non-kinship-based managers, the enhancement of managers' power often resulted in the conflict between family members and non-kinship-based managers. In the cases of Cornerstone and Roaring English, such conflict led to the ousting of non-kinship-based managers and more entrenched family control.

UNTENABLE LOCAL COOPERATION AND THE NEW FRONTIER OF OPPORTUNISM

The stumbling managerial revolution of these leading SEOs narrowed their options for cross-region expansion. The need for growth and local market saturation spurred market leaders to expand to cities outside of the home city of their headquarters. Some old opportunist SEOs, such as Roaring English and United IELTS, adopted the franchise model. They chose the franchise model partly because this model could accelerate the cross-region expansion without incurring much cost and it was gaining popularity in other service industries in China. Another reason for adopting this model was the shortage of managerial resources: the lack of trustworthy non-kinship-based managers and the limited number of family members dimmed the hope for building directly managed branch schools. The franchise model became an expedient choice. Conversely, the franchiser headquarters could not provide much central support or product standardization without a strong managerial team. Accordingly, much coordination was left to each franchisee organization.

The lingering ambiguity of the Education Industry also narrowed SEOs' options for cross-region expansion to franchise and/or other informal forms of local cooperation. Although China passed the Non-State Education Promotion Act in 2002 and state regulators sent encouraging signals about for-profit operation, it was still unclear whether SEOs could operate as for-profit companies. Most notably, for-profit companies were allowed to set up branches in other cities but education bureaus banned SEOs from establishing branch schools. The education bureau of each city implemented this ban by requiring founders and legal representatives of SEOs to be local residents. Under these requirements, expanding SEOs had no choice but to look for franchisees or other forms of local collaborators. As a former senior manager and veteran branch school president at Supernova recalled,

> It was absolutely forbidden to open up branch schools in other cities. So you would break the law if you opened one. . . . They [education bureau people] would make sure the founder was local and that he or she had the right identification. Even if you had local residency, it would be a problem if your home was in a different district from where you wanted to register your school.
>
> (Informant No. 37)

There were also rampant local protectionism and nepotism in the Education Industry in the 2000s. The Education Industry had long succumbed to local protectionism: education bureaus often favored local SEOs rather than acting as impartial referees in disputes between a local franchisee and an outsider franchiser. Furthermore, it was not uncommon for friends and relatives of education bureau officials to operate local SEOs. In such cases, local education bureaus restricted market entry of nonlocal brands in order to protect the interests of friends and relatives. Common practices by local education bureaus included claiming market saturation and denying licenses to new applicants (Informants No. 37, No. 64).

Given this climate, finding a local franchisee or forming a partnership with local residents was imperative. These strategies serve the function of circumventing the ban on cross-region expansion and dampening local protectionism. The franchise-based cooperation, however, became the new hotbed for opportunistic practices because franchisees frequently violated agreements.[7] This is not because the franchise model is inherently incompatible with the Education Industry. Many leading SEOs in the United States, Canada, and Japan, such as the Princeton Review, Sylvan, and Kumon, adopted the franchise model to spread their businesses nationwide and overseas (Aurini and Davies 2004).

The sustainable function of the franchise model, however, is based on two critical conditions: first, local regulators and the legal system have to be relatively mature and impartial; second, the franchisers should be able to provide strong branding, standardization, and other forms of central support. Unfortunately, neither condition was met in the early 2000s. Refusal to pay agreed-on franchise fees was also prevalent. A former manager at Roaring English recalled how Duan Ping, the founder, was struggling with franchisees:

> All the branch schools of Roaring English were franchisees. Whether these franchisees paid a franchise fee to Roaring English basically depended on those franchisees' good will and conscience. In most cases, those franchisees just fooled the Roaring English people. The branch school in Beijing, for example, was operating relatively well. It was also a franchise school and those franchisees just refused to pay the franchise fee. But Duan could not do anything to the franchisees. He had to ask his sister to establish a directly managed school in Beijing. . . . You know, Roaring English did not have a lawyer or any management. So there was a time when numerous people in different places just used the Roaring English brand name and recruited students. After they recruited enough people, they would ask Duan to fly over and give a lecture. They told Duan "we could split the bread if you come over."
>
> (Informant No. 49)

As this quote demonstrates, Duan faced a dire situation in collecting franchise fees from his franchisees. This quote also exposes another opportunistic practice by some of his partners: first they used Roaring English's brand to recruit local students without Duan's permission. Then these people approached Duan and asked him to teach the recruited students. In other words, these people not only forced Duan into cooperation but also took advantage of Duan's brand for their own financial benefit. Duan, the victim of brand misuse, often had no choice but to cooperate if he wanted to claim part of the tuition revenue.

In some other cases, local franchisees' opportunistic practices further undercut the franchiser's competitiveness. The founder of Scholastic Times—an SEO that was expanding in the early 2000s—recalled how its franchisees "stole" teachers:

> We had cooperation with two local brands [in Shenzhen]. After two or three years, they wanted to decouple from us. You know, I was not there and wasn't supervising what they were doing. So they figured that [cooperation] was not a good deal for them. In the beginning, I often went to their place. Later, I just sent two teachers to stay there and teach for them. So those [franchisee] people thought I was just laying back and making easy money. So they stopped working with us and the two teachers switched to their school. Later, these two teachers left again and went to other schools. Now looking back, I should have shuffled my teacher team more often, replacing these two teachers with

someone else so they wouldn't hang out with local people so closely. We gave much help [to our local partners], you know. At the very beginning, their business started after I sent the two teachers to help them. Some people are just not thankful.

(Informant No. 72)

Opportunism could also emerge even if a market leader rejected the franchise model and instead employed local residents as branch school presidents or legal representatives. One of the founding members of Blue Ocean recalled how such opportunistic practices unfolded:

For policy reasons, it was extremely difficult to expand to other places. For example, when we wanted to open up a branch school in Heilongjiang Province, we were required to register at the local education bureau. There was a similar requirement for founders of any SEO: he/she had to be an associate professor or above and had to have a local resident's *hukou*. So once we invested money into these local schools, we found that our management could not follow. We could not send everyone from headquarters to those branch schools. What we could do was train an employee for one or two weeks, and then send him/her to be the president of that local school. But you can imagine how loyal this person could be with only one week of training.

The legal representative was also a local guy. So we basically made an investment and let this guy run the branch school by himself. This kind of situation is tricky. If the branch school were running well, it would belong to the legal representative. Legally speaking, the school would be the representative's! He or she could ask our headquarters to pay him/her a large fee, or else he or she would take over the school.

Another thing [that could happen] is when you send someone who is not loyal. Nowadays people pay tuition by card. Back then, people all used cash. If a local guy recruited five thousand students and put them into ten classes, you [headquarters] would never know what the real number was. If there had been 480 people in a class, he or she might say there were 420 and then keep the difference.

(Informant No. 8)

His quote reveals that opportunistic practices of local representatives ranged from embezzling tuition revenue to taking over the branch school.

The Exception Track: Supernova's Managerial Revolution and Its Decentralized Model of Cross-Region Expansion

Supernova was an exception among leading opportunist SEOs founded before the 2000s. Although it started as a family business, it had undergone a managerial revolution by the mid-2000s. Supernova's relatively successful managerial revolution was associated with two factors: moving away from family control and its decentralized model of cross-region expansion.

MOVING AWAY FROM FAMILY CONTROL

Like its contemporaries, Supernova began as a family business. From 1991 to 1995, Su's wife, mother, sister, sister-in-law, and brother-in-law all held top managerial positions: his wife was responsible for finance, though she had not received any financial training previously; his mother was in charge of logistics and his brothers-in-law were heads of other departments such as book publishing. There were few managerial ranks. In most departments, there was only two or three staff as subordinates.

Supernova's transition to an informal partnership kicked off the long and winding road for diminishing family control. During 1995 and 1996, Su persuaded three of his former teachers and friends from college—Wei An, Dai Bin, and Kang Chun—to return from North America and join his business. Facing the government ban and the impossibility of registering a corporate structure, Su devised a verbal agreement of informal partnership with each of them.

According to the partnership, each returnee would start a new business under the brand of Supernova, and they would not tap into TOEFL/GRE training that was under the control of Su's family. Returnees could retain 85 percent of the revenue from their individual businesses but had to give 15 percent to Su as a management fee. Under this informal partnership, Su was pleased with his control and expansion of the Supernova brand, while the three returnees as minor partners enjoyed financial benefit and a high level of autonomy.

Despite its initial success, the informal partnership soon proved unsustainable. As business expanded, the division of territories under the partnership became unfair. Some territories expanded faster than others. Furthermore, minor partners felt increasingly insecure under the informal partnership because, without a formal contract and legal protection, Su could "put an end to the agreement anytime he wanted" (Informant No. 17).

To deal with these problems and prepare a corporate structure for an IPO, Su Leidong launched a corporatization process that went hand in hand with reducing family control. In 2000, Su and his partners terminated their partnership and established Supernova Corporation. Former minor partners and a few exceptional teachers became the ten minor shareholders. Su was the major shareholder with 45 percent of Supernova shares.

Now that Su's territory and others' had merged, Su felt that the ground for a family business had been shaken and it would no longer be appropriate for his family members to hold top managerial positions. From 2000 to 2002, Su asked his sister, brothers-in-law, and other family members to leave Supernova. Most of Su's family members left, although his mother remained on the payroll and controlled food-vending services for a short while before also quitting.

One of the reasons Su was determined to remove his family members was the push from a few minor shareholders, especially Wei An and Dai Bin. As the earliest returnees from the North America to join the Education Industry, these shareholders openly opposed family control and called for moving Supernova toward a modern enterprise. More importantly, Wei and Dai enjoyed greater power and superior social status over Su within their own circle. Their superiority over Su extended back to their shared college years. During those years, Wei An was in the same department and cohort as Su. A popular student leader, Wei was also the student president of Capital University's art troupe, for which Dai was also the supervising faculty member. During his college time, Su earned little respect from these fellows because of his rural accent, two failed College Entrance Examination experiences, and unimpressive GPA.

Not surprisingly, Wei and Dai had held a higher status within their circle ever since college. Under the push from Wei and Dai, Su was determined to relocate Supernova's power center away from his family members. As one can expect, some of Su's family members, especially his mother, were resistant to the change. Su's family members and minor shareholders even broke into intense conflicts, as I will elaborate in the next chapter. As Su recalled, "In 2000, the greatest problem was not about the business but the conflict between my family members and others" (Supernova Archive No. 5, 110). As Su was leaning toward minor shareholders over his family members and his determination grew, Supernova transitioned out of family control.

SUPERNOVA'S DECENTRALIZED MODEL OF
CROSS-REGION EXPANSION

Supernova was among the earliest SEOs to establish a clear standard for promoting managers: selecting teachers from within rather than inviting managers from outside. An analysis of the biographical data of fifty-one senior educational managers promoted from 2003 to 2010 in table 6.1 shows that at least forty-six started as Supernova teachers (Supernova Archives No. 65–116).[8]

TABLE 6.1. Top Leaders and Branch School Presidents at Supernova from 2003 to 2010

Manager's Number	Highest Rank (Year First Promoted to Be Senior Manager)	Was a Branch School President?	Was a Teacher before Becoming Manager?	Taught at a Branch School (outside Beijing) before Becoming Manager?	Was a Department Head at Branch School?
1	Executive President (2003)	Y	Y	–	N
2	Senior Vice President (2006)	Y	Y	–	N
3	Senior Vice President (2006)	Y	Y	–	Y
4	Vice President (2006)	Y	Y	–	Y
5	Vice President (2008)	Y	Y	–	Y
6	Vice President (2010)	Y	N	–	N
Percentage of YES		100%	83.3%	–	50%
7	Branch School President (2000)		N	N	N
8	Branch School President (2002)		Y	N	N
9	Branch School President (2002)		Y	Y	N/A
10	Branch School President (2002)		Y	N	N
11	Branch School President (2002)		Y	N	N
12	Branch School President (2003)		Y	N	N
13	Branch School President (2003)		Y	N	Y
14	Branch School President (2004)*		Y	N	Y
15	Branch School President (2004)*		Y	Y	N
16	Branch School President (2005)		Y	Y	Y
17	Branch School President (2005)		Y	N	N

18	Branch School President (2005)	Y	Y	Y
19	Branch School President (2005)	Y	N	Y
20	Branch School President (2005)	Y	N	N
21	Branch School President (2005)	Y	N	N
22	Branch School President (2005)*	Y	Y	Y
23	Branch School President (2005)*	Y	Y	Y
24	Branch School President (2005)*	Y	Y	Y
Percentage of YES		94.4%	38.9%	47%
25	Branch School President (2006)*	Unknown	N	Y
26	Branch School President (2006)	Y	Y	Y
27	Branch School President (2006)*	Y	Y	Y
28	Branch School President (2006)	Y	Y	Y
29	Branch School President (2006)	Y	Y	Y
30	Branch School President (2006)	Y	Unknown	Y
31	Branch School President (2006)*	Y	Y	Y
32	Branch School President (2006)*	Unknown	Y	Y
33	Branch School President (2006)*	Y	Y	Unknown
34	Branch School President (2006)	Y	N	Unknown
35	Branch School President (2006)	Y	Y	Y
36	Branch School President (2007)*	N	N	N

continues

TABLE 6.1. (continued)

Manager's Number	Highest Rank (Year First Promoted to Be Senior Manager)	Was a Branch School President?	Was a Teacher before Becoming Manager?	Taught at a Branch School (outside Beijing) before Becoming Manager?	Was a Department Head at Branch School?
37	Branch School President (2007)		Y	Y	Unknown
38	Branch School President (2007)		Y	N	Unknown
39	Branch School President (2007)*		Y	Y	Y
40	Branch School President (2007)*		Y	Y	Y
41	Branch School President (2007)*		Y	Y	Y
42	Branch School President (2008)*		Y	Y	Y
43	Branch School President (2008)		Y	N	Unknown
44	Branch School President (2008)*		Y	Y	Y
45	Branch School President (2008)		Y	Y	Y
46	Branch School President (2009)*		Y	N	Y
47	Branch School President (2009)*		Y	Y	Y
48	Branch School President (2009)*		Y	Y	Y
49	Branch School President (2009)*		Y	Y	Y
50	Branch School President (2010)*		Y	Y	Unknown
51	Branch School President (2010)		Y	Y	Y
Percentage of YES			96%	77%	95.2%

Note: * Indicates that the branch school president is not the founding president.

Sources: Supernova Archives No. 65–116 (No. 65–105 are Supernova's internal documents announcing the appointments, promotions and other position changes of managers. The rest are based on Supernova's website that contains a series of interview summaries with managers).

The managerial revolution at Supernova was intertwined with its approach of cross-region expansion. As family members left and former partners and teachers grew to be managers, Supernova used its managerial resources to build a national network of directly managed schools. Su pushed the formation of this national network earlier and more aggressively than did Doo & Cool. By 2005, when Doo & Cool was still in its nascent development, Supernova was already operating a network of fifteen non-Beijing branch schools.

Su adopted a decentralized approach to expand its directly managed branch schools. By decentralized model of branch schools, I mean giving branch school presidents outside of Beijing a high level of autonomy and tremendous power in finance, human resources, and other strategic decisions. This decentralized model had two stages. In the first stage (2000–2003), the model was an extension of its informal partnership. Branch school presidents resembled feudal lords so much that some people called it a "feudal system."[9]

During this stage, Su gave branch school presidents at Shanghai and Guangzhou a high level of autonomy partly because Supernova Corporation had just been founded. The corporation wielded little central coordination. To ensure control, Su was the only one who enjoyed the authority to select and appoint a branch school president. For example, he appointed two high school classmates to lead the first branch school outside of Beijing—the Shanghai Supernova School. Su trusted their loyalty because they had admired Su as a leader since high school.

Under the feudal system, branch schools had to rely on themselves for resources, support, and operation. Before 2005, the corporation only provided the initial capital and teaching resources. For example, the founding presidents of Shanghai and Guangzhou each received a half million RMB startup fund from the corporation before founding the two branches. The corporation did not provide branch schools with standard or centrally prepared educational content. Neither did the corporation initially help recruit or train local teachers. When the Shanghai and Guangzhou schools were founded, the corporation simply sent four teachers to Shanghai and another four to Guangzhou for TOEFL/GRE classes. Every two weeks, the two teams flew to the other city to cover different classes (Informants No. 37, No. 74).

Without formal rules to coordinate the relationship between the corporation and branch schools during this early stage, the level of resources a branch school could obtain from the corporation largely depended on the personal connections of the branch school president. A former Supernova branch school president described how different personal connections led to disparate levels of resources:

At that time. . . . those people [from the corporation] just let you live or die by yourself. The only support we could get [from Beijing] was the TOEFL/GRE teachers Su sent to us. . . . At that time, IELTS was not part of Su's territory. It was territory of another partner. My personal connection with this partner was OK, so he sent some IELTS teachers to help us. It was because of our personal connections. You know, the president of Shanghai did not get along with this partner. So this partner never sent any teacher to support Shanghai. Even Shanghai's books were different from others'.

(Informant No. 37)

In the absence of a strong central coordination from the corporation, early branch school presidents as "feudal lords" had considerable autonomy in disposing of revenue and profit. The earliest branch schools in Shanghai and Guangzhou only needed to submit 50 percent of their profit to the corporation and could retain the rest.

Even during the second stage (2003–10), Supernova branch school presidents still possessed tremendous power in hiring, training, and promoting their subordinate managers. Supernova branch school presidents enjoyed much higher autonomy than did their counterparts at Doo & Cool. Moreover, Supernova's branch school network was highly decentralized in the sense that branch schools outside of Beijing became major pools for future managers. This is very different from Doo & Cool's centralized model where the vast majority of branch school presidents were sent down from its power center—Doo & Cool's headquarters and Beijing School.

Whereas branch school presidents at Doo & Cool were sent from the top down, their counterparts at Supernova increasingly emerged from below. Here, the analysis of the biographical data of fifty-one senior managers at Supernova sheds light on this bottom-up pattern. Table 6.1 shows that branch school presidents were increasingly chosen from teachers of non-Beijing schools. According to the middle rows (Nos. 7–24), only 38.9 percent of branch school presidents who were appointed between 2000 and 2005 had teaching experience at non-Beijing schools prior to their managerial experience. The majority of branch school presidents appointed during this time used to be teachers at Beijing School and sent from Beijing. Things have changed for those who were appointed between 2006 and 2010. As shown in the bottom rows (Nos. 25–51), the number of branch school presidents who had teaching experience at non-Beijing schools increased to 77 percent.

Accordingly, a branch school presidency increasingly became the springboard for top leadership positions, such as CEO, president, or vice president. Among those who rose to top leader positions between 2000 and 2005, only one was promoted from a branch school president position outside of Beijing. The majority of top leaders during that time had served as teachers or department heads at the Beijing School prior to being promoted to top leadership positions. Now let us turn to the top rows of table 6.1 (Nos. 1–6). For those who were appointed between 2006 and 2010, every single one first served as a branch school president before becoming a top leader.[10]

This decentralized model greatly shaped the course of the managerial revolution at Supernova, especially through the transformation of the critical rank of branch school president. Under the decentralized model, even though Supernova could not provide much training to its branch school presidents, it offered them ample opportunities for learning by doing on a wide variety of managerial issues, such as finance and government relations.

A comparison on how branch school presidents dealt with local governments between Doo & Cool and Supernova branch school presidents offers a clue. Doo & Cool branch school presidents outside of Beijing never had to worry about government relations. Its strong Beijing-based headquarters shouldered this responsibility. When a local competitor filed a report to the education bureau in Shenzhen alleging the Doo & Cool Shenzhen Branch as an unregistered school, Doo & Cool defused the situation by sending its government relations representatives from the headquarters to Shenzhen (Informant No. 67).

Things were different at Supernova under the decentralized model. Without any formal training, Supernova's branch school presidents had to learn by themselves how to deal with government officials. Multiple branch school presidents agreed that what they had learned most while being presidents was relationship with local governments in China (Informants No. 32, No. 33, No. 38, No. 44).

Since the majority of branch school presidents were teachers and had few experience in dealing with government officials, the learning curve was steep for many. This is especially true for those who had no local connections. Often they learned how to manage government-related issues through making mistakes and trial-and-error. A former branch school president from Guangdong reflected on a hard lesson he learned as a new president:

> I only got to understand how the Chinese government works after this incident. So first of all, there was a big fire at a nearby bar. I heard almost 40 people died. The central government was mad. Local officials had to hurry up and check the fire safety of all institutions. They closed more than ten thousand institutions within a few days. You know, lots of these institutions were not meeting the fire safety standards. They had gotten away by giving money to the local officials, but this time the government was serious. . . .

The director of the subdistrict office (*jiedao banshi chu*) was responsible for the checkup. Only then did I know that the subdistrict office was a level of government. It was the lowest level of government [in China]. It is like a comprehensive public safety agency that can command local police and firefighters.

Anyway, our case was even more complicated. . . . Of course we had all the licenses, including the one for fire safety, but after that big fire, every government agency was out to inspect us. There was a kindergarten, and the kindergarten was under the supervision of the subdistrict office, not the education bureau. But the people at the education bureau had gone to inspect the fire safety of that kindergarten and had decided to close it because it did not meet the standards.

So people from the subdistrict office wanted revenge on the education bureau. They decided to put us under the knife. Well, part of the reason was that I did not take them seriously. I was not there [to throw them a welcome] when they came to inspect. You know, I did not give them enough respect. I did not know the internal strife between these government agencies. I thought we had all the paperwork.

(Informant No. 33)

In contrast, branch school presidents with rich local connections were more capable of dealing with local governments. Another former Supernova branch school president fleshed out how his local connections and family background helped him deal with an aggressive local government in Hubei province:

I started operating without a license. I was fearless basically because there was so little I knew. I learned a lot about the government through operating the SEO. Government people came to me right away [after we began operating] and told me that I was operating illegally without a license. They told me that this was serious. They said, "First, we will forfeit all illegal income; second, you will have to pay a fine equal to two to ten times the amount of the illegal income; third, for those who directly participated in the decision-making and illegal activities, they will be transferred to the legal department if they had broken any criminal laws."

Well, I told them that I did not know [that operating without a license was illegal]. But the [major] thing was I was not afraid. An important reason was that our SEO had been a cooperative venture with the party school (*dang xiao*) of the local [Chinese Communist] Party Committee. The head of the party school was the vice secretary of the committee. When I had such a person as my collaborator, would I be afraid of the education bureau' bluffing? No, of course not.

The second reason why I was not afraid was because I had majored in law. It hadn't been long since I had graduated, so I blurted out all the laws.

The third thing was my family background. I was not from a family of high-ranking officials. But I had this confidence: as long as I was dealing with people in my own province, and as long as I was not conducting criminal activities, I could get things done. If the Supernova brand name could not get things done, my relatives could.

(Informant No. 32)

Under the decentralized model, becoming a branch school president was a leap forward in career development. The know-how of being branch school presidents were so different from midlevel managerial positions that a former branch school president described the experience as "transforming" (Informant No. 38).

OPPORTUNISM FROM WITHIN AND SU'S RESPONSES

The decentralized model is fragmented and chaotic. There was substantial disparity among branch schools in terms of strategies and procedures. Different branch schools used different financial systems. Even the logos for different branch schools were different. A former senior financial manager recalled how chaotic the system was in 2005 when Supernova had already built over ten branch schools:

At that time, we already had over ten branch schools but each school ran on its own system. Each branch school used a different financial system. . . . I remember our financial managers spent three or four days on each branch school, checking all the books and preparing for IPO. We had not even done a single internal audit yet. Auditing by external professionals would be unimaginable if branch schools couldn't even pass our internal auditing. . . . The financials were a mess. Basically, a branch school president could do whatever he or she wanted. The accountants there could not balance the accounts. It was horrible to see that even an accountant could not balance the accounts.

(Informant No. 41)

Such a fragmented and chaotic system emboldened branch school presidents; some felt that they could do anything they wanted. Opportunistic practices by branch school presidents took a variety of forms. Some branch school presidents took advantage of the poorly coordinated financial system and embezzled their schools' money and properties. According to the same senior financial manager I just quoted, a branch school president in Shenzhen made a fortune selling his personal items to his school:

When we went to this branch school, we saw an astonishing thing. The branch school president had sold his used refrigerator to the school and brought the money back home. He just made up an excuse and did that. He sold much of his own stuff to the school at a price he decided. We were completely astonished. There were many things like this. No one knew and no one was responsible.

(Ibid.)

Another opportunistic practice adopted by branch school presidents was recruiting students in the name of Supernova without reporting these enrollment figures to Supernova Corporation. In so doing, these presidents were able to put relevant tuition revenue into their own pockets. A former branch school president in Shenyang, a major city in northeastern China, discussed how his predecessor mobilized a whole team to fill up his own pocket:

> When he was the president, there were all kinds of disgusting things. The financial managers [at the branch school] just split the money with him. For example, they opened up classes in a nearby city and recruited students, but they did not route the tuition money into the system. They just split the money and took it home themselves. They went to another nearby city and collected hundreds of thousands of RMB for each class. Sometimes they put the information in the system but changed it a bit. An associate of the president once called a financial manager and said, "Didn't I tell you to add RMB 50 for each student's tuition? That money is our president's money. Are you stupid or what?" They talked like that in public! Of course, he gave all those associates and managers good money so they did not report him. Those people even gave him good scores when there was an internal evaluation.
>
> (Informant No. 48)

Apparently, this branch school president shared financial benefits with his subordinates so that their opportunistic practices could be kept in secrecy for a long time. In addition to embezzling, this president took kickbacks by choosing construction and facility management firms. He was able to cover up his corrupt behaviors until he left.

In the face of these opportunistic practices, Su Leidong had to depend on various forms of informal practices. He used practices that deviated from cooperation norms and other informal means to secure loyalty from branch school presidents who were all over China. These practices started with the personal selection and appointment of branch school presidents. Despite the existence of a human resources department and written standards for selecting branch school presidents, all that mattered in the selection process was the one-on-one interview with Su (Informants No. 63, No. 64). To make the process personal and retain all decision-making power, Su often reached a decision after heavily drinking with candidates. Using these approaches allowed Su to establish personal connections with candidates and rely on his "intuition in judging their reliability" (Informant No. 64).

Another informal practice of Su, and also a response to opportunism, was to tolerate and even encourage rank-and-file teachers and staff members to snitch on branch school presidents. Su frequently wrote emails to every teacher and staff member at Supernova, and encouraged them to reach him. These rank-and-file teachers and staff members became Su's eyes and ears in the vast network of branch schools all over China. In addition, Su took these secret reports seriously. Despite managers' oppositions, Su often took these secret reports more seriously than reports through formal channels (Informants No. 29, No. 48, No. 64). As a former branch school president said, "It often took Su a long time to reply to our emails, but if a staff member or teacher wrote an email to Su, Su would reply immediately" (Informant No. 29).

Su made strategic use of the secret reports and was reluctant to disregard them. He did not always believe every snitch report or punish his branch school presidents based on these reports. As a former branch school president described, Su acted like a Chinese emperor with seasoned political moves (Informant No. 48).[11] For example, when he felt that the reported action was not egregious, he would erase the name of the snitcher and forward the message to the relevant branch school president without saying anything. The former branch school president I just quoted described a dramatic incident of this type:

> At that time, our school was performing well. But there was still this one unhappy guy. Well, there might have more, but this is the one I knew about because Su forwarded his emails to me. Of course, Su did not disclose this guy's name. Su's message was basically "look, reform is difficult. Someone is pouring dirty water on you." At that time, I did not understand Su's intentions. I was thinking, "Why would you forward this email to me if you did not believe what he wrote?" Now I understand. It was part of the big boss's techniques of taming people. It was just too difficult for him to know what was going on in each of these schools. He would use these incidents to remind you that you should not do this or that. Basically, that email was complaining about my corruption. This unhappy guy mentioned that we had rented a classroom at the rate of RMB 60 per square meter but other people could get it at RMB 45.
>
> So my first reaction was to put this email on the table during an internal meeting [of my branch school], and I said, "Look, people will say bad things about you no matter what you do." Do you know what happened then? That unhappy guy wrote another email to Su, asking Su why he had forwarded his secret email to me. He told Su, "Don't you know I might get grilled [by the branch school president]?" Then Su called me and scolded me. Su was like,

"How can you sell me out?" I couldn't understand him at that time. I thought
he was crazy. Our school was doing really well. He could have checked all the
data in the system. Why would he believe this crazy stuff? He should have
deleted emails like this directly.

(Informant No. 48)

As we can see from this quotation, Su forwarded secret reports to branch
school presidents to demonstrate his knowledge of each faraway branch school.
In the wake of rampant local opportunism, Su used informal strategies to keep
local branch school presidents in check.

OPPORTUNISM AND THE MANAGERIAL
REVOLUTION AT SUPERNOVA

Opportunistic practices by branch school presidents and Su's informal responses, together with the decentralized model, exerted further impact on
the managerial revolution at Supernova. On the one hand, the prevailing
opportunistic practices by branch school presidents and the decentralized
model prompted Su to strengthen central coordination and push for formalization. To alter its status as a weak center, Supernova Corporation took various measures. For example, it made multiple attempts in the mid-2000s to relocate the evaluation power for local financial managers from branch school
presidents to the corporation.

In addition, Supernova strengthened the power of the corporation by re-
locating senior and well-performing branch school presidents to the corporation. In late 2005, Su promoted four branch school presidents to be regional
vice presidents, each supervising a number of nearby branch schools. Since
these regional vice presidents used to be branch school presidents, they were
knowledgeable about opportunistic practices in branch schools. Promoting
well-performing branch school presidents accelerated shifting the power center toward the corporation.

On the other hand, Su's informal and occasionally opportunistic responses
undercut the effort to advance formalization. After the launch of regional vice
president positions in 2005, Supernova formally required all managers to not
skip the report line. Teachers and staff were asked to report to their department managers and branch school presidents, instead of reaching directly to
Su. All branch school presidents were supposed to report to their regional
vice presidents. Despite senior managers' strong opposition, however, Su Leidong still maintained his close contact with rank-and-file teachers, staff, and
branch school presidents. A former branch school president gave an example:

A candidate just filed an application for the position of branch school president. . . . He should have talked with the regional vice president [about which
school to take over]. But this candidate called Su directly. In front of a few
people, Su was asking this guy, "If you don't want to go to this city, what about
another city? I can talk to the regional vice president for you." You know, he
should have followed the report line, right? This was a business of the regional
vice president. The regional vice president must have talked to the candidate
first and told him to go to a city, say, Guangzhou. But this guy wanted to go to
Shanghai. Now Su intervened. He promised to help the candidate get what the
candidate wanted by talking to the regional vice president.

(Informant No. 64)

There was a tension between Supernova's formalization effort and Su's
informal responses. This tension had long-lasting effects on the managerial
structure and the career trajectories of managers. First, this tension catalyzed
the evolution of the managerial structure. Shortly after promoting regional
vice presidents and implementing the regional management model in late
2005, Su felt that this model stymied his direct control over branch schools
and that this model had the potential to breed factions led by regional vice
presidents. In 2007, Supernova abolished the regional management model
and implemented a multidivisional structure. In 2009, Supernova further
evolved into a matrix system. In four years, Supernova experimented with
three types of fundamentally different managerial structures.

This tension between Supernova's formalization effort and Su's informal
responses was also associated with a mass exodus of senior managers. Formalizing and empowering the corporation elevated the power of former regional
vice president to a level close to that of Su, but at the same time Su's informal
responses constantly undercut their power. Emboldened with a massive influx
of global capital, development of new technology and the increased tension
with Su's informal style, many Supernova senior managers decided to launch
their own SEOs. By 2015, three of the five top leaders mentioned in the top rows
of table 6.1 had left Supernova. In addition, these top leaders mobilized more
than a dozen branch school presidents to leave together and join their startups. More than forty-five out of the fifty-one branch school presidents had left
Supernova by 2015. This is a much higher turnover rate than that of Doo &
Cool branch school presidents.

Several factors related to the aforementioned tension galvanized managers
into a mass departure. First, strengthening the corporation through empowering regional vice presidents put a large number of branch school presidents
under direct influence of the regional vice presidents, thus increasing the like-
lihood of faction formation. The formation of these factions, in turn, made the

tension worse because Su felt more inclination to skip over the regional vice presidents. When several regional vice presidents launched their startups, those managers who fell into their factions were likely to join these startups.

Furthermore, the decentralized model had trained a large team of managers whose well-rounded managerial tool kits enabled their entrepreneurial acts. As a veteran Doo & Cool senior manager said, "Our managers are not competent enough to build their own businesses. But look at Supernova. Their managers are so capable. Each one of them looks like a versatile hero. The result? They have all left" (Informant No. 53).

Conclusion

This chapter discusses the complex coevolution between SEOs' managerial revolution and their cross-region expansion. I identify three tracks along which the managerial revolution and the cross-region expansion interacted with each other differently.

From a selection versus adaptation perspective, the fast track tells a story of selection. It means that new market leaders had a smooth managerial revolution partly because they were imprinted with characteristics of the environment that were more compatible with the rise of managers. This is also a story of institutionalization in the sense that new market leaders brought in managers from other industries and imitated the ways in which other corporations were operated. In contrast, the slow track presents a story of failed adaptation: some surviving market leaders, mostly opportunist SEOs, could not develop a functional managerial team even if the institutional environment pressured them to do so. Their adaptation was impeded by not only entrenched family control but also rampant opportunistic practices during the cross-region expansion process.

Despite the difficulty in adaptation, there were exceptions. My findings for Supernova suggest that transition out of family control prepared the ground for adaptation. Moreover, Supernova's path of managerial revolution led to a decentralized model and opportunistic practices from within, both of which in turn shaped its unique course of managerial revolution.

Who Cares about Tuition Money

[The Education Industry] used to be a profitable industry. It required solid and rigorous [work]. Now all the profits are gone. . . . These people have made this industry into a bubble just like blowing up a balloon. Everyone, every underdog, wants to go IPO.

(Informant no. 8)

In terms of the series A round investment, we might have been one of the earliest. . . . Before 2012, if you had a concept that could go "viral," you could get tons of money from venture capital. . . . Now, the tide has shifted. People ask you if you can do "ground promotion (*di tui*)." This was how we got to the series D round and got a good valuation (*gu zhi*).

(Informant no. 64)

The epigraphs for this chapter offer a glimpse of the financial revolution that took place between the mid-2000s and 2018. As the first quotation suggests, the Education Industry before the mid-2000s was an organizational field where market leaders enjoyed high profit and excellent cash flow. The whole industry at that time had little connection with the financial sector: the vast majority of SEOs relied on family savings to start their businesses, capital from banks was unheard of, and most importantly, not a single SEO was listed on stock market and very few were busy courting venture capital or any other investors.

When I was conducting the fieldwork in 2014 and 2015, several encounters made me realize how much had changed: as the second epigraph illustrates, some interviewees kept using American-flavored financial terms, ranging from series A, series D, and stock market valuation to angel investors, P/E ratio, and Sarbanes-Oxley Act; in a ceremony in March 2015, I witnessed how

Le-We-Me, a newly established high-tech SEO based in Beijing, announced
that it had set a new record for Chinese corporations' series A round investment even though it had not made any profit (field notes, 3/30/2015); and in
a closed-door meeting in April 2015, a Doo & Cool cofounder proudly introduced his investment plan, which included acquiring domestic SEOs and US
for-profit colleges (field notes, 4/29/2015).

Behind these encounters was a financial revolution that upended the landscape of the Education Industry. This financial revolution started with the
Supernova IPO in 2006 and subsequent IPOs of other market leaders. As
this revolution unfolded, global capital poured into the Education Industry.
This revolution changed how SEOs operated in the following ways. First, the
idea that founding an SEO presupposed securing venture capital investment
became the new norm, and the number of venture capital–related investment
cases soared.[1] As the first epigraph suggests, some SEOs drastically increased
spending in order to lure in investors. Second, some market leaders started
to generate profits through investment. They have kicked off the transition
from educational service providers to investors. For example, Doo & Cool
invested in 106 domestic and global SEOs between 2010 and 2018. Third, a
few SEOs have expanded overseas to make use of global capital as well as the
global job market.[2]

This chapter traces the early process through which the upper echelon of
the Education Industry became globally financed.[3] Since IPOs on overseas
stock markets predated and galvanized other forms of investments, the first
part of this chapter focuses on IPOs, especially the industry's first wave of
IPOs.[4] I will show that this first wave unfolded partially as a selection and
institutionalization process.[5] Some newly established opportunist SEOs, such
as Doo & Cool and Duvell, were imprinted with organizational repertoires
that prepared the ground for IPOs. More specifically, the IPOs of these two
market leaders unfolded as an isomorphic process as they imitated the actions of Supernova—the first publicly listed SEO.[6]

Despite this selection process, the very first IPO of the first wave—Supernova—was primarily the fruit of adaptation. Under lingering ambiguity, underdeveloped institutional demands were not sufficient to act as supraorganizational forces and materialize Supernova's IPO. The second part of this
chapter notes how Supernova's intraorganizational conflict facilitated its IPO.
A watershed event, Supernova's IPO triggered the rest of the first wave of
IPOs. As Supernova and its competitors embarked on overseas stock markets, they accelerated the formalization of their structures and procedures.
Being listed on stock market further sustained the leadership statuses of these
opportunist SEOs.

The last part of this chapter reorients our attention to the implications of the first wave IPOs for the persistence and development of opportunistic practices. After the first wave of IPOs, global investments poured in the Education Industry. Global capital became the key resource for SEOs' survival and growth. SEO Entrepreneurs became increasingly keen to secure investments, and such a situation led to a spiraling escalation of opportunism. New opportunistic practices flourished and old-fashioned opportunistic practices resurfaced. These opportunistic practices were associated with many failed IPOs, forced delisting, and withdrawals from stock markets.

The Selection: Being Listed on Overseas Stock Markets as an Institutionalization Process

By 2018, a vast number of market leaders in the Education Industry had evolved into corporations that were globally financed. A clear sign of being globally financed is the growing number of SEOs publicly listed on overseas stock markets. Figure 7.1 documents this change over time. Before 2006, no Chinese SEO was publicly listed on any stock market. Supernova's IPO on the New York Stock Exchange in 2006 was a watershed event. After Supernova's IPO, more and more SEOs had IPOs on overseas stock markets. By the end of 2018, dozens of leading SEOs had listed themselves on stock markets outside of mainland China. Now the upper echelon of the Education Industry is owned and financed by investors all over the world.

The first wave of IPOs was an institutionalization process because environmental changes and institutional factors pressured and prepared SEOs for connecting with the financial market. Following Supernova's IPO in 2006, global venture capital firms and financial analysts rushed to the Education Industry as a new gold mine. As we shall see, these institutional actors had not only ignited entrepreneurs' motivation to go public but also brought financial personnel and financial concepts into the Education Industry.

The institutional environment also matters in the sense that the overseas IPO route through the variable interest entity (VIE) structure had already proved its feasibility in other industries before this route was adopted in the Education Industry.[7] After the first VIE-based overseas IPO among Chinese firms in 2000, dozens of Chinese high-tech, state-owned, and private enterprises used the VIE structure to go public on overseas stock markets. The knowledge about and personnel for setting up VIE structures had permeated among Chinese corporations. Taking this route to list a company on overseas stock markets had been recognized among Chinese entrepreneurs as a safe and legitimate process for IPOs.

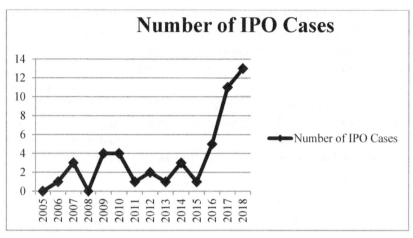

F I G U R E 7.1. The Number of the Education Industry's IPOs on Overseas Stock Markets
Source: Deloitte (2012–2018)

Except for Supernova's IPO, the first wave of IPOs was primarily an institutionalization process also because the new listings materialized under less functional need for investment than institutional pressure for legitimacy. Among the SEOs that had IPOs between 2007 and 2010, four were major competitors of Supernova. They launched IPOs in response to, and as an imitation of, Supernova's IPO. One example was United IELTS, Supernova's primary competitor in the IELTS submarket. The founder and CEO of United IELTS said that "Supernova's IPO means a great leap in advancement ahead of United IELTS in terms of reputation and capital, which might cause the loss of (our) good teachers" (Li Haoyu et al. 2015, 66–67). He decided to turn to the financial market, so that his company's "accounts can have some money, and can store some spare food to go through the winter" (ibid.). United IELTS launched its IPO plan even though the top financial manager was the founder's wife who had no training or experience in finance. United IELTS went public on Nasdaq in 2010 but was soon delisted (Informant No. 90).

The IPO of Doo & Cool in 2010 was also primarily a response to, and an imitation of, those of Supernova and other competitors. Like United IELTS, Doo & Cool leaders felt the threat and uncertainty associated with Supernova's IPO. To defend themselves against real or imagined threats, they decided to imitate Supernova and go public. As a veteran Doo & Cool senior manager said,

> Supernova's IPO changed everything. Our boss got nervous. You know, in K–12, we started earlier than Supernova, but their IPO might have put them on the fast track. Their IPO turned the situation around completely. . . . Right

after Supernova's IPO, which I think was 2006 or 2007, other schools started getting investment. Hercules SEO [which was a major competitor of ours in Beijing] got investment and used that money to steal five of our best teachers. At that time we were young and inexperienced, so we started wondering, "What if they use the money to steal all our teachers?"

So we also started looking for investment. . . . We asked around and looked for venture capital investments, and our big boss wanted to find the same venture capital firm that Supernova had used. . . . Our boss just gave one order, "find out which venture capital firm did IPO for Supernova". . . . He said that it had to be this firm because people in this firm would know how to get us on the stock market. . . . So we also went to Taurus.[8] Right after Taurus entered, Duvell went public on a US stock market. So we figured we had to speed up our IPO. We managed to accomplish it in a few months. The general manager of Taurus was astonished by our speed.

(Informant No. 53)

To respond to Supernova's IPO and considering the state's ban on SEOs being listed domestically, some SEOs went so far as to use shell companies for IPOs on domestic stock markets. In 2014, Spotlight Education, a Shanghai-based SEO and Supernova's competitor, filed applications to go public through this route. When commenting on his rationale for going public, the founder said "seeing Supernova's IPO made us anxious. We started to think about going public too" (Li Haoyu et al. 2015, 129). After presenting their case multiple times to, and being denied by, China's Ministry of Education and the Securities Regulatory Commission, Spotlight finally won approval, and its shell company went public on the Shanghai Stock Exchange. Although this IPO was not on the overseas stock market, it again demonstrates competitors' motivation to imitate Supernova as a key rationale for IPO. The success of Spotlight's IPO also indicates a bottom-up institutional change: as more and more SEOs went public on overseas stock markets and as pressure built up from below, state regulators loosened the ban and acquiesced domestic listing of SEOs.

The Adaptation: The First IPO and the Engine from Within

Although the first wave of IPOs was largely a process of institutionalization and selection, the very first of the first wave—Supernova's IPO in 2006—unfolded mainly as an adaptation process. To be sure, Supernova's IPO was facilitated by institutional actors, such as consulting firms, and this IPO also used the typical VIE route to go public in the US stock market. However, the institutional environment and institutional actors were insufficient to make the first IPO happen.

Supernova faced a more unfavorable and uncertain situation than its fol-
lowers. Most notably, the fundamental institutions for listing SEOs on a stock
market, such as private ownership and corporate governance, were underdeveloped in the Education Industry in the early 2000s even though they
had taken root in many Chinese for-profit industries.[9] Moreover, by that time
there had been no precedent in the Education Industry for going public. Domestic and foreign investors had no idea about the prospect of the Education
Industry or the risk of investing in this industry in China. Last but not the
least, by the early 2000s the Chinese state had not lifted the ban on listing
SEOs on domestic stock markets. In other words, the state as a powerful institutional actor was against the public listing of SEOs.

In this environment when the institutional drives were falling short, intraorganizational dynamics played a critical role. In what follows, I will show
how the internal conflict of Supernova served as an engine from within. I will
first show how the ambiguity of the industry and Supernova's partnership
sowed the seed for internal conflicts. Internal conflicts led to IPO through two
processes: deadlock and professionalization.

THE CONSULTING FIRM AND THE ORIGIN
OF THE IPO IDEA

Let us recall that Supernova rose to prominence in Beijing's TOEFL/GRE
submarket in the mid-1990s. During 1995 and 1996, Su's former classmates
and teachers—especially Wei, Dai, and Kang—joined Supernova. Afterward,
Supernova was organized as an informal partnership.

The contact with a renowned Chinese consulting firm brought to light
the idea of an IPO. In 2000, after being introduced by a Supernova student,
Supernova founder Su Leidong became acquainted with the leader of Kunlun
Consulting. When they met, the Kunlun Consulting leader told Su and his
partners that Supernova was worth RMB 5 billion on the stock market. This
valuation meant that Su and his partners would become billionaires after an
IPO, so they were excited about the idea of an IPO.

On the other hand, Supernova leaders were skeptical of the IPO plan because there had been no IPO precedent in the Education Industry. Supernova
did not even have a corporate structure in 2000, not to mention functional
corporate governance. This is why Supernova leaders were surprised when
the Kunlun Consulting leader brought up the IPO idea (Supernova Archive
No. 40). Supernova leaders did not believe it was possible for their noncor-
porate entity to have an IPO. Their suspicion and lack of confidence slowed
down the progress. Some Supernova senior managers bluntly noted that it

was the Kunlun Consulting people who were pushing for the IPO. As one of the earliest eleven shareholders of Supernova recalled, "Kunlun people invited us to a hotel to discuss the plan every week. They just brainwashed us. That was when the idea of IPO was planted in our heads" (Informant No. 35).

Despite the uncertainty of and skepticism toward the plan, Supernova leaders agreed that they needed to establish a corporation in order to phase out the informal partnership and test the water for an IPO. The direct result was the founding of the Supernova Corporation and the termination of the partnership in 2000. Su, seven minor partners, and three star teachers became the initial eleven shareholders of the Corporation. Su held 45 percent of Supernova shares on behalf of his family, the other ten shareholders held 45 percent, and 10 percent was left for future shareholders.

Since the education bureau did not allow corporate operation, Supernova Corporation was registered under the Administration of Industry and Commerce. Initially, the corporation did not generate any revenue. The Beijing Supernova School served as the major supplier of cash flow. Supernova leaders expected to pump the Beijing Supernova School's revenue to Supernova Corporation through "affiliated transactions," also known as "contractual arrangements" in Supernova's IPO prospectus (Supernova Archive No. 1).[10]

THE INTENSE CONFLICT

Although initially enacted to solve problems, this corporatization process created new problems. It catalyzed intense and prolonged internal conflicts. To begin with, this corporatization process triggered conflicts between minor shareholders and Su's family members. Corporatization blurred the territorial boundaries among shareholders, and it also eliminated the buffer zone between minor shareholders and Su's family members. The two groups broke into open conflict. Minor shareholders advocated for deepened formalization because they considered formality crucial to institutionalizing their economic gains. Minor shareholders who had overseas experience strongly advocated for moving away from family influence, replacing it with the institution of modern corporate governance (Lu 2002; Informant No. 9).

In contrast, Su's mother and other relatives of his advocated for filial piety and other family values. They took it for granted that Su, as a son, should obey his mother. Moreover, a group of relatives gathered closely around Su's mother because Su's previous actions toward family members—forcing his wife and two brothers-in-law to quit Supernova to create positions for nonfamily partners—made them skeptical of Su as a champion for family interest.

The ambiguity in ownership exacerbated this family-friends feud. Given the ambiguity on the dimension of ownership, no private individual was the legal owner of the cash cow—the Beijing Supernova School. The corporatization process magnified the negative effects of ambiguity because minor shareholders now became formal owners of Supernova Corporation even though they were not owners of the Beijing Supernova School. To make things even worse, family members did not consider minor shareholders owners. Before corporatization, all minor shareholders' businesses constituted approximately 30 percent of the total revenue. Su's TOEFL/GRE business, with the support of his family members, accounted for more than 60 percent (Informant No. 9). From the point of view of Su's mother and other family members, providing minor partners with a large portion of shares was like "stealing the property from the family" (ibid.).

Another reason that family members did not consider minor shareholders owners was because Supernova Corporation relied on the Beijing Supernova School for revenue. Su and his family members had much greater influence over teachers and managers at Beijing Supernova School than did minor shareholders. For family members, minor shareholders' shares did not mean anything if Su quit with "teachers and managers to open a new school" (Informant No. 17).

Family members and minor shareholders engaged in open conflict. Each side blamed Su for his allegedly preferential treatment of the other group. During an argument with Su and minor shareholders, for example, Su's mother took down the Beijing Supernova School's license from the wall and threatened to tear it apart. She considered herself the legitimate person to do so because she was the one who had obtained the license from the education bureau and hers was the legal representative's name (Informant No. 9; Lu 2002). On other occasions when the conflicts were intense, she "used an ax to cut the table corner" (Informant No. 9). Since Su held dear to the value of filial piety, he obeyed her in most cases. He sometimes even kneeled before her when other shareholders were present. Such behavior elicited harsh criticism from minor shareholders, especially those overseas returnees. Wei and Dai both threatened to quit because, according to them, Su was already a successful entrepreneur but he could not even step beyond his mother (Lu 2002).

The most severe conflicts broke out between Su and minor shareholders over the issue of dividends. After the informal partnership was terminated in 2000, economic returns for minor shareholders decreased because they could no longer receive their 85 percent revenues attached to their own territories under the partnership. Although they enjoyed six-figure salaries from Supernova Corporation, their income was not as good as it had previously been. With only noncirculating shares, no one knew how much his or her shares might be worth. At this moment, Su's unfortunate decision to not distribute dividends ignited the fuse.

Ambiguity of the Education Industry gave each side a vast amount of room for interpreting the same situation in one's own favor. According to Su, distributing dividends was not allowed at that time due to legal and technical barriers. The education bureau indeed required tuition payments to be retained within schools, forbidding the distribution of tuition as corporate dividends (Supernova Archive No. 5, 124). There were also technical barriers for distributing dividends as financial managers were still trying to figure out how to transfer revenue from the Beijing Supernova School to Supernova Corporation.

Minor shareholders, however, interpreted the situation differently. Two former minor shareholders said that the only problem was that Su did not *want* to give money to minor shareholders. One of them said, "Supernova used to be Su's family business. If I were him, I wouldn't have wanted to distribute the dividends either" (Informant No. 5). The other reasoned that Su's refusal to distribute dividends was because "we won't play with Su anymore once we get rich. That is why Su only fed us half-full" (Informant No. 19). Still others went so far as to conjecture that the whole process—terminating the partnership and transitioning to a corporate structure—was Su's hoax to get rid of minor partners' financial entitlements under the partnership (Lu 2002).

The fact that these conflicts unfolded along multiple interrelated lines contributed to fluid coalition building. Although the general line of dividing coalitions was between Su (including his family members) and other minor shareholders, minor shareholders constantly shifted their alliances depending on the issue and even fought against each other (Supernova Archive No. 5, 130; Informant No. 18). This complex situation meant that shareholders "did not know what they were fighting for" and Su "did not know how to satisfy them" (Supernova Archive No. 5, 125). There were recordings of frequent verbal confrontations. Some people smashed glasses and overturned tables during meetings. Others felt so helpless that they started hugging each other and crying. Several shareholders and senior managers said they felt that Supernova could collapse at any time (Informants No. 9, No. 39, No. 41).

EXHAUSTION OF MUTUAL TRUST AND EMERGENCE OF DEADLOCK

In the face of the entrenched problems and conflicts after incorporation, Supernova's founders and shareholders resorted to a series of conventional solutions. But none were successful. The first solution involved the informal distribution of dividends at the school level. The idea was to collect a large sum of receipts and distribute dividends to minor shareholders in the name of reimbursement. This type of action was common in China in the 2000s, but it often required obtaining receipts directly from the tax bureau and paying a small amount of tax. A former shareholder and senior manager described how this solution was carried out and how Su called it off:

> People started to propose that we could perhaps have some sort of "dividend" at the school level. But to make distributions in the name of a dividend presented a legal problem plus a high tax rate. It was something like 40 percent, if I remember correctly. People wanted the money, but they did not want to pay the tax. If the sum was not large, we could find receipts from other expenses to deduct the tax. But the sum was large! Where could we find so many receipts? So they asked Su to figure it out. Su made the financial manager ask officials at the tax bureau. Some officials said we could pay another type of tax that had a lower rate and obtain enough receipts. But that financial manager later did not bring money to the tax bureau. Instead, he went to street vendors to buy receipts at a low cost and embezzled the money that should have gone to the bureau. Su found out and said we should stop this. So he called it off.
>
> (Informant No. 73)

As the financial manager's corruption was exposed and Su called off the plan, minor shareholders still could not receive a dividend. The first solution failed. Confrontation and conflicts further escalated.

Since another focal point of conflict was the doubt over the value of the shares, Su turned to internal pricing of shares as a new solution in May 2001. He proposed to buy shares from minor shareholders at the price of RMB 1 million per 1 percent share, but no one accepted his offer. The reasons minor shareholders refused to sell their shares were twofold. First, Su's offer made them realize that their shares were now worth good money, which also meant that keeping those shares could bring even greater fortune in the future. Second, they were unhappy about Su's aggressiveness in pushing them to accept the price he set (Informants No. 17, No. 18). They felt that they were coerced to sell and therefore refused to cooperate. This solution also failed.

Similarly, all the other solutions attempted during 2001 and 2002 failed. Intense conflict and failure to find solutions critically damaged the mutual trust among shareholders. Minor shareholders and Su no longer trusted each other. They worked to undermine each other and undercut each other's agendas. Minor shareholders also overthrew Su from his position as chair of the board. After Su stepped down, the chair position rotated among Wei, Dai, and other people. However, "no matter who became the chair, other people soon became discontent and would seek to overthrow [the chair] again" (Supernova Archive No. 5, 131).

Despite all the conflicts, minor shareholders refused to depart Supernova. One of the reasons was that minor shareholders were fully aware of the 40–50 percent annual growth rate and the substantial financial returns possible in the future (Supernova Archive No. 1). Leaving Supernova meant giving up a bright financial future. Neither did conflicts lead to the collapse of Supernova. Shareholders tacitly "kept the door closed" whenever they were fighting against each other (Supernova Archive No. 5, 29). Therefore, most teachers did not know shareholders were in fighting. Thus, the educational services were not interrupted by the conflict.

Since shareholders fought against each other but no one could leave, Supernova at the shareholder level entered a stage of organizational deadlock. Under deadlock, shareholders could not advance their agenda or pull themselves out. Su and others started to ask the question, Were there any solutions that could help minor shareholders depart Supernova with compensation? In addition, the IPO started to present a new meaning to shareholders. Previously, an IPO only meant a shortcut to becoming billionaires. But now, an IPO started to make sense to internal actors as a new, and perhaps the only, way out of the deadlock.

THE PROFESSIONALIZATION OF
FINANCIAL MANAGEMENT

Another way in which internal conflict led to Supernova's IPO was through professionalization of financial management. Intense conflicts were associated with the depletion of mutual trust among shareholders. As shareholders no longer trusted Su, the former group pushed to oust the financial manager who was Su's family member. This kicked off a fast succession of financial managers at Supernova and their professionalization, which culminated in the improvement of the organization's readiness for an IPO.

During the partnership period (1996–2000), the financial manager was one of Su's relatives. He had no professional financial training or any prior experience therein. His loyalty and familiarity with negotiating with tax bureaus were all that Su needed at that time. During the partnership period, minor partners did not care about who the Beijing Supernova School's financial manager was, because the income of each partner was only associated with his own business. However, as corporatization blurred the lines between each partner's business and as conflicts escalated, minor shareholders no longer trusted this financial manager. As a former senior financial manager at Supernova observed,

> The oldest financial manager only knew how to keep a record of the expenses. People called him "the Old Third." He was Su's relative and whatever he said about how much we made, that was it. When you were just starting a business, it was most reliable to go with your family members, right? You cannot trust other people. This is very common for those who start with their bare hands. But because you're not operating professionally, other shareholders get suspicious: are the numbers you give us reliable? You say that I should be given this amount of money, is that all that I should be given? Are there any other revenues that you did not reveal to us? . . . The old manager did not even have a channel to present financial data, or he simply did not even have accurate number or financial statement. So minor shareholders felt unsafe and they demanded a new financial manager.
>
> (Informant No. 41)

The second financial manager, however, turned out to be a poor hiring decision. Without any knowledge about financial managers, shareholders at Supernova relied on the recommendation of Kunlun Consulting. This newly hired manager was the one who later embezzled the funds for receipts. He lost the trust of the top leadership and finally had to leave. Afterward, the succession of professional managers further accelerated. The third and fourth managers were professionally trained; the fourth even held a senior financial managerial position at a major technology firm (Informants No. 9, No. 41, No. 73). Later, two financial managers from the United States joined Supernova. Together, these financial managers set up an offshore company in the Cayman Islands as the entity to be listed on overseas stock market. With the two-level "contractual arrangements" in place, as figure 7.2 shows, Supernova evolved into a VIE structure (Supernova Archive No. 1, 3).

The eroded trust among shareholders also fueled the formalization and standardization of Supernova's financial statements. No longer trusting financial numbers prepared by Su's relative, minor shareholders demanded that more professional accounting firms be hired. Two US accounting firms were hired. One was hired to provide accounting and consulting services; the other was responsible for auditing. These two firms, both among the world's Big Four accounting and auditing, produced professional statements for three consecutive years. According to minor shareholders, Su would not have considered hiring these firms, because they cost Supernova a large portion of its annual gross profit (Supernova Archive No. 9). In the early 2000s, even highly resourceful Chinese state-owned enterprises rarely used US accounting firms

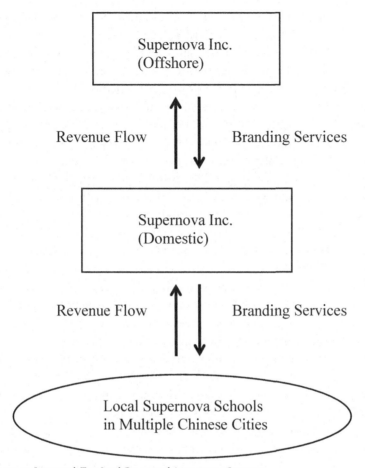

FIGURE 7.2. Supernova's Two-Level Contractual Arrangement Structure

(ibid.). But the distrust among shareholders necessitated hiring US firms despite their high cost.

ON THE EVE OF THE IPO

Since Chinese regulators did not allow IPOs of SEOs on the domestic stock market and since the US stock market is often associated with high valuation, Supernova leaders were considering an IPO on the US stock market. To make this happen, a US venture capital firm seemed indispensable. To begin with, since US investors had little knowledge about the Education Industry or the risk of investing in this industry, a US venture capital could help bridge the information gap. Furthermore, Supernova leaders had little knowledge of, or experience with, IPOs, let alone an IPO on an overseas stock market. The entry of a US venture capital can help Supernova leaders overcome the cultural, information, and knowledge barriers to being listed on the US stock market.

Given this context, it was unsurprising that Supernova advanced to secure investment from Taurus Global, a US venture capital, in 2004. Initially, the leader of Taurus China was doubtful of the prospect of this investment because no organization in the Education Industry had ever demonstrated the basic level of financial professionalism. After the initial contact with Supernova, however, she was surprised by the professionalism of all the financial statements and auditing reports. Soon after confirming that the Big Four had prepared all financial reports, this Taurus leader immediately agreed to invest US $30 million for a 10 percent stake of Supernova.

After the investment by Taurus, an IPO increasingly made sense to Supernova shareholders as an innovative and feasible solution to the deadlock. With a clear agenda to cash out through an IPO, Taurus convinced minor shareholders that an IPO was now within reach and could be their last chance to exit the deadlock with decent compensation. According to Taurus, an IPO was a more open and transparent platform compared to other failed solutions and, most importantly, it was an option Su could not control or manipulate. Moreover, the entrance of Taurus created a powerful coalition. Minor shareholders started to push hard toward an IPO and became allies of Taurus. Previously, all minor shareholders held a total of 45 percent of shares, the same percentage as that held by Su himself. With the entrance of Taurus, their total shares reached 55 percent—10 percent higher than Su's.

Although Su initially welcomed the investment of Taurus and an IPO, he became increasingly opposed to going public because he gradually learned the meaning of the IPO for him: substantial loss of control. Despite Su's opposition, the momentum to go through with an IPO had become unstoppable due to the new alliance between minor shareholders and Taurus. It finally became clear to Su that without an IPO, "there would be no way out of this mess" and that "anyone blocking the way of an IPO would be doomed" (Supernova Archive No. 5, 140). Eventually, Su agreed to go public. Supernova filed the application for an IPO and went public on the New York Stock Exchange in 2006.

The Contradiction: Formalization and the Escalation of Opportunism

To be sure, the IPOs of Supernova and other SEOs entailed circumventing the state ban. Preparing for an IPO sometimes also involved breaking cooperation norms with business partners or colleagues.[11] Overall, however, being listed on overseas stock market meant standardization and compliance with formally written overseas regulations.

For example, Supernova built up its formal structure and procedures that accorded with US stock market requirements during the IPO preparation. A former senior manager at Supernova recalled the systematic effort Supernova managers made in order to comply with US stock market standards:

> I took over this branch school when Supernova started to prepare for [its] IPO. We started to follow a series of rules and procedures. We went through a long and winding process of restructuring called 404 reforms.[12] The idea, if I remember correctly, was to comply with the Sarbanes-Oxley Act. I think the whole idea was to strengthen internal control. The Big Four US accounting firms came to do auditing. They selected a few branch schools for examination. If someone got selected but failed, he would be blamed for ruining the IPO process. . . . So that meant we needed to reform a lot of internal procedures. We needed to change the way we did purchases. For example, the standard procedure required that the manager responsible for purchases and the manager responsible for reimbursement should not be the same. Also, you cannot ask the same person to do both finance and accounting. You need to separate the job on money from the job on booking. You know, these are just the basic standard procedures. But we just had not been doing that before.
>
> (Informant No. 64)

Supernova's IPO was a turning point for the Education Industry. It became clear to all SEOs that IPOs come with huge material benefits and reputational gains. Other SEOs also found that legal and institutional barriers were possible to overcome, and they became cognizant of every necessary step for overcoming those barriers. Furthermore, the first IPO showed Wall Street and other global investors that the Education Industry was a gold mine. Domestic and foreign venture capital firms flocked into the industry to look for the next Supernova.

The entrance of massive amounts of capital altered the behaviors of entrepreneurs and managers in the Education Industry, contributing to a spiral escalation of opportunism. Entrepreneurs became interested in not only collecting tuition payment but also securing investment. Some SEOs even dramatically increased their spending in order to impress investors. One of the founding members of Blue Ocean lamented the changed behaviors of investors and entrepreneurs after Supernova's IPO:

> I think Supernova's IPO in 2006 was a watershed event in the Education Industry. Domestic and international capital all rushed here. . . . They totally

messed up this industry. All they cared about was wrapping up SEOs with new covers for IPOs and expanding to new niches quickly. . . .

Once the investment is in, the salaries for executives and staff can double. But where do you get the revenue? So they have to expand rapidly. Their management and quality control cannot adapt to the expansion. They run deficits. They lose what they made. They also lose investors' money. You know, without Supernova, no one ever would have thought about going IPO. Neither did investors think about investing in Chinese SEOs. This industry has been doomed since Supernova's IPO. The vitality of this industry has still not recovered yet.

(Informant No. 8)

Apparently, founders, managers, and investors changed their behaviors in the wake of the first wave. Some of them unlocked new forms of opportunistic practices, and others brought back opportunistic practices that had disappeared. Some of these practices, such as pulling students away, violated both cooperation norms and state regulations. In what follows, I use a few examples to discuss three typical approaches of opportunistic practices related to securing investment.

OPPORTUNISTIC PRACTICES BY ENTREPRENEURS

The two most common opportunistic practices adopted by entrepreneurs were securing investment through deception and breaching agreements after investment. In both cases, entrepreneurs intentionally violated cooperation norms. A former senior manager of Roaring English recalled how Roaring's founder, Duan Ping, breached agreements with investors and put the investment money into Duan's own pocket:

At that time Duan told others he wanted to go IPO. He also invited a US firm to do auditing. It looked serious, right? Some of the local investors, like the Holy Wood Group in Guangzhou, invested millions. But soon after they gave Duan the money, Duan no longer obeyed the rules they agreed on. It was not the first time, you know. A few years ago, another investor came in but soon Duan and these people broke up. Duan had zero respect for the rules. People in the Holy Wood Group asked him, "You guys need to be transparent for your finance and you cannot just take money away from the company." Well, that was exactly what Duan did. He just took their money home. He was like a child.

Finally, people from the Holy Wood Group confronted him and asked him what happened. Duan could not even name where he spent all the money. . . .

The Holy Wood Group people never realized that Roaring English did not even have a basic shareholder structure. It was just Duan's personal company. Yes, it looks like Roaring English had accountants [who] were not Duan's relatives. But they were Duan's ex-girlfriend's parents. And her parents naively thought that Duan would marry their daughter someday.

(Informant No. 49)

OPPORTUNISTIC PRACTICES BY MANAGERS

With their growing power and influence within SEOs, managers found room for opportunistic practices during the investment process. Some managers saw investors as their coconspirators and used the entrance of investors as opportunities to oust entrepreneurs. Instead of using formal methods such as voting in board meetings, these managers resorted to deceptive measures.

What happened to Blue Ocean in the late 2000s was most revealing. Blue Ocean had been a family business controlled by Gao Wenbo and his family. As part of the effort to transition his SEO out of family control and empower managers, Gao Wenbo promoted Song Jian, a manager with a doctorate degree, to the second most powerful position. To Gao's surprise, his SEO slid out of his control after he took a study trip to the United States. One of the founding members of Blue Ocean recalled how Song gained control with deceit and how the whole plot was interwoven with a major investment plan:

In 2007, Gao went to the US for further study. He signed a one-year contract-out agreement with Song Jian. . . . Basically, this agreement says that Song should give Gao [a certain amount] money each year. . . . But the idea was that Blue Ocean still belonged to Gao and his family. Gao gave Song all teachers, staff, and everything before leaving. . . .

But in one year, Song somehow changed the clauses into a company transfer contract. Gao was restricted to use the name Blue Ocean and was even forbidden to enter into the Chinese Graduate Exam business. What happened was that before Gao left, an investor would like to invest some money in Blue Ocean. Gao asked Song to talk with the investor. Gao knew that Song was very good at telling stories.

So Song came up with an idea. He registered another company with RMB 300,000 to hold shares of Blue Ocean. Then he hooked up with the investor to pump money into his own company. You know, some people in that investor's company knew about this and they said, "Hey, we were investing in Blue Ocean, not this unknown company." So Song used the chance of Gao's studying abroad to change the clause and gained the control of Blue Ocean.

(Informant No. 8)

MORE CONCERTED OPPORTUNISTIC PRACTICES

In some cases, there were opportunistic practices coordinated by entrepreneurs, managers, and investors. Their concerted practices were most often
aimed at tricking another group of people, such as entrepreneurs and managers of their acquisition target. Let me use Arrow Education's IPO as an example. Its entrepreneur, managers, and early investors disguised Arrow as an
organization that had completed a large number of mergers and acquisitions
in a short period of time so that the stock market investors and regulators
would buy the story and give the green light to an IPO.

A returnee from the United States founded Arrow in 2000. In 2010, Arrow
shares began being traded on the New York Stock Exchange after it acquired
twenty-three K–12 schools and SEOs in China. Arrow was able to launch such
a large-scale merger and acquisition after securing US $150 million from vari-
ous investors. But its success story took a sharp turn in 2013, only three years
after the IPO. Multiple entrepreneurs from the acquired SEOs filed reports to
auditing firms and the US Securities and Exchange Commission (SEC) and
accused Arrow of fraud.

A close examination reveals that Arrow acquired many SEOs through opportunistic practices by its entrepreneur, managers, and early investors. A key
opportunistic practice was promising everything with nothing. According to
one of the complaints filed with the SEC, Arrow used half cash and half stock
to purchase 100 percent of the operation and revenue rights of a K–12 school
in Hunan province. After the acquisition, Arrow became the holding company for the Hunan school, and the founder of the Hunan school became the
shareholder of Arrow.

In a secret deal, Arrow promised the Hunan school founder that Arrow's
stock after the IPO would surge and make the founder a billionaire. In return,
Arrow asked the founder to return the cash he had received from Arrow in
the name of software sales. In other words, Arrow gave the founder money
but asked him to send the money back secretly, so that Arrow could obtain
an asset with nothing but a promise of future stock price. Shortly after, Arrow stock began trading on the New York Stock Exchange. But since its stock
price plunged, the founder of the Hunan school lost the prospect of becoming
a billionaire. He felt that the whole thing was a hoax, and he filed complaints
against Arrow to auditors and regulators.

Complaints against Arrow came from multiple directions. Another complaint to the SEC accused Arrow of violating the promise of keeping tuition
steady. According to the complaint, Arrow increased tuition in order to impress investors with a better financial statement before the IPO. In light of

these complaints, a court in the Cayman Islands, where Arrow's VIE was located, weighed in. This court ordered Arrow into provisional liquidation. In 2014, Arrow was forced into insolvency. Although Arrow was out of spotlight after that, its capital-dependent merger and acquisition model did not die out. In 2015, a group of former Supernova senior managers inherited this model and founded Whooshing Education. By 2018, Whooshing had been listed on the US stock market.

THE RETURN AND DEVELOPMENT OF
THE OLD TRICKS

The escalation of opportunism since the first IPO wave entailed not only the emergence of new opportunistic practices but also the resurfacing and rebranding of old tricks. For example, there was a return of pulling students away. As investment poured into the Education Industry, there came a wave of entrepreneurship by former teachers and managers of market leaders, such as Supernova. Like those who pulled students away in the 1990s, new entrepreneurs stole students from their former employers. What made the new practice of pulling students away distinct was that these new entrepreneurs were less interested in the tuition of students than the role of student enrollment in securing investment. For example, Supernova teachers and managers staged a massive exodus in the 2010s, and some of them and especially TOEFL/GRE and SAT teachers pulled students away from Supernova. A former manager at Supernova who became a "solo" entrepreneur himself explained what rationales were behind this opportunistic practice:

> There were some people who pulled students away from Supernova. If you take a look at the profiles of those teachers, you will see that most of them did not come from the K–12 department, but from TOEFL/GRE, SAT, and IELTS. Before [the 2010s], very few Supernova teachers went out to do entrepreneurship. This is because they earned as much as what they could do by themselves and they did not have to worry about recruiting students. There was no incentive. Why would they go out and face the fierce competition?
>
> Now things are different. Now under the one-on-one or small class model, a TOEFL/GRE or SAT class asks for about RMB 1,200 per hour. If you go on solo, you can probably earn RMB 800 per hour. So you only need a few students from Supernova to show investors that your business is sustainable.
>
> (Informant No. 14)

Another opportunistic practice that resurfaced was engaging gang members to occupy the market. Gang members were involved to cause disorder of competitors and increase student enrollment in a short period of time, both of which can help capture the hearts of investors. To secure investment, Blue Ocean launched attack on Blue Wings, a major competitor of Blue Ocean, in 2008. When Blue Wings was delivering a demo class in a college, Blue Ocean mobilized a group of gang members to storm into Blue Wings' classroom (Informant No. 8). These intruders handed out Blue Ocean pamphlets and demanded that all students leave immediately. When being confronted by Blue Wings' staff, Blue Ocean people swung fists and chairs at those staff. Six people were injured and two of them suffered broken noses. The violence did not stop there. After the fight, Blue Ocean and Blue Wings engaged in a number of standoffs. Combining gang violence with investment was a new development of the old opportunistic practice.

The third opportunistic practice that came back to life was SEO entrepreneurs absconding with collected tuition. As mentioned in chapter 2, such incidents occurred in the 1980s and 1990s and students had deep-seated worries about such incidents then. According to two veteran entrepreneurs in the Education Industry, the problem of absconding became pricklier after the Education Industry was connected to the financial market in the 2010s (Informants No. 4, No. 61). There are several reasons for this.

First, SEOs in the 2010s were under tremendous pressure to increase spending in order to lure investors, which added to their financial burden and increased the risk of capital chain rupture. To impress investors, some SEOs rented lavish office buildings and used fancy decorations. These aggressive spending practices sent some profitable SEOs into deficit. In such situations, any tiny enrollment reduction or environmental volatility could fracture the capital chain of an SEO. Second, SEOs were encouraged to profit more from investment instead of tuition, which further added to their financial risk. Indeed, SEOs of the 2010s charged much higher tuition than did the early SEOs, and the former were also likely to demand a long-term tuition payment. These practices had the effect of increasing cash flow, but since SEOs were interested in reaping greater financial benefits from investing tuition, financial risk in fact increased.

When capital chain rupture or bankruptcy was on the brink, some entrepreneurs chose to disappear with the remaining tuition. The rising number of absconding cases was the context for the case mentioned in chapter 2: the education bureau asked some large SEOs to accept students from another SEO whose founder ran away (field notes, 6/10/2014). The exacerbation of the situation was the major reason why, in 2018, state regulators started to forbid SEOs from collecting tuition for more than three months.

OPPORTUNISM AND THE COURSE TO CONNECT
WITH FINANCIAL MARKETS

Partly due to such prevailing opportunistic practices, leading SEOs' attempts
to embark on global financial market were not short of failures, such as failures for IPOs. For example, Blue Ocean, Blue Wings, and Roaring English
kicked off IPO plans but were not able to land on stock markets after multiple
attempts. Although their failures could be attributable to diverse causes, opportunistic practices between managers and investors were one of the major
contributors for the failures. Again, let me illustrate this point with the case of
Blue Ocean. Song Jian, the hired top manager of Blue Ocean not only tricked
the founder but also deceived an investor. The whole drama culminated in a
conflict between Song and the investor. One of the founding members of Blue
Ocean described how Song and the investor fought against each other:

> Song just knew how to trick investors. He wanted to go IPO and wanted to
> show off to investors. At that time, our annual revenue was about RMB 6 mil-
> lion. But Song told investors we made about 400 million a year. He also moved
> Blue Ocean to a high-end office building. That was very expensive. The cost
> went up like a rocket. . . . Those investors did not do anything to stop him.
> You know how investors made money, right? They would help you go IPO, but
> regardless of whether the IPO pulls through, investors will earn their commis-
> sions. . . . Eventually those people who gave money to the investors were the
> unfortunate guys.
>
> Later, Song and the investor fought against each other. The investor crafted
> the paperwork very well, leaving only 9 percent of shares to Song. They also
> had a valuation adjustment mechanism. Basically Song had to promise how
> much revenue and profit he had to show to the investor, otherwise the inves-
> tor can claim more shares. But Song controlled Blue Ocean and did not give
> up the shares. Finally the investor went with a lawyer and argued with Song.
> You know what happened? Song hit the investor and the investor had to call
> the police.
>
> (Informant No. 8)

After the fight, the relationship between Blue Ocean and the investor was
damaged. Due to the deteriorating relationship with investors and other factors, Blue Ocean's IPO plan went sour.

For SEOs that had already been listed on overseas stock markets, engaging
in opportunistic practices cost them dearly. Some SEOs ended up being delisted or withdrawn from stock markets. During the first wave of IPOs from
2000 to 2010, more than ten Chinese SEOs landed on overseas stock markets.

However, six of them had been delisted or withdrawn by 2020. Some of the six SEOs, such as United IELTS and Duvell, withdrew from stock markets for a variety of reasons, such as governance issues and financial crisis worsened by their poor stock performances. But there were three SEOs, including Arrow, that were delisted from stock market by regulators due to fraud or deception. As the case of Arrow shows, complaint reports alleging opportunistic practices provide sufficient support for US regulators to remove an SEO from the stock market.

Conclusion

This chapter investigates how the Education Industry became deeply embedded in the global financial market from the mid-2000s to 2018. I focused on the early IPO processes of market leaders. I found that environmental changes and institutional demands were indeed major catalytic factors for IPOs that came after Supernova's. At the center of this institutionalization process was isomorphism: market leaders imitated Supernova and each other. Because more and more overseas IPOs succeeded and some Chinese SEOs started to pressure the Chinese state for policy changes, the state finally opened domestic stock markets to SEOs. This is also a classic example of how bottom-up changes characterized the marketization of the Education Industry.

Again, Supernova was an exception since its IPO followed a unique trajectory. Its IPO was primarily driven by its adaptation rather than environmental selection. Specifically, intraorganizational dynamics played an indispensable role in Supernova's IPO. The intraorganizational conflict pushed Supernova to move toward stock markets through deadlock and professionalization.

Being connected with global stock market helped SEOs formalize their structures and procedures. But formalization and compliance with rules were only part of the picture. As an immense amount of capital flooded the Education Industry, there was also a return and new development of opportunistic practices. Entrepreneurs, managers, and investors broke cooperation norms when dealing with each other. The Education Industry's financial revolution took two seemingly contradictory routes: institutionalization and an escalation of opportunism.

Conclusion

Studying "social embeddedness," we claim, means not the denial of agency, or even groups, but rather an appreciation for the localized, ambiguous, and contradictory character of these lives.

JOHN PADGETT AND CHRISTOPHER ANSELL (1993, 1310)

[The] state often took actions that blunted the course of a given conception and thereby opened up the possibility for a new course of action.

NEIL FLIGSTEIN (1990, 21)

This book tells a story of change and continuity. I start with the research question about how and why the Education Industry privatized and marketized in the last four decades despite the state's restrictive policies. I answer this question by closely examining this industry's twenty-eight market leaders with interviews, archives, and observation data. In addition to looking at how macro institutional demands imposed changes from top down, this book puts more analytical weight on how opportunists and their entrepreneurs pushed changes from below under two-dimensional ambiguity. This bottom-up trajectory constitutes not only a distinct path of education privatization and marketization but also a new account of how China's private sector has emerged and thrived right under the nose of a giant state sector.[1]

There is another question I asked in the introduction of this book: Why do today's students and their parents seem to experience ever-growing anxiety for education despite more options of formal and supplemental education to choose from than before? This anxiety has clearly been felt across contemporary Chinese society. Its specter has also begun to hover over many other countries. Let me still use China as a case study and show what we can learn from it. Throughout this book, I have provided a clue by focusing on education's supply side. Since I have been highlighting the role of opportunist SEOs and their opportunistic practices, it might seem to readers that this book considers these SEOs as culprits of the heightened anxiety.

Indeed, the opportunism of SEOs has played a nonnegligible role in further escalating the level of anxiety among students and their families. We have seen how SEOs adopted a variety of opportunistic practices, such as hunger marketing strategies, to make students more anxious about SEO classes. The tightened coupling between supplemental education and the financial market since the mid-2000s also unleashed a new torrent of opportunistic practices. These practices not only met the rising demand but also manufactured new demand and intensified competition among students, thus helping increase the level of anxiety.

Having said that, SEOs are far from the sole culprit of sowing the seeds of anxiety. Even if we limit our discussion to opportunism's anxiety-inducing effect, this book has made it clear that there are structural issues that are underlying the societal anxiety. One of the major petri dishes for opportunism is ambiguity. The state's unclear policies, their frequent oscillations, state regulators' lax enforcement, and regulators' lack of considerations for consequences have all exacerbated the ambiguity and the prevalence of opportunism. More importantly, we should not gloss over the societal anxiety induced by the broad social transformations in China and around the world in the last forty years. In other words, Chinese SEOs have not been the major producers of anxiety. They have been riding on the waves of societal anxiety. Moving beyond the supply-side-only storyline, but without diving deep into China's political changes, below I briefly discuss how its state and social transformations are related to the heightened anxiety.

Some scholars see the deepened anxiety in education as a result of "the theater effects." Students are like an audience in a theater. Initially, they are all seated to view the show; however, if a small group decides to stand up to watch, those in the back seats have no choice but to stand up as well. Eventually everyone stands up, but no one gains a better view of the show. Similarly, when some students and their families break the norm by overly engaging themselves in competition and supplemental education, others feel obliged to follow suit.

Despite the popularity of the theater metaphor, which does not account for actions of the state, some scholars consider the lack of government intervention as the root cause of the theater effects. According to Yang Dongping (2018), the renowned Chinese educator previously cited, the rule-less and chaotic theater described in the theater theory is only seen when theater regulators allow the audience to stand up in the first place. Applying this logic to the issue of supplemental education, the culprit for anxiety is the lack of intervention of the state, especially the lack of effective governance on degree-oriented formal education. Since supplemental education is a shadow of the formal education sector, Yang reasons, the chaos in the Education Industry simply mirrors the problematic values and ineffective governance of China's predominantly state-led formal education system.

More fundamentally, the state is partially accountable for the ever-growing anxiety because of its retreat and its problematic approach to reversing the retreat. In the last forty years, China and many other countries witnessed the retreat of the state in education and health care. Naturally, the state retreat created a vacuum. The demand surge for supplemental education, according to some scholars, is nothing but filling the vacuum (e.g., Yuan and Zhang 2015). Although the retreat of the state in the past created problems, reentrance of the state right now does not necessarily redress those problems. It is doubtful if anxiety will subside if the state simply reverses the course by increasing the supply for state-run schools and prolonging students' school time. The effects of such policy reversal are questionable not only because the socioeconomic context has changed dramatically but also because the unintended consequences of state policies deserve closer studies than do the intent of these policies. Moreover, the findings of this book show how frequent changes in policy priorities give rise to greater anxiety. Without addressing the complex underlying conditions for education inequality and education burden, calling for another campaign-style war against inequality and burden is likely to create more confusion and chaos, which are hotbeds for opportunism.

In addition to the state, myriad social factors matter in the production of societal anxiety for education. I have mentioned in previous chapters about the uneven allocation of educational resources and the East Asian cultural factors—meritocracy, Confucianism, and "contest rules." Another crucial social factor is the changed class structure, especially the rise of the urban middle class since China's market transition. In recent years and around the world, middle-class families face an ever-growing financial burden but try to catch up with elites and upper-middle classes (e.g., Koo 2016). Supplemental education has become a means for the middle class to maintain and elevate their class status. Furthermore, the one-child families as the dominant family structure, when coupled with the rise of the middle class, causes the anxiety to spiral. The middle-class families are known for translating monetary capital into cultural capital through supplemental education, and the one-child family structure requires intensive resources into the only child. Unsurprisingly, demand for supplemental education is concentrated in families with only one child (Yuan and Zhang 2015). In sum, these social and cultural factors interacted with each other to push the anxiety level ever higher.

Implications and Takeaways

IMPLICATIONS FOR UNDERSTANDING THE STATE
AND STATE POLICIES

My findings enrich our understanding about the state, especially its relationship with opportunism. To many economists, state regulations are futile in curbing opportunistic practices.[2] Sociologists, on the other hand, are more likely to suggest that state regulation is crucial in disciplining opportunistic practices in the market. For example, sociologist Mitchel Abolafia (1996, 11) argues, "As restraint increases, opportunism declines."

My study captures a more complex role for the state, particularly the Chinese state during the market transition. I show how, under ambiguity, the state's restrictions on opportunistic practices often unintentionally favored opportunists, facilitating the creation of a highly marketized industry. Fligstein (1990, 21) once said that the state's restrictions often block one course of action and thereby open up the possibility of another course, as I cited at the beginning of this chapter. This is true even under ambiguity. Without addressing the ambiguous situation, therefore, imposing all-out restrictions is most likely to be met with unintended consequences. In short, a market filled with opportunism could develop not only in spite of but also because of state restrictions.

My book also has implications for state policies. When there is ambiguity, state policies against opportunism often fail to accomplish their original goals and occasionally lead to consequences that are contrary to the policy's initial intent. Having said that, I am not suggesting lax regulation or deregulation. The problem is not regulations, per se, but the mechanism by which they are enforced: Do regulations deal only with opportunism, or do they also address ambiguity and its underlying conditions? Two underlying conditions are at stake here: ambiguity-inducing policies and mismatch.

By ambiguity-inducing policies, I mean that state policies themselves are a major source of ambiguity. As we clearly see in the Education Industry, ambiguity is a social condition under which regulations operate, but the former is also the fruit of the latter. In other words, state policies are a direct underlying condition for ambiguity, which in turn, affects state policies. As for mismatch, I am referring to the situation where the state espouses socialist philosophies but does not provide adequate support for those philosophies. In China's education in general, the state is usually a champion for the socialist style of equity, but inadequate state resources are invested into underfunded areas, such as childcare. There is also an unequal allocation of state resources across different regions and different types of schools.

When these two underlying conditions are unaddressed, ambiguity tends to linger and opportunism tends to prevail. These situations are seen in some other public goods–related sectors where privatization and marketization have not advanced as far as the Education Industry. China's state-run medical system is a case in point. Some studies have criticized this system as being privatized and marketized (e.g., Blumenthal and Hsiao 2005). Indeed, Chinese state hospitals often rip off patients with expensive and unnecessary checkups. The state also played an important role in pushing hospitals to the market.

It is noteworthy, however, that the marketization and privatization levels are restricted in some areas of this system. The visit fees and salaries of physicians, for example, have been kept low. This is because the state mandated that the medical system keep a socialist public goods nature, even though the state substantially reduced financial support for hospitals and pushed hospitals to the market (Yao 2017). As hospitals faced such ambiguity and felt financial pressures, they put revenue-seeking responsibilities on physicians. During this process, the emerging market force and the strong state power further undermined the already weak professionalism and professional associations in China's medical system, as happened in the legal and education systems.[3] In such a medical system, a wide variety of opportunistic practices by physicians, such as asking for gift-like money in red-pockets, are fruits of both promarket policies and ambiguity-inducing policies.

TAKEAWAYS BEYOND THE EDUCATION INDUSTRY

One of the takeaways from this book is how ambiguity benefits opportunists. I illustrate how opportunistic organizations in the Education Industry rose to market leaders and maintained such status under ambiguity. This rise-of-opportunists-under-ambiguity phenomenon is observable in other industries and outside China. The US rideshare industry is a case in point. This is an ambiguous industry because it has been unclear whether ride share firms are platforms or employers. Despite recent policy proposals in California, the ambiguity of the industry is likely to persist for some time. This ambiguity provided opportunists plenty of options for expanding. Uber, for example, has been famous for its noncompliance with local regulations: even if it knows that a city bans rideshare programs, it enters the city to operate without filing any paperwork. This opportunistic strategy proved highly effective in this ambiguous industry. Uber has been able to exploit this ambiguity and grown to be a giant in this industry.

This book is empirically grounded on an industry under two-dimensional ambiguity, but it is plausible that the affinity between opportunism and ambiguity is not limited to the two aforementioned dimensions. The US rideshare industry is ambiguous on a different dimension. To be sure, more studies are needed to justify this affinity. Some pioneering studies have already explored the linkages of the two. Padgett and Ansell (1993), for example, detail how Medici's ambiguity—not pursuing any specific goal—is driven by his flexible opportunism.

Another major takeaway is that opportunism is generative and productive. Opportunism entails deviance from existing rules and norms. One might argue that it is no new idea to include defying professional or technological norms as innovation. After all, innovation involves creative destruction (Schumpeter 1976). To date, however, few studies have gone so far as to consider violations of laws or cooperation norms as innovation. Except for some early functional studies on corruption,[4] researchers usually assume that violations of trust and formal regulations are destructive to market order. Opportunistic practices are said to contribute to crisis, not the boom of an industry (Fligstein and Roehrkasse 2016). Even though Abolafia (1996) admits that opportunism can make markets, he advocates that opportunism needs to be tamed and restrained.

This book, however, argues that under certain social conditions, opportunism, rather than norms and rationality, is the engine for the initial formation of an industry and its subsequent transformations. Opportunism facilitates these changes because opportunists are structurally positioned to introduce resources and organizational repertoires from unrelated social spaces into a nascent industry, as shown in the first three empirical chapters. In addition, opportunists can rapidly exploit the rising demand, spatial concentration and other opportunity windows in an emerging organizational field, thus contributing to the expansion of the industry's external boundary and reshuffling of its internal boundaries.

Another way in which opportunism produces changes and innovation is through the replacement of overly opportunistic organizations with more formalized ones. As mentioned in the empirical chapters, the initial success of opportunists is also associated with their high failure rates, especially by highly marginal entrepreneurs and among those that center their practices on violating laws and regulations. This means that institutional fields that were dominated by opportunists are likely to face drastic reshuffling as these fields institutionalize. When opportunistic organizations founded by highly marginal entrepreneurs die out, vacancies will appear. Newly founded organizations will move fast to occupy those vacancies, and their new practices also enter the field. Having said that, opportunism does not necessarily die out when institutionalization picks up steam. The development of opportunism can shape the course of institutionalization. Conversely, institutionalization on one level can spur the development of opportunism to another level.

Theoretical Implications: Organizational and Institutional Change

THE R–K TRANSITION AND ITS IMPLICATION FOR OPPORTUNISM AND SELECTION-ADAPTATION

I propose to use the r- and K-strategies, initially put forward in bio-ecological studies, to further develop the selection-adaptation paradigm as well as expand the meaning of opportunism. The potential of this proposal lies in developing a micro-level organizational ecology theory.

According to bio-ecological studies,[5] r-strategy species—such as insects and rats—can quickly occupy a resource-rich ecological niche (e.g., tropical islands) with quantity-based reproduction. This is in stark contrast with K-strategy species, such as human beings, that compete in a resource-scarce ecological niche with quality-based reproduction. Notably in these studies, r- and K-strategists are two distinct species, and there is no way for one to transition into another in a short term. These two species follow different environment selection mechanisms. These studies fall into a selection paradigm.

When applying the r- and K-strategy species to organizational studies, population ecologists adopt this selection paradigm.[6] As one of the earliest scholars to introduce the r–K species, Brittain and Freeman (1980) consider r-strategists first-mover organizations. In contrast, K-strategists are, according to them, organizations that compete with efficiency and more elaborate structures. Drawing on the semiconductor industry in the United States, Brittain and Freeman (1980) show that r-strategists are the dominant form due to having first-mover advantage in an industry's early stage when there is low population density of organizations and high technological volatility. When the industry evolves to the later stage and becomes densely settled, K-strategists gain greater survival advantage and succeed as the dominant form. In this succession of the dominant forms, selection trumps adaptation as the primary mechanism.

I propose to modify the existing r–K theory to enrich our understanding of opportunism and the selection-adaptation debate for several reasons.

First, considering r-strategy as an equivalent of opportunistic practice enriches our understanding of both r-strategy and opportunism. Zhao (2001, 64–65) points out that r-strategies are essentially opportunistic. In this sense, r-strategies should not only include first-mover actions but also encompass short-term actions that rapidly occupy an ecological niche with little regard for principle. Combining this insight with my empirical findings, it is safe to conclude that r-strategies enjoy advantages when the environment is volatile, resource-rich, and ambiguous. With regard to the meaning of opportunism, its close relationship with short-term action should be highlighted. After all, unprincipled and amoral economic actions are usually associated with pursuing short-term interests.

Second, linking r–K theory with opportunism offers new insight into the selection-adaptation debate. For biological theories and existing studies on r–K strategists, r-strategy organizations cannot adapt to become K-strategists. For biologists, this is because r-strategy and K-strategy species are entirely different and cross-species evolution is almost impossible in the short term. For organizational theorists, their refusal to consider the possibility of r–K transition is due to their belief in organizational process as a Darwinian selection process.

This book, however, shows how we can approach this debate differently. My findings about the early dominance of r-strategies and their waning dominance during formalization suggest that whether r- or K-strategists dominate a niche is indeed primarily governed by selection. Since opportunists can be considered r-strategists, my findings about the difficulty in opportunists' adaptation support existing studies' conclusions on the limitation of adaptation.

Having said that, my findings about a few exceptions—especially Supernova's adaptation described in chapters 6 and 7—suggest the possibility of an r–K transition in the Education Industry. My findings also point to internal conflict and other intraorganizational dynamics as engines for the transition. Whereas classic population ecology accepts a Darwinian assumption, the significant role of learning, culture, and leadership means that the r–K transition is essentially Lamarckian.[7] By using the r–K transition to bridge selection with adaption, I am proposing modifying organizational ecology and reviving the tradition of the micro-macro link: although traditional organizational ecology only operates on the population and other macro level, r–K transition of individual organizations is micro-level ecology. As chapter 7 shows, the micro-level adaptation even triggered macro-level selection. This also points to the direction of the firm-form interaction: we should be *specific* about whether we are talking about firms or forms, but that does not mean we should *separate* them in our analyses.

Since the 1970s and 1980s, new institutional theory and population ecology have redressed previous studies' substantive and methodological pitfall that is caused by overreliance on the internal dynamics of individual organizations. By emphasizing supraorganizational forces, new institutional theory and population ecology remind us of the limitation of only looking at intra-organizational dynamics.

Over the years, however, new institutional theory has given much more focus to supraorganizational factors than to intraorganizational dynamics. Although some early versions of new institutionalism have expressed interest in individual organizations, their internal conflicts and their roles in effecting broader changes (e.g., Tolbert and Zucker 1983), later versions explicitly oppose examining intraorganizational dynamics (e.g., DiMaggio 1991, 268)

Recently, institutional scholars have launched reform agendas for new institutional theory. One of the major reform agendas on institutional logics and institutional complexity, as mentioned previously, is to question new institutionalists' claim about the prevalence and benefits of a single coherent institutional logic. The uniqueness of interinstitutional spaces, according to this reform agenda, is the multiplicity of normative and cognitive systems within these spaces (Thornton, Ocasio, and Lounsbury 2012, 3–4).

Despite their recognition for the complexity in institutional spaces, studies under this reform agenda still tend to "imply way too much consensus in the field about what is going on and why and way too little concern over actors' positions, the creation of rules in the field that favor the more powerful over the less powerful, and the general use of power in strategic action fields" (Fligstein and McAdam 2012, 11). In other words, the strands of institutional logic and institutional complexity have glossed over the power imbalance and competition among multiple types of organizations.

On another front of reform agendas, there have been continuous efforts by institutional theorists to look into institutional entrepreneurs and institutional work in order to explore the role of organizations in institutional change.[8] This book specifies opportunists as institutional entrepreneurs when there is ambiguity. Opportunists are institutional entrepreneurs not only because they break from existing ways of organizing but also because the rise of opportunists is based on two enabling conditions for institutional entrepreneurs: the ambiguity of an industry and the marginality of entrepreneurs (Battilana, Leca, and Boxenbaum 2009, 67).

My book joins these reform efforts to depict how institutional changes took place as institutional entrepreneurs pushed changes from the bottom up. Furthermore, this book supports these reform agendas by locating the micro origin of institutional changes in the intraorganizational dynamics of institutional entrepreneurs.[9] Although this book is supportive of these reforms, I place greater weight on interorganizational-model competition and heterogeneity of organization models and their diverse access to organizational repertoires. Although this emphasis on intermodel competition seems like a field theory approach, my findings move away from the field theory's prediction on the state's capacity in supporting its allies (Fligstein and McAdam 2012). Specifically, I show that different approaches in building allies with the state led to different competition consequences: SEOs affiliated with the state were strong allies of the state and they also tapped into organizational repertoires of the informal economy, but they quickly lost their competitiveness. In comparison, opportunist SEOs founded by moderately marginal entrepreneurs started as weak allies with the state and were more closely associated with the informal economy, but their relatively solid connections with the state proved to be vital in their sustained success.

INSTITUTIONAL CHANGE WITH CHINESE CHARACTERISTICS

The Education Industry and other ambiguous Chinese industries have gone through a distinct path of institutional change: their formalization and corporatization did not follow a linear progression toward the Western rationalized model, as some new institutional studies describe (e.g., Guthrie 1999; Nee and Opper 2012). Neither is the opposite argument, that Chinese enterprises are inherently irrational, correct. The fact that Chinese enterprises seem to be rule breaking does not mean these enterprises are inherently amoral or lawless. Many Chinese enterprises share a distinct pattern of working with or working around morality and laws. That Chinese enterprises do not conform to the Western rationalized model does not mean these enterprises are trapped in the lasting influence of *guanxi* network and political connections.

As we have seen from the Education Industry, opportunistic organizations that became market leaders in the 1990s did not boast powerful political connections. In fact, these opportunistic organizations fell behind state-affiliated organizations in terms of social and political connections. In sum, the pattern of institutional changes seen in the Education Industry is neither advancing toward the Western model nor reversing to the traditional model.

This pattern—Chinese enterprises not complying with a Western rationalized model but complying with nontraditional institutional templates—is also observed in other Chinese enterprises. Rural Chinese enterprises of various industries thrived in the 1980s and early 1990s when their socially marginal entrepreneurs made full use of weak market institutions and developed their own informal adaptive strategies (Tsai 2007; Ang 2016). Over the years, Chinese organizations have generally marched toward greater conformity with formal rules and market norms, but compliance with formal rules has not overtaken spontaneous informal norms in priority (e.g., Zhou 2017).

In a nutshell, this path of institutional change urges us to rethink whether it is appropriate to directly apply the tenets of new institutionalism—supraorganizational pressures, norm compliance, clear and coherent institutional templates—to the complex Chinese reality. Of critical importance is the absent convergence of Chinese organizational forms to the so-called world society as well as the lack of an overwhelming normative or cognitive system as the foundation for new institutions (e.g., Meyer et al. 1997). Assuming that there will be convergence or an overwhelming normative system is, in fact, contradictory to a Weberian tradition that is the intellectual root of new institutionalism: different cultures are associated with different meaning systems that motivate social actors to seek economic interests in starkly different ways.

This book calls for more studies to discuss the possibility of an institutional change with Chinese characteristics. New studies should set aside the teleological agenda of a rationalized model, and they need to capture the winding road of formalization and professionalization that push Chinese organizations increasingly away from traditional *guanxi* paradigms. To set aside the teleological agenda, we need to keep an open mind toward how opportunistic practices are institutionalized. Scott (2002, 72) notes that "corrupt practices may become institutionalized in the sense that the beliefs underlying them are widely shared and provide guidelines about how to act in uncertain situations. But other norms and standards are also being crafted to support participants seeking to behave in morally responsible ways." The key question, according to him, is "How can we explain these differing trajectories? Why is it that in some situations, norm condoning corruption develops, whereas in others, codes reinforce honest actions?"

To further develop Scott's argument, I argue that institutionalization in China does not necessarily translate into the waning of opportunism. Under certain social conditions, new opportunistic practices keep popping up and old practices come roaring back. Such a spiral escalation of opportunism differs from the cyclic perspective that predicts the repetition of the same opportunistic practices (Abolafia 1996). This escalation process is not necessarily at odds with an institutionalization process.

Two caveats should immediately follow my proposal for investigating institutional changes with Chinese characteristics. First, we should be wary of the pitfall in overemphasizing the uniqueness of the Chinese culture. Of course, Fei (1992) has pointed out that Chinese culture tends to look at the collective-versus-individual conflict from a more relative approach.[10] From this perspective, the Chinese culture is indeed flexible with regard to non-compliance with rules and norms. Nevertheless, this book has made it clear that an overemphasis on culture is neither adequate for explaining temporal change nor appropriate for understanding regional variation in China.

Second, exploring institutional changes with Chinese characteristics is not only for understanding China. Gaining more knowledge about China's economic and organizational transformation is rewarding. But the key here is using the Chinese case to generate theoretical insight on the complex interactions between ambiguity, opportunism and institutionalization. Geertz (1973, 22) once said, "Anthropologists do not study villages. They study *in* villages." It is with this spirit that we carry out and carry on the exploration of institutional changes with Chinese characteristics. Even though there is a limit in generalizing local knowledge, keeping an open and broad theoretical agenda while treasuring the Chinese context will produce more intellectually stimulating results.

Acknowledgments

Sociologically investigating the social world where one used to be an insider is both exciting and challenging. It is exciting because conducting such an investigation is like discovering a familiar world with a new pair of eyes. It is challenging because the investigator needs to turn the cold blade of analysis onto the warm memory of the past. Writing this book has been just such an experience, both exciting and challenging. It is a book on China's supplemental education industry, in which I worked as a teacher and manager before my graduate study. Covering this vast industry's evolution over nearly four decades, this book is not free from errors and limitations, for which I am the sole bearer of responsibility. Standing at this project's finishing line right now, I feel not only the gravity of being responsible but also the joy of finally being able to give appreciation.

This book could never have been completed without the guidance and support of numerous informants, teachers, colleagues, friends, and family members. They helped me cast doubt on what I thought I knew. They reminded me of the pitfalls of relying on my past experience. Most importantly, they lifted me to reach more exciting heights and helped me overcome the most challenging obstacles. My deep gratitude goes to all of them.

My first debt is to all informants who shared their stories. Without their help, my goal of capturing an industry's complex dynamics would have been impossible. My interviewees, many of whom are veterans, leaders, and legendary figures in China's supplemental education industry, spent long hours with me and opened their worlds to me. Some interviewees voluntarily introduced me to other informants. I wish I could show my appreciation to key informants by listing their names here. To protect their identities, however, I have to be consistent with the rest of the book and conceal their names. As I am wrapping up this book project and writing acknowledgments in the summer of 2021, state regulators just hammered this industry with a new round of harsh restrictions. An academic work with a gestation of longer than ten years, this book has had no influence on, and has not been influenced by, the new regulations. Although in the current policy environment this book's cold analytical blade might disappoint some informants, I still hope my informants can join me and other readers in rediscovering the past and finding the nonjudgmental nuance in my arguments.

I have incurred enormous debt to my dissertation committee members who helped me bring an earlier version of this project to life. Since my first day at the University of Chicago, Andy Abbott has demonstrated how an intellectual works and what the beauty of knowledge production looks like. During our conversations over tea, he also taught me the importance of combining open-mindedness with brute force in research and kept reassuring me of the value of what I was about to tell. Dingxin Zhao led me into the fantastic world of sociology and shaped my taste in social science research. I am grateful that he pushed me to live up to the standard of approaching validity in both theory and story and doing sociological research both as a science and as an art. I am fortunate and thankful to have Lis Clemens on my committee. Her vision and professionalism were especially helpful when I was learning how to sharpen research questions and build analytical skills. Many times she guided my works' theoretical direction based on combing empirical details with me. Kimberly Hoang joined my committee at a most needed time. She brought fresh intellectual nourishment, new angles, and strong emotional support. When I doubted the potential of my project, Kimberly could immediately lift me up by saying how my research had "blown her away."

I also thank my fellow students, friends, and scholars who provided guidance and support during my transition from a student to a junior scholar. This book and its earlier versions were improved through various writing workshops with Yan Long, Laura Doering, Valentina Assenova, Chengpang Lee, Ling Han, Wen Xie, and Yuhao Zhuang. I thank Yang Zhang for never being shy about sharing his sociological imagination, which helped my research for this book project at various stages. At several American Sociological Association and Society for the Advancement of Socio-Economics annual conferences, Heather Haveman, Sebastien Lechevalier, and many other scholars offered thought-provoking comments on my chapters and papers related to this book.

At the University of Hawaii's Department of Sociology, I am lucky to have been in the company of wonderful colleagues and students. Their intelligence, caring, and aloha spirit have given me an intellectual home. When

I was writing this book and especially when the pandemic and other unexpected incidents disrupted my writing plan in the last two years, Jen Darrah, David Johnson, Aya Kimura, Krysia Mossakowski, Ashley Rubin, Manfred Steger, Pat Steinhoff, Myungji Yang, and Wei Zhang provided invaluable support and encouragement. At the Asia and Pacific Workshop, I enjoyed lively discussions with, and learned a lot from, Sun-Ki Chai, Hagen Koo, Rumika Suzuki, Yuki Asahina, Yusuke Tsukada, and Keqing Zhang.

My appreciation also goes to individuals and institutions that helped me smooth the data collection and book writing process. I would like to thank Shizheng Feng, Baijing Hu, and Ling Zhang, who introduced me to a number of legendary and otherwise elusive figures in China's supplemental education industry. At various points, Henry Levin, Mark Bray, Yuan Zhang, and the ETS provided guidance and help in collecting valuable data. The University of Chicago Center in Beijing provided venues, facilities, and other logistical support that any fieldwork scholar would envy. I also thank the American Council of Learned Societies for granting me a one-year postdoctoral fellowship, which afforded me the luxury of focusing on writing for a year.

I feel fortunate to have worked with excellent editors at the University of Chicago Press. I am grateful to Elizabeth Branch Dyson for her trust in a first-time author. Her warmth, professionalism, and responsiveness guided me through all stages of writing. Mollie McFee and Dylan Montanari provided all-around support and helped bring this book to final fruition. I am also thankful to the two anonymous reviewers who offered constructive and contextualized suggestions to the first draft of this book.

Words can hardly express my gratitude to my family. My mother's love for nature, respect for curiosity, and quest for a clear mind sowed the seeds in me for a scholarly career. Overcoming many challenges in this decade-long project was only possible with the optimism and perseverance she taught me. My father taught me the intrinsic value of observing as well as the importance of living an interesting life through storytelling, sports, music, and a minimalist lifestyle. My heartfelt appreciation and love go to my wife. Her encouragement and support are behind every line of this book. Through her and my son's efforts, strange cities were turned into homes. My stepfather, in-laws, aunt, and half brothers have also provided an immense amount of help throughout the years. Last but not least, I thank my four grandparents. It is through discovering their footprints that I became surer of walking on a less traveled path. They have long passed away, but their caring for me in my childhood and their life stories have always been significant sources of courage for me. This book is dedicated to the memory of them.

Appendix: List of All SEOs and Data Source

SEO Names	Locations of Fieldwork	Interviews	Archives	Observations	Secondary Sources
Supernova	Beijing, Guangzhou, Shanghai	Yes (founder, managers, teachers, staff)	Yes	Yes	Yes
Doo & Cool	Beijing	Yes (founders, managers)	Yes	Yes	Yes
Pioneers	Beijing	Yes (founder, teachers)	No	Yes	Yes
Blue Ocean	Beijing	Yes (founder)	No	Yes	Yes
Roaring English	Beijing, Guangzhou	Yes (managers, teachers)	Yes	Yes	Yes
Nova Academy	Beijing	Yes (founders, founders' family member, manager)	Yes	No	Yes
United IELTS	Beijing	Yes (managers, teachers)	Yes	Yes	Yes
Lingua Fun	Hangzhou, Shanghai, New York	Yes (founder, managers, teachers)	Yes	Yes	Yes
Whooshing	Beijing	Yes (founder, managers)	No	Yes	Yes
Le-We-Me	Beijing	Yes (founder, managers)	No	Yes	Yes
7Study-Up	Beijing	Yes (founder)	No	Yes	Yes
ABCKID	Honolulu[a]	Yes (teachers, students' parents, industry analyst)[b]	No	No	Yes
Ding Dong	Guangzhou	Yes (founder, teachers)	No	Yes	Yes
Duvell	Beijing	Yes (managers)	No	No	Yes
Central College SEO	Beijing	Yes (teachers)	No	No	Yes
Capital University SEO	Beijing	Yes (teachers)	No	No	Yes

SEO Names	Locations of Fieldwork	Interviews	Archives	Observations	Secondary Sources
Arrow Education	N/A	No	No	No	Yes
Shining	Shanghai, Chicago[c]	Yes (student)	No	Yes	Yes
Blue Wings	N/A	No	No	No	Yes
Questing	N/A	Yes (teachers)	No	No	Yes
Seven Swords	Beijing	Yes (teachers)	No	No	Yes
Cornerstone	Beijing	Yes (teacher)	No	No	Yes
Scholastic Time	Guangzhou	Yes (founder)	No	No	Yes
English Excellence	N/A	No	No	Yes	Yes
Spotlight	N/A	No	No	No	Yes
Hercules	N/A	No	No	No	Yes
Nasdaka English	N/A	No	No	No	Yes
Sea Dragon	N/A	No	No	No	Yes

[a] The author conducted all ABCKID-related interviews in Honolulu via telephone, Skype, and WeChat.

[b] The author interviewed thirty-seven ABCKID teachers but only included here those who went beyond their individual employment issues and discussed the organizational structures and procedures of ABCKID.

[c] The author conducted this interview with a former student of Shining who lives in Chicago.

Notes

Introduction

1. See Baker et al. (2001) about outside-school learning and related educational services.

2. See Aurini and Davies (2004), Bray (2009), and Ventura and Jang (2010). Supplemental education is also known as supplementary education or supplemental educational service (Koyama 2010; Aurini, Dierkes, and Davies 2013; Yi 2013). Other names that have been used to designate this industry and related organizations include "cram schools" (e.g., Roesgaard 2006) and "the for-profit testing and tutoring industry" (e.g., Koyama 2010). The existence of multiple names reflects the fluidity of supplemental education's boundaries. While some names capture key characteristics of supplemental education, others include only a particular feature or dimension of this industry. For example, the term *shadow education* epitomizes the tight connections between supplemental education organizations and the formal education sector, as well as the fact that the former often mimics the structure and practices of the latter (e.g., Stevenson and Baker 1992; Bray 2009; Mori and Baker 2010). However, there are various supplemental education organizations, such as those specializing in foreign language tutoring, that do not necessarily mirror the formal education sector of a given country. Similarly, the term *cram schools* exclude supplemental education organizations that do not specialize in test-preparation services. Therefore, this book uses the broadly defined supplemental education to include any organizations that provide educational services outside formal education.

3. For example, Koyama (2010, 57–60) lists a whole gamut of misconducts by US SEOs. Misconducts are also prevalent in non-US countries. Yi (2013) associates examination cheating by Korean students with malpractices of Korean SEOs. In Egypt, according to Sobhy (2012), the expansion of supplemental education is associated with the verbal and physical intimidation of teachers. For reports that cover lawsuits about cheating in standardized tests that involve Chinese SEOs and students, see Pan (2001). Fish, Parris, and Troilo (2017) also list various ways in which Chinese SEOs cheat customers. For a rebuttal to the cheating allegation, see Lu (2002).

4. See Aurini, Dierkes, and Davies (2013).

5. See, for example, Stevenson and Baker (1992); Baker and LeTendre (2005); Buchmann, Condron, and Roscigno (2010); Lee and Shouse (2011); Byun and Park (2012); Y. Zhang (2013); Matsuoka (2015); Zhang and Xie (2016); and Tsiplakides (2018).

6. For example, Aurini (2006) analyzes the legitimation of learning center franchises in Canada. When it comes to supplemental education in East Asia, Dierkes (2010) writes about the

entrepreneurs of Japanese SEOs (*jukus*), and Trent (2016) focuses on the professional identities of SEO teachers in Hong Kong. Despite the admirable efforts of these studies, each of them only focuses on one submarket of the supplemental education industry, and with the exception of Dierkes (2010), they are largely ahistorical.

7. For the top status of Chinese SEOs, see LEK Special Report (2019). It is important to note that this report uses stock market capitalization in 2018 to measure status. The wealth of billionaires (in US dollars) in education, as reported in the Hurun Report (2020), is also measured by stock market capitalization in 2020. Of course, stock market capitalization values are volatile and may not reflect the revenue or size of SEOs. For most of the 2010s and according to multiple financial statements, however, the two top Chinese SEOs as measured by stock market capitalization have also been the world's top two in terms of revenue and enrollment.

8. See Deloitte (2018, 2019).

9. See *China Daily* (2016). KPMG (2011) also reports that the number of SEO students was already near 100 million in the early 2010s. It is worth noting that these reports are possibly based on overall attendance rather than distinct attendees. Since it is plausible for one student to attend SEO classes multiple times, the actual number of students might be smaller than what has been reported.

10. See 21st Century Education Research Institute (2012) and Xue and Fang (2019).

11. See Lu (2002).

12. I will return to this question in the conclusion chapter. For now, note that Chinese urban residents clearly feel anxiety in education. A search on Google in 2021 with the two Chinese keywords *jiaoyu* (education) and *jiaolü* (anxiety) yields over 35 million results. Among these results, the top came from influential media and government agencies. For an example, see An, Jin, and Li (2021), an article that was originally published on *Guangming Daily* and later cited on the official website of the Ministry of Education at http://www.moe.gov.cn/jyb_xwfb/xw_zt/moe_357 /2021/2021_zt01/baodao/202103/t20210311_519047.html.

Similarly, participating in education has increasingly become an anxiety-inducing experience in Korea. Koo (2016) documents how Korea's middle class has become anxiety ridden, with education cited as a major stressor.

13. I was a full-time teacher at one of the largest SEOs in China from 2003 to 2007, and I also acted as a manager in this SEO from 2004 to 2006. After I came to the United States for graduate study, I taught part time at this SEO in the summers of 2008 and 2009.

14. These corporations are private not only because private entrepreneurs control them but also because shareholders are entitled to legally protected private ownership. In this sense, there is no contradiction between these corporations being private and some of them being publicly listed on stock markets. It is worth noting that the private ownership has been banned in the Education Industry, although SEO entrepreneurs figured out ways to circumvent some state restrictions after the early 2000s.

15. For example, *juku* in Japan have always been for-profit business enterprises instead of education entities (Dierkes 2010). In the United States, 63 percent of SEOs are for-profit and 25 percent are not-for-profit (Koyama 2010, 51).

16. Of course, opportunism exists far beyond China's supplemental education. During the 1980s and early 1990s when China's market transition just took off, opportunistic practices were prevalent across industries. Opportunism is also widely seen in other countries and regions, especially those that have undergone rapid social changes. In this sense, this book is about discovering patterns rather than tainting the image of any particular industry, country, or culture.

17. Despite this consensus, the next chapter will show how diverse the existing definitions of opportunistic practices are and how different my conceptualization of opportunism is from existing ones.

18. Opportunism, according to existing studies, stands opposite trust-based activities (e.g., Williamson 1993; Granovetter 1995; Lyons and Mehta 1997). Opportunism also deviates from trust-based cooperation that allows multiple parties to benefit through reciprocity. This is why Nee and Opper (2012, 21) adopt Axelrod's (1984) idea of cooperation and consider some Chinese private entrepreneurs' compliance with reciprocity and cooperation as signs of "abstention from opportunism." In dialogue with Nee and Opper (2012), this book uses their term *cooperation norms* to indicate all norms that are based on trust, reciprocity, and cooperation.

19. By systematically, I mean not only deviating from all the aforementioned three major dimensions but also conducting more kinds of such deviations and doing so more frequently than others. To be sure, any SEO might be compliant with certain rules and norms while being noncompliant with others. The key is that opportunists are *more* noncompliant than others. In other words, this book conceptualizes opportunists from a comparative perspective.

20. I chose these starting and ending years for several reasons. Although the Chinese state started to encourage private individuals to found SEOs and schools in the late 1970s, most cities did not have an operational regulation for SEOs until 1980. Wen (1983) illustrates how the situation was in Beijing. As for the end date, I chose 2018 because that is the year the Chinese state started to impose a new round of restrictive regulations and because I had completed most of the data collection by the end of that year.

21. The informal economy, also known as the second economy in transition economies, can be defined as the sum total of income-earning activities with the exclusion of those that involve contractual and legally regulated employment (Gábor 1979; Portes and Sassen-Koob 1987). To be more precise, a second economy is different from an informal economy in that the former is not only deviant from the formal bureaucratic processes but also conducive to social change (e.g. Stark 1989). Since China has gradually transitioned from a socialist economy into market capitalism, I use *informal economy* to describe both the second economy before the transition and the informal economy afterward. See subsequent chapters for more details.

The organizational repertoires of a given organization are the set of organizational models that are culturally and experientially available (Clemens 1993). They can also be conceptualized as all the available ways in which a given organization is operated.

22. Marginal entrepreneurs here refer to those who are excluded to enter a market, and many of these entrepreneurs possess low social statuses. Despite the state's stringent regulations on SEO founders' social backgrounds, a large number of SEO founders were university staff members, junior faculty members, graduate students, and even people who had never worked in the state education system. They were marginal entrepreneurs because they were not qualified as founders according to state regulations. They entered the Education Industry by circumventing state regulations.

23. In general, institutionalization refers to the process by which organizations move beyond technical requirements and adopt what the environment and others perceive as rational. See Scott and Davis (2003, 73), and Aldrich (2008, 50). This book also discusses specific institutionalization processes in terms of increased conformity to rules and cooperation norms as well as the formalization of organizational structures and operating procedures. For formalization of Chinese enterprises and its relationship with rationalization and institutionalization, see Guthrie (1999, 43–44).

24. In the existing literature, education privatization and marketization can refer to a variety of processes, ranging from the diffusion of voucher and other school choice plans (Friedman 1962; Carnoy 1998; Levin 2002) to the industrialization of scientific knowledge and the higher-education system (Mok 1999; Slaughter and Rhoades 2009; Berman 2012). Although the processes described in some of these studies are different from what the Education Industry has experienced, I consider these studies relevant because many of their cases and mine share similar underlying structural changes, such as globalization.

25. Even in economic sectors, findings about the state's role in developing the private economy have been mixed. See Oi (1992, 1995), Walder (1995), and Blecher and Shue (2001) for the role of China's local developmental state in promoting local private enterprises. On the other hand, the intent of the state has been ambivalent toward formal private ownership and the growth of the private sector (Tsai 2007; Y. Huang 2008; Nee and Opper 2012).

26. Also known as the "welfare sector" in socialist societies (Kornai 1997, 272), education and health care used to be considered socialist public goods in the sense that they provided affordable services to urban residents, promoted egalitarian ideologies, and manifested socialism's welfare advantages when compared to capitalistic societies.

27. Neoliberal policies in education reached their peak in the late 1990s, when China launched the "Industrialization of Education" campaign. In the early 2000s, neoliberal policies continued in the education sector, but China's overall policy agenda shifted away from neoliberalism, partly due to the top leadership succession (e.g., Gallagher 2005; Naughton 2007, 108). Chapter 5 will further illustrate how the expansion of the K–12 submarket benefited from the quasi-egalitarian policies of the early 2000s.

Having said that, this book does not oppose educational equity or other egalitarian policy agendas. What is problematic is not egalitarianism itself but rather the haphazard or piecemeal implementation of egalitarian policies without addressing some of the underlying structural issues, such as the concentration of resources in elite schools and the heavy emphasis on "contest rules" in East Asian education (e.g., Turner 1960; Stevenson and Baker 1992).

28. See Vogel (1990), Davis (2000), and Zhao (2001, 4) for examples.

29. I consider Chinese SEOs as more active not only because the number of publicly listed Chinese SEOs is higher but also because leading Chinese SEOs, such as Supernova and Doo & Cool, were the world's most valuable education corporations measured by stock market capitalization during the late 2010s.

30. Nonstate SEOs, commonly known as *minban* SEOs in Chinese, are educational organizations that are operated by private entrepreneurs not affiliated with any state institution and supervised by a particular department under local education bureaus. Since formal private ownership has been forbidden in the Education Industry, operation by private entrepreneurs does not mean these SEOs are private.

31. See the next chapter for a systematic discussion on new institutionalism. For an introduction, see Meyer and Rowan (1977), and DiMaggio and Powell (1983).

32. For a review on the definitions of organizational form, see Romanelli (1991).

33. For the argument on temporal order being the hallmark of historical sociology, see Abbott (2001) and Zhao (2015, 4–5).

34. As Ragin (2009, 8) points out, case studies run on multiple levels and an investigation of an industry includes inquiries on the levels of its submarkets and organizations therein. Submarkets are also known as segments or niche markets.

35. To be precise, this submarket also serves students preparing for other North America-oriented standardized tests that were introduced to and became popular in China before the 2000s, such as the Graduate Management Admission Test and the Law School Admission Test. For the sake of simplicity and since the patterns found in TOEFL/GRE providers can also be applied to organizations of these other tests, I use TOEFL/GRE to indicate the entire submarket.

36. IELTS is the equivalent to TOEFL for the British Commonwealth.

37. Having said that, these chapters will also inquire if the patterns found in Beijing's TOEFL/GRE can be applicable to other submarkets, such as the Chinese Graduate Exam and spoken English.

38. For current market leaders and especially those that are publicly listed, I use publicly available revenue data to assess if they are market leaders. For SEOs that were previously active and those that have not been publicly listed, I use enrollment to assess their statuses. This is because educational products among different SEOs were relatively undifferentiated in the early stages. Enrollment was a good indicator for revenue and market share when SEOs used similar products and similar unit price. Compared to revenue, profit, or market share, enrollment data was also easier to obtain.

39. This is not a problem because my research questions primarily concern leading organizations, their competition for market dominance and their influences on the entire industry. My purposive sampling also moves beyond random sampling in the sense that random sampling runs the risk of missing important cases that have shaped or are shaping this industry's landscape.

40. According to Hannan and Freeman (1989, 26–27), one of the methodological issues for only including successful cases is called "sampling on the dependent variable." This happens when researchers only use successful cases to infer the causal factors behind the successes. The issue lies in the difficulty in ruling out the possibility that failure cases might hold the same characteristics as the successful ones do. For a critique on the overemphasis on the issue of "sampling on the dependent variable" in historical analyses, see Adams, Clemens, and Orloff (2005, 25).

41. Also known as paired comparison (Ragin 2014, 38–41), balanced comparison means giving each case equal weight in the analysis. When there are a small number of cases, a balanced comparison runs the risk of determinism, a lack of degree-of-freedom and a narrow scope of research questions (Lieberson 1991; Zhao 2015, 24–25). For an organizational study, a balanced comparison of multiple organizations has the potential problem of neglecting rich and complex internal dynamics that are only seen in a single organization. In addition, balanced comparison often focuses on generating a universal causal model through comparison. Although this book aims to specify important explanatory factors, each empirical chapter usually gives more weight to specifying a process than providing a causal explanation.

42. For a book that includes several nationally and globally influential brands, complete anonymity is impossible. The idea that organizations and individuals can be de-identified in research is based on the assumption that all research subjects are randomly selected and therefore not substantially distinct from each other. For studies that are not based on random sampling, however, organizations and individuals under study are usually selected because of their distinct characteristics that tend to make them identifiable. Researchers also need to highlight these distinct characteristics to clarify the importance of the study and justify the choice of cases. In addition, organizations and individuals in nonrandomized studies often enjoy their unique market and social statuses. In such a case, it is difficult to make de-identification work without omitting

critical information about research subjects. There is no way a market's dominant player can be de-identified as an average organization. Furthermore, a nonrandomized study might need to use newspaper and online data to increase the validity of certain claims, but using these data increases the chances of making research subjects identifiable.

Despite the fact that completely de-identifying subjects is impossible, this book adopts pseudonyms for all my informants and their organizations (e.g., SEOs, universities and colleges in China) to protect their identities. To create additional buffers for my informants and make the names consistent throughout the book, I changed some titles in the references when real organization names are used in the original titles. I also put two reference items into the category of archives, because the authors of these items are SEO entrepreneurs and the real names of these SEOs are included in the original titles. Moreover and whenever possible, I made serious attempts to de-identify organizations and individuals by omitting certain highly specific information, such as the exact leadership position of an informant in an SEO, especially when doing so does not obscure the reality or my argument.

43. The four cities are Beijing, Guangzhou, Shanghai and Hangzhou. As mentioned earlier, Beijing is the most important research site because it has bred the largest number of market leaders. Guangzhou is the city where Roaring English started its business and housed its headquarters. Shanghai and Hangzhou are used primarily as points of comparison with the other two cities. Although Shanghai and Hangzhou have enjoyed economic prosperity, they did not contribute to any nationally influential brands until the mid-2000s when the K–12 segment flourished.

44. With that said, I make sure there are informants and/or secondary data for the majority of other organizations. In so doing, I reduce the problem of underrepresentation of archives associated with these organizations.

Chapter One

1. In general, this book follows the Chinese tradition by putting last names first for Chinese individuals' names. For scholarly works that are published in English in the West, however, I keep the Western name order as shown in the publication.

2. Institutional logics are socially constructed cultural symbols and beliefs that shape the behaviors of social actors (Friedland and Alford 1991; Thornton and Ocasio 1999; Thornton, Ocasio, and Lounbsury 2012). The study of institutional logic has been "at the forefront" of breaking from institutional determinism while simultaneously linking macro-level institutions with organizational strategies and practices (McPherson and Sauder 2013, 166).

3. In other words, Chinese SEOs possess ambiguous organizational identities. According to Polos, Hannan, and Carroll (2002), Zuckerman et al. (2003), and Hsu and Hannan (2006), organizational identity is audience based. An organization's identity ambiguity can be measured by the level of perception disparity by different stakeholders (e.g., state and consumers).

4. Across China's education sectors, the core of the socialist public goods lies in the degree-oriented and state-run formal education system. This is why I consider supplemental education, an extension of the system, as emerging on the peripheries of the public goods.

5. Informants No. 5, No. 6, No. 8, and several others described such experience. Such an account is in line with the idea that it requires certain structure-conditioned prior knowledge to discover entrepreneurial opportunities (Shane 2000).

6. Coined by Zuckerman (1999), illegitimacy discounts are used to describe the problems of resource shortage, stigma, and lack of legitimacy of ambiguous organizations.

7. It is worth noting that nonstate enterprises suffered from stigmas not only because they had unclear ownership but also because they emerged as a prototype of private enterprises when being private was naturally associated with political stigma during the socialist era. See Tsai (2007, 51).

8. See, for example, Lieberthal (1992).

9. According to Fligstein (1996), private ownership and corporate governance are critical because these institutions enable actors to organize themselves to compete and cooperate.

10. For example, the *Merriam-Webster Dictionary* emphasizes "taking advantage of circumstances" and "with little regard for principles or consequences" when defining *opportunism*. Indeed, the conceptualizations of opportunism offered by *Oxford Dictionary* and *Britannica* highlight a few slightly different qualities, such as making false promises, misrepresenting intentions, reneging on agreements, and lack of long-term planning. Arguably, however, these different qualities are compatible with each other in the sense that practices that prioritize self-interest over principles are short of long-term planning.

11. Having said that, Williamson (1993) joins Lyons and Mehta (1997) in recognizing that trust/distrust has many different forms.

12. It is worth noting that value neutrality does not mean value nihilism. As Weber (2011) argues, being value neutral only stops authors from being judgmental. It does not prevent authors from embedding their values in selecting topics and terms.

13. According to Fligstein and Roehrkasse (2016), opportunistic behaviors, malfeasance, and fraud are closely related to each other.

14. To be precise, Supernova by the end of the 1990s did not seek cross-region expansion outside of Beijing. Neither did Supernova launch any nationwide advertisement campaign. As chapter 4 shows, students from other cities came to Supernova's Beijing classes through the word-of-mouth effect. In this regard, therefore, Supernova did not violate the state's cross-region ban.

15. I am aware of the fact that existing studies consider it difficult for a group of similar organizations to adapt to environmental changes, but these studies do not rule out the possibility for any individual organization to undergo successful adaptation. It might seem that my findings do not add anything new to these studies. But as I go on to show, my findings reveal how the adaptation of a market leader catalyzed the changes of the whole upper echelon in the Education Industry. My contribution, therefore, lies in the linkage between the adaptation of individual organizations and the selection of organizational forms.

Chapter Two

1. To date, the highest contribution has come from an entrepreneur who founded the largest SEO in tutoring students for contemporary China's Civil Service Examination.

2. In a book published in the early 2000s (Lu 2002), a famous Chinese investigative reporter narrated how Su Leidong, after being publicly censured by Capital University, quit his lectureship from the university and began his entrepreneurship in the Education Industry. According to this narrative, the reason why Su quit from Capital University was because he was organizing his own informal SEO classes. Making money through these classes under the name of a Capital University faculty member allegedly violated university regulations. Although this narrative seems to make sense, a different storyline emerged in the 2010s in Su's TV interviews and his memoires: Su recalled that he had to quit because his recruitment of students within Capital University conflicted with SEO classes organized by the Capital University's English Department, but he did not specify the conflict and how the conflict led to his departure.

My triangulation efforts started with speaking to multiple informants during my fieldwork in 2014. From their accounts, I found that numerous faculty members at state universities used their state university faculty member titles when organizing SEO classes on a part-time basis (Informants No. 9, No. 10, No. 11, No. 16). One informant mentioned that state universities usually turned a blind eye to faculty members working as part-time entrepreneurs (Informant No. 10). This is consistent with what entrepreneurs of other SEOs said and what I read from newspaper articles and archives.

One informant who was a former colleague of Su at Capital University corroborated my speculation and provided rich details with regard to Su's conflict of interest (Informant No. 9): the director of the English Department was unhappy and jealous that Su was making money. This director asked Su to stop organizing his own classes and to help the department's SEO classes. When Su refused, the university publicly censured and sanctioned him. In China's early reform era, to be sanctioned by one's *danwei* and disliked by supervisors meant the loss of all kinds of benefits, including housing. Su had no choice but to quit.

3. I also use the Chinese Graduate Exam to assess whether the TOEFL/GRE pattern is applicable to other submarkets in the Education Industry.

4. For a review on the changes of China's education during this period of time, see X. Lü (2005).

5. The Chinese state started to encourage private individuals to establish nonstate schools and SEOs in the late 1970s when the Third Plenary Session of the Eleventh Central Committee of the Chinese Communist Party was held. Beijing passed its first regulation—The Temporary Regulation on School Operation by Private Individuals—in 1980. See Wen (1983).

6. In the 1980s, the supervising agency was called the Adult Education Bureau. The regular education bureau at that time was a separate government agency only responsible for formal education. In the 1990s, the Adult Education Bureau merged with the education bureau. For simplicity, hereafter I use *education bureau* to designate the supervising agency for SEOs regardless of timing.

7. See Institute of International Education (1980–1990).

8. See Zhao (2001) and Miao (2010).

9. Despite phenomenal economic growth in the early 1980s, the Chinese society was plagued with high inflation and corruption in the mid- and late 1980s. These economic and political crises culminated in the Beijing Student Movement of 1989. Students' confrontation with the government and the government's hardline response made prospective students increasingly worried about not being able to study abroad, which hastened their decisions to take tests.

As the situation intensified, there were rumors that the government would close the gates of China again and suspend studying abroad. These situations led students to conclude that they needed to leave China before it was too late. Students rushed to test centers and waited in long lines until midnight in order to secure test opportunities (Zhao 2001, 131). Moreover, one of the consequences of the government's crackdown of the movement was that many college students became disillusioned about China's future. They became determined to escape from the country. Students who were hesitant about going abroad made up their minds as the movement developed.

Another often-neglected role of the 1989 Student Movement was the increase of free time for a large number of students and teachers. University classes were suspended from April to August 1989. Multiple informants reported that they started organizing TOEFL/GRE classes in the summer of 1989 because as faculty members, they had no classes to teach, and students were craving for test-preparation classes (Informants No. 4, No. 9, No. 61).

This association between social movements and the expansion of supplemental education is also observable in other countries. For example, Dierkes (2010) shows that a large number of owners of small SEOs (jukus) in Japan had the background of being student activists during 1960s.

10. Here leading the market refers to being the top three players in terms of enrollment. Please see the introduction for the reasons for using enrollment as the key measure for market leadership.

11. This situation is similar to what Stark (2009, 46) describes as "bringing the second economy inside socialist firms."

12. This memoir is a published book. Including it in the reference list will reveal the names of the entrepreneur and his SEO. To protect their identities, I include this memoir as an archive.

13. Supernova was known as Nova Academy's division on English from 1991 to 1993. Nova in this period had a complicated structure. Nova Academy's top leaders were six retired professors, but its division on English was a relatively autonomous entity led by Su Leidong. A marginal entrepreneur, Su needed to subcontract this division under Nova in order to enter the market. In other words, this division was an opportunist SEO inside an intellectual SEO. Su broke away with Nova Academy and established Supernova as an independent SEO in 1993.

14. There are three clear indicators for the privatization and marketization: the state's passing of Non-State Education Promotion Act in 2002, public listing of SEOs on domestic stock markets in the early 2010s, and state categorizing SEOs into for-profit and not-for-profit ones during the 2010s. See Tao and Wang (2010) and S. Wang (2011).

15. See Tao and Wang (2010, 117–20).

16. This is the Chinese government agency that has the power to regulate all revenue-generating organizations.

17. Literally, what Su Leidong said should be translated as "people in the society" (*shehui shang de ren*). In Chinese, it refers to those who did not have stable jobs, especially those who did not have jobs associated with the state. Sometimes people also use this phrase to refer to gang members or hooligans.

18. Except for Su's division, Nova Academy was primarily an intellectual SEO. Although its title suggests a degree-oriented institution, this former entrepreneur confirmed that Nova had always been an SEO. After Su Leidong left Nova Academy in 1993, this SEO explored English and English-related classes in its Fifth Division (Informant No. 16).

19. See the previous chapter for a series of legitimacy challenges for nonstate organizations under two-dimensional ambiguity. In a nutshell, the state and consumers considered nonstate education in China as less legitimate than state education in the 1980s and early 1990s. Even in the 2000s when China's private sector has grown much stronger than before, SEO entrepreneurs were hesitant to register SEOs as nonstate since this label would hamper student recruitment (Informant No. 37).

20. *Hukou* refers to China's local household registration permit. For major cities such as Beijing, local *hukou* has been difficult to obtain for immigrants.

21. *Ganqing* means affect or sentiment in Chinese. According to Wank (2001, 168), enhancing *ganqing* through chit-chats, exchanging cigarettes, and bonding with business partners and officials is arguably less risky than giving kickbacks.

22. I should note that obtaining past test questions is different from the student-organized cheating that became popular after 1999 when computer-based GRE tests were implemented. Student-organized cheating was based on some test takers memorizing test questions and sharing them in online forums and others memorizing these test questions with hopes of running into them during computer-based tests.

23. SEOs did not have to pay any corporate income tax (*qiye suode shui*) until 2004 (Tao and Wang 2010, 118; Informants No. 20, No. 28). With regard to the sales tax (*yingye shui*), the story has been complicated and controversial. While some entrepreneurs contend that sales tax was minimal and often not collected until the 2000s (e.g., Informant No. 28), others claim that such tax was implemented at about 3 to 3.5 percent in the 1990s (e.g., Informant No. 20). Given the ambiguity of the Education Industry, no official document provides a timeline on the evolution of the taxation system.

24. Besides these entrepreneurs' preferences to negotiate tax rates, the absence of formal policy and formal procedures in tax bureaus also provided room for negotiation. Such a high level of informality also existed in other state agencies, such as electric power bureaus. Even in the 2000s, some Supernova branch school presidents were still able to negotiate electricity price in capital cities of northeastern provinces (Informant No. 64).

25. See chapter 1 for an example on how cross-region expansion practices became widely accepted in the Education Industry and how such rule-breaking practices escaped the radar of state regulators. The diffusion of cross-region expansion practices accelerated the formation of a nationally integrated market for supplemental education.

Chapter Three

1. Although this book is primarily concerned about opportunism on organization level, both organizations and individuals participate in opportunistic practices. For small organizations, organizational opportunism is often manifested in the opportunistic practices of entrepreneurs. Therefore, examining opportunistic practices by entrepreneurs, employees, and other individual stakeholders is relevant for understanding opportunism on organization level.

2. State SEOs also suffered from teachers' departing and operating on new enterprises. But on average, state SEOs encountered fewer teachers' opportunistic practices such as dumping classes and pulling students away. This is partly because the majority of teachers who taught at state SEOs were employees of the host universities. In other words, these teachers were subject to the pressures and incentives of these universities as well as peer pressure.

3. See N. Lü (2008) on the evolution of employment contracts in China since the late 1970s.

4. Unlike employment contracts, service contracts were originally meant for short-term and project-based relationships. In Chinese, employment contracts are known as *laodong hetong*, while service contracts are called *laowu hetong*.

5. This informant said so because Teacher Cheng was once beaten by a group of gang members hired by the founder of Sea Dragon.

6. Specifically, a veteran teacher who taught at Nova Academy/Supernova in the early 1990s and who was familiar with multiple parties involved in this event said that these accounts were rumors (Informant No. 39). On the other hand, another veteran teacher who taught at multiple SEOs said that he found this account trustworthy because he heard about a similar story (Informant No. 66).

7. Hold-up does not only occur within organizations. See Williamson (1981) for an analysis on interorganizational hold-up.

8. It is worth noting that using coercion on teachers violates not only cooperation norms but also state laws.

9. Yuan Shikai (袁世凯) was a top official and military officer of the Qing/Manchu Empire (1644–1912). To many ordinary Chinese, Yuan was known as a traitor because it is said that he

first promised to help revolutionaries against the Qing/Manchu Empire but then sold out these revolutionaries to the empire.

10. See note 6 of this chapter for the mixed findings.

11. See Davis (2000).

12. Having said that, these Supernova teachers also agreed that too much entertainment and too little substantive educational contents would hurt evaluations.

13. By subject, I mean a particular section of a standardized test, such as TOEFL listening, TOEFL grammar, or GRE vocabulary.

14. According to Burawoy (1982), some capitalistic employers organize game-like competition among workers. Through encouraging workers to compete for prestige and tangible bounties, these games have the effect of generating senses of satisfaction and belonging among workers.

Chapter Four

1. See Lafargue (1972).

2. In other words, the early stages of the competition within the group of opportunist SEOs and the late stages of the intermodel competition among opportunist, intellectual and state SEOs transpired simultaneously. Of course, even during the high tide of intermodel competition, individual opportunist SEOs also competed with each other. But what was at stake in those early years was which model became dominant.

3. A teaching norm only concerns what to include as educational content and how to deliver it. In comparison, a teaching model not only includes a teaching norm but also encompasses teacher management, price strategy, and other organizational repertoires.

4. Accordingly, the taken-for-granted teaching norms in this emerging market were similar to those for teaching English. Teachers who had been trained in English had legitimate control over how to teach test-preparation courses in TOEFL and GRE. Although the GRE is designed to be an aptitude test, rather than a language test, it was primarily considered a test of English in China at that time, with the exception of the quantitative reasoning section.

5. Crystallization can be conceptualized as relevant organizational repertoires being locked in. Some studies, including those in the tradition of theory of ambiguity, criticize locking in as a situation where innovation is restricted (Page 2007; Stark 2009, 177). Their assumption is that innovation is based on exploring divergent elements and retaining long-term flexibility, whereas exploiting existing organizational repertoires curtails innovation (e.g., March 1991).

Indeed, being locked in may lead to a static or compromised situation. But locking in also means exploiting existing organizational repertoires to such an extent that relevant repertoires are molded into a stable configuration. This is no easy task in an ambiguous industry where organizational actors were navigating uncertainty and conducting trial-and-error strategies. In this sense, the process for reaching locking in is also innovative.

6. *Meili* is the pronunciation for the Chinese equivalent of charisma.

7. For example, superstar teachers are widely seen in SEOs in Hong Kong, South Korea, and Taiwan (e.g., Ng 2009). Some SEOs in these areas and Vietnam also resort to large class size and motivational stories (e.g., Dang 2013, 106). Yet few use these elements so systematically as did Supernova teachers. Neither do other SEOs crystalize these elements into a stable configuration.

8. This Chinese idiom portrays a situation in which a person is determined to carry out his/her current project due to a lack of alternatives.

9. For a more comprehensive discussion on performative pedagogy, see Lin (2020).

10. It should be noted that the implementation of performative pedagogy proceeded not because the top leader of Supernova explicitly required teachers to use such pedagogy. Rather, it was Supernova's adoption of the market-based evaluation system and the coteaching model that indirectly locked its teachers into using performative pedagogy.

11. There are some social contexts in which Supernova adopted nationalist discourses. See Lin (2020) for more details.

12. Su's life stories in this paragraph are reconstructed from Lu (2002), Supernova Archive No. 5, and multiple interviews.

13. In China, there has been a popular idea that undergraduate institutions are a better indicator of one's academic excellence than graduate institutions.

14. This Chinese idiom describes a person who is knowledgeable but is incapable of conferring that knowledge to others.

15. The wuxia novels are a popular genre of fiction in China. As indicated by its name in Chinese, these novels feature people with superb kung-fu (*wu*) skills and hero spirit (*xia*). Jin Yong's wuxia novels are considered one of the best of the genre.

16. When new teachers copied others' motivational stories or nationalist comments, embarrassment sometimes arose: multiple teachers could be telling the same story to the same group of students and each teacher would act as if he or she was the creator of the story.

17. Having said that, there was substantial variation across different seasons and different types of classes. Average students-to-teacher ratios were often higher than 100 during summer and winter sessions. Multiple informants confirmed that it was common for a Supernova class in TOEFL/GRE to have more than five hundred students (Informants No. 5, No. 7, No. 9).

18. According China Statistical Yearbook (1990–2000), the monthly per capital disposable income for the Chinese population was under RMB 1,000 throughout the 1990s.

19. Five hundred students aren't always necessary to produce a touching class. What is more important than the class size is how packed a classroom is. Therefore, Supernova managers often preferred to pick smaller classrooms to create the atmosphere of packed classrooms (Informant No. 37).

20. Of course, this does not mean that Supernova controlled 100 percent of the market share. Other SEOs were still able to enroll students. For Supernova and these SEOs, some students signed up for classes but did not take the tests. In other words, it is not surprising that the total number of TOEFL/GRE students in the Education Industry exceeded that of TOEFL/GRE test takers. With that said, it is not easy for any single SEO to enroll more TOEFL/GRE students than the total number of test takers, especially considering the fact that there are test takers who do not attend any SEO classes.

Chapter Five

1. South Korea experienced a similar process. See Bray (2009).

2. According to Stinchcombe (1965) and Johnson (2007), imprinting is a process by which organizations' structures and procedures are stamped with the environmental characteristics of a given time, and these structures and procedures tend to persist. Imprinting is largely a selection mechanism, especially the so-called second stage when organizations are bounded by structural inertia. This is why Johnson (2008) claims that imprinting means nonadaptation of organizations. Interestingly, the first entrepreneurial stage Johnson (2007, 2008) describes seems to be highly adaptive because the organization she investigates was constantly reshaped as new elements were incorporated.

3. See the website of Ministry of Education of the People's Republic of China (www.moe
.gov.cn).

4. With that said, China's *overall* policy agenda in the early 2000s switched to emphasize
egalitarianism and independence from market forces, in part due to the succession of China's
top leadership (Gallagher 2005; Naughton 2007, 108).

5. *Affiliated transactions* refer to purchases and sales within a corporate group in order to
legitimize revenue and profit, from an accounting perspective. For example, Supernova's corporate entity does not generate any revenue or profit, and state regulators do not allow Supernova's
schools to distribute tuition payments as profits. However, Supernova devised affiliated transactions under which the corporate entity provided branding, training, and other services to
Supernova schools so that the former could collect payment from the latter.

6. In Chinese, "playing Tai Chi" means making a situation murky, shirking responsibility, and
passing the buck to others.

7. See the report by Zhong (2012).

8. Doo & Cool has been a leader not only in the K–12 submarket but also across the Education Industry. Its leadership can be measured in multiple ways. First, its revenue has been
the highest among Chinese K–12 SEOs since the mid-2000s. By 2010, when Doo & Cool was
publicly listed on the New York Stock Exchange, its total annual net revenue had reached
$69.6 million. Second, Doo & Cool's market share has been the largest in the K–12 submarket.
The K–12 submarket in China has been more local and fragmented than some other submarkets,
such as that for the TOEFL/GRE. In 2009, Doo & Cool had a 0.26 percent market share in China
and a 4.5 percent market share in Beijing, higher than its competitors such as Supernova and
Duvell. Third, Doo & Cool's stock market capitalization value surpassed that of Supernova in
2017 and was the highest among all Chinese SEOs between 2017 and 2018 (Doo & Cool Archives
No. 1, No. 2).

9. See Bjork (2015) for Japan's movement toward relaxed education.

10. Its Chinese term is *suzhi jiaoyu*. It is also known in English as "quality education" or
"education for quality." For a critical review of quality-oriented education (*suzhi jiaoyu*), see
Kipnis (2006).

11. See Xue and Ding (2009).

12. See P. Li (2017).

13. For example, the number of high-net-worth individuals, defined as those with over RMB
10 million in liquid financial assets, increased from 180,000 to 1.6 million from 2006 to 2016. See
Bain & Company (2017).

14. The literal translation for seat-occupying classes is "toilet-occupying classes" (*zhankeng
ban*); therefore, Yang claims that the name of these classes is disgusting.

15. See Xue and Ding (2009) and Xue and Fang (2019).

16. See Hannan and Freeman (1977, 1989). Put it simply, generalist organizations are those
that operate in multiple markets, whereas specialist organizations focus primarily on one particular submarket.

Chapter Six

1. Guthrie (1999, 43) shows that formalization is intricately connected with the rise of a rational bureaucracy within corporations. A system of rational bureaucracy includes, but is not limited to, a team of managers. Although family members of founders can also serve as managers,

the formalization process is most often associated with the decline of kinship-based managers because formalization requires moving away from personal connections (Guthrie 1999, 63). Moreover, Chinese family firms are well known for their lack of formal rules and procedures (Kiong 2005).

2. Of course, it is not uncommon for Chinese family firms to hire and empower non-kinship-based professional managers (Zhang and Ma 2009). Market and institutional factors also pressure family firms to develop managerial structures. However, the conflict between founders' families and non-kinship-based managers is prevalent among Chinese family firms for the following reasons. First, founders' families usually tend to retain control of their firms and prevent takeovers by "outsiders" (Chung and Luo 2008). Second, there is often much trust among family members within these family firms but little trust for professional managers (Zhang and Ma 2009). Third and as mentioned previously, family control is based on personal connections, whereas empowering non-kinship-based managers means moving toward impersonality.

3. Managerial revolution refers to the processes described by A. Chandler (1993): the rise of full-time and salaried managers in power and influence, the formation of managerial hierarchies, and the clarification of managers' career paths.

4. Besides teaching-intensive SEOs, there are service-intensive SEOs, such as Duvell.

5. See Fligstein (1990).

6. An organization is defined as "in the hands of a founder's family" if three or more strategic managerial positions, including CEO and top financial managers, are held by family members.

7. Of course, some franchisers also employed opportunistic practices against franchisees. In the late 2000s, it was not uncommon for SEO franchisers to violate agreements with franchisees, and in some instances, this happened despite the fact that franchisees honored agreements regarding marketing and student recruitment. See the report by Wang, Zhao, and Zhao (2010). This chapter does not discuss these cases in detail because I am focusing on the obstacles for franchisers' cross-region expansion.

8. This includes all branch school presidents and top leaders such as vice presidents but excludes Su Leidong and senior managers in noneducational departments such as finance and human resources.

9. Lu (2002).

10. Of course, some might argue that the difference is due to the fact that there were only a few branch schools from 2000 to 2005, and therefore, there were few branch school presidents to promote. This is a valid argument. My point here, however, is not about how things were during those early stages but about the changes afterward—becoming a branch school president outside of Beijing has increasingly become a necessary step before being promoted to top leadership.

11. Lu (2002, 200) also documents that Su Leidong likes reading strategic novels, such as *Romance of the Three Kingdoms*, and learning political strategies from them.

Chapter Seven

1. The total number of venture-capital-related investment cases in the Education Industry was in the single-digits before 2005, but the number increased to 86 between 2005 and 2010 (Deloitte China 2011, 2012). This number kept its upward trend into the 2010s. In the first six months of 2018, the Education Industry saw 137 venture-capital investment deals, while the number was 65 in 2016 and 90 in 2017 (Deloitte China 2018).

2. As the average labor cost rose in China in the 2010s and as Western labor forces struggled with wage stagnation during this period, hiring teachers and managers from the United States and other countries became not only possible but also financially desirable. Two top managers at Lingua Fun's New York Office told me that it only cost about US $42,000 to $45,000 per year to hire a teacher/education consultant from liberal arts programs of elite, private US universities such as Columbia University (Informants No. 82, No. 84). In some other cases, new technologies were used to connect global capital with the global job market. One of the examples is ABCKID, a Beijing-based English-learning digital platform that connected about 60,000 North American contractors with 500,000 young Chinese children by 2019 (Informants No. 87, No. 88; Lin 2021).

3. This global and transnational process consists of multiple dimensions, such as IPOs on overseas stock markets and investment by global venture capital firms.

4. The first wave refers to the twelve IPO cases on overseas stock markets from 2006 to 2010.

5. Here, institutionalization is used to indicate three interrelated processes. First, supraorganizational and institutional demands pressured SEOs to shift toward financialized operation. Second, the financialized form of operation was diffused not by each individual SEO's rational choice but rather through imitating market leaders and competitors and conforming to what is perceived as the legitimate form. Third, the two aforementioned processes were accompanied with a formalization of the structures and procedures of SEOs, as I will elaborate in the next section.

6. See DiMaggio and Powell (1983) about the isomorphic process.

7. VIE refers to a set of financial transactions and arrangements that link domestic firms to their newly established offshore companies. Many Chinese high-tech companies, such as Alibaba, used this structure to circumvent regulations of the Chinese state and went public on overseas stock markets.

8. Taurus is a US-based venture capital firm that invested in Supernova and benefited financially from the latter's IPO.

9. See Fligstein (1996). These fundamental market institutions started to take root in manufacturing industries after the passing of China's first Company Law in 1993. See Kang, Shi, and Brown (2008).

10. According to Informants No. 4, No. 28, and No. 41, for a long time Supernova's financial managers could not figure out how to financially link Supernova Corporation with Supernova schools. Between 2000 and 2004, these managers gradually came to understand how to realize "contractual arrangements"—using the corporation as the provider of branding and training services to schools all over China, with the former receiving revenue from the latter accordingly.

11. For example, it is said that some Supernova shareholders tricked a former top manager who was fired in the 2000s to sell his shares to other shareholders before the IPO, so his grievances and actions would not have hampered the IPO process (Informant No. 73).

12. Section 404(b) of the Sarbanes-Oxley Act requires a publicly listed company's auditor to attest to, and report on, management's assessment of its internal controls.

Conclusion

1. Until recently, the three major accounts for understanding the rise of China's private sector were the following: clear private property rights, state-led accounts, and bottom-up accounts. Since the private sector flourished long before the state's formal recognition of private ownership, economists' emphasis on clear private property rights as a precondition for

capitalistic development does not hold water (e.g., North 1981; Sachs 1991). The absence of the state's direct support also challenges the top-down development path described by various state-led models (e.g., Oi 1995; Walder 1995; Blecher and Shue 2001). Due to the state's ambivalent stance, China's private economy has three points of origin with corresponding developmental trajectories: privatization of state-owned enterprises, development of individual businesses, and most importantly, privatization of ownership-ambiguous enterprises such as township and village enterprises.

In light of the state's limited role, recent studies have shifted to a bottom-up entrepreneurial perspective (Tsai 2007; Y. Huang 2008; Nee and Opper 2012). A common theme across these bottom-up accounts is that China's private economy emerged below the state's radar in distant rural areas.

Moving beyond existing bottom-up accounts, this book shows that two-dimensional ambiguous industries did not emerge below the state's radar in rural areas. Rather, these industries thrived right under the state's nose in metropolitan centers. They flourished within and grew out of the shadow of the state. In addition to state-owned enterprises, ownership-ambiguous firms and small individual businesses, industries facing two-dimensional ambiguity constituted a fourth origin for China's private sector.

This account also implies that China's private economy has grown far bigger and deeper than was previously realized. Since no study of China's private economy has included these public-goods-related industries, even the studies with the highest figures about the size and economic impact of the private sector tend to be understatements (Dollar and Wei, 2007; Dougherty and Herd, 2005). This is especially true for the pre-2000 period, when the vast majority of ambiguous enterprises had not reregistered as corporations. Even in the early 2010s, there were nineteen thousand to twenty-one thousand privately operated SEOs that remained as educational entities rather than corporations (China Statistical Yearbook 2010, 2011, 2012).

2. See Fligstein and Roehrkasse (2016) for a discussion on these economists and the role of reputation in preventing fraud.

3. See, for example, Liu (2006) and Yao (2017) for the lack of professionalization in China's legal and medical systems. Compared to these systems and the formal education sector, the professional associations in the Education Industry are even weaker and less developed. This is also one of the reasons why self-regulations on opportunism by professional associations do not work.

4. See Osrecki (2017) for a discussion on the functionalist studies of corruption.

5. See, for example, MacArthur and Wilson (1967) and Pianka (1970).

6. See, for example, Hannan and Freeman (1989) and Aldrich (1999).

7. See Zhao (2015).

8. See DiMaggio (1988), Fligstein (1997), and Battilana, Leca, and Boxenbaum (2009) for definitions of institutional entrepreneurs. For discussions on institutional work, see Lawrence, Leca, and Zilber (2013).

9. For the definition of the micro origin of institutional changes, see Kellogg (2011, 7).

10. For a closer reading of Fei's influence in social sciences and economic sociology, see Hamilton (2015).

References

Abbott, Andrew. 2001. *Time Matters: On Theory and Method*. Chicago: University of Chicago Press.

Abolafia, Michel Y. 1996. *Making Markets: Opportunism and Restraint on Wall Street*. Cambridge, MA: Harvard University Press.

Adams, Julia, Elisabeth Clemens, and Ann Shola Orloff. 2005. "Introduction: Social Theory, Modernity, and the Three Waves of Historical Sociology." In *Remaking Modernity: Politics, History, and Sociology*, edited by Julia Adams, Elisabeth S. Clemens, and Ann Shola Orloff, 1–72. Durham, NC: Duke University Press.

Akerlof, George, and Paul Romer. 1993. "Looting: The Economic Underworld of Bankruptcy for Profit." *Brookings Papers on Economic Activity* 2: 1–73.

Aldrich, Howard E. 1999. *Organizations Evolving*. London: Sage Publications.

———. 2008. *Organizations and Environments*. Stanford: Stanford University Press.

An, Shenglan 安胜蓝, Jin Haotian 晋浩天, and Li Danyang 李丹阳. 2021. "Rang jiaoyu jiaolü shao yixie, rang renmin manyi duo yixie" 让教育焦虑少一些，让人民满意多一些 [Let there be less anxiety for education, and let there be more satisfaction by the people]. *Guangming ribao* 光明日报, March 11, 2021.

Ang, Yuen Yuen. 2016. *How China Escaped the Poverty Trap*. 1st ed. Ithaca, NY: Cornell University Press.

Apple, Michael. W. 2001. "Comparing Neo-Liberal Projects and Inequality in Education." *Comparative Education* 37 (4): 409–23.

Astley, W. Graham, and Andrew Van de Ven. 1983. "Central Perspectives and Debates in Organization Theory." *Administrative Science Quarterly* 28 (2): 245–73.

Aurini, Janice. 2006. "Crafting Legitimation Projects: An Institutional Analysis of Private Education Businesses." *Sociological Forum* 21 (1): 83–111.

Aurini, Janice, and Scott Davies. 2004. "The Transformation of Private Tutoring: Education in a Franchise Form." *Canadian Journal of Sociology* 29 (3).

Aurini, Janice, Julian Dierkes, and Scott Davies. 2013. "Out of the Shadows? An Introduction to Worldwide Supplementary Education." In *Out of the Shadows: The Global Intensification of Supplementary Education*, edited by Janice Aurini, Julian Dierkes, and Scott Davies, xv–xxiv. Bingley: Emerald Group Publishing Limited.

Axelrod, Robert. 1984. *Evolution of Cooperation*. New York: Basic Books.

Bai, Limin. 2006. "Graduate Unemployment: Dilemmas and Challenges in China's Move to Mass Higher Education." *China Quarterly* 185: 128–44.

Bain & Company. 2017. *2017 China Private Wealth Report*. August 11, 2017 https://www.bain.cn /news_info.php?id=715.

Baker, David P. 2020. "An Inevitable Phenomenon: Reflections on the Origins and Future of Worldwide Shadow Education." *European Journal of Education* 55 (3): 311–15.

Baker, David P., and Gerald K. LeTendre. 2005. *National Differences, Global Similarities: World Culture and the Future of Schooling*. Stanford: Stanford University Press.

Baker, David P., Motoko Akiba, Gerald K. LeTendre, and Alexander W. Wiseman. 2001. "Worldwide Shadow Education: Outside-School Learning, Institutional Quality of Schooling, and Cross-National Mathematics Achievement." *Educational Evaluation and Policy Analysis* 23 (1): 1–17.

Battilana, Julie, and Silvia Dorado. 2010. "Building Sustainable Hybrid Organizations: The Case of Commercial Microfinance Organizations." *Academy of Management Journal* 53 (6): 1419–40.

Battilana, Julie, Bernard Leca, and Eva Boxenbaum. 2009. "How Actors Change Institutions: Towards a Theory of Institutional Entrepreneurship." *Academy of Management Annals* 3 (1): 65–107.

Becker, Gary S., and Richard A. Posner. 2009. *Uncommon Sense: Economic Insights, from Marriage to Terrorism*. Chicago: University of Chicago Press.

Berman, Elizabeth Popp. 2012. *Creating the Market University: How Academic Science Became an Economic Engine*. Princeton, NJ: Princeton University Press.

Besharov, Marya L., and Wendy K. Smith. 2014. "Multiple Institutional Logics in Organizations: Explaining Their Varied Nature and Implications." *Academy of Management Review* 39 (3): 364–81.

Bjork, Christopher. 2015. *High-Stakes Schooling: What We Can Learn from Japan's Experiences with Testing, Accountability, and Education Reform*. Chicago: University of Chicago Press.

Blecher, Marc, and Vivienne Shue. 2001. "Into Leather: State-Led Development and the Private Sector in Xinji." *China Quarterly* 166: 368–93.

Blumenthal, David, and William Hsiao. 2005. "Privatization and Its Discontents—The Evolving Chinese Health Care System." *New England Journal of Medicine* 353 (11): 1165–70.

Boisot, Max, and John Child. 1999. "Organizations as Adaptive Systems in Complex Environments: The Case of China." *Organization Science* 10 (3): 237–52.

Boli, John, Francisco O. Ramirez, and John W. Meyer. 1985. "Explaining the Origins and Expansion of Mass Education." *Comparative Education Review* 29 (2): 145–70.

Bray, Mark. 2009. *Confronting the Shadow Education System: What Government Policies for What Private Tutoring*. Paris: UNESCO Publishing and IIEP Policy Forum.

———. 2017. "Schooling and Its Supplements: Changing Global Patterns and Implications for Comparative Education." *Comparative Education Review* 61 (3): 469–91.

Bray, Mark, and Magda Nutsa Kobakhidze. 2014. "The Global Spread of Shadow Education: Supporting or Undermining Qualities of Education?" In *Qualities of Education in a Globalized World*, edited by Diane Brook Napier, Clementina Acedo, and Allan Pitman, 185–200. Rotterdam: Sense Publishers.

Bray, Mark, and Chad Lykins. 2012. *Shadow Education: Private Supplementary Tutoring and Its Implications for Policy Makers in Asia*. Mandaluyong City, Philippines: Asian Development Bank.

Brittain, Jack, and John Freeman. 1980. *Organizational Proliferation and Density Dependent Selection: Organizational Evolution in the Semiconductor Industry*. Berkeley: Institute of Industrial Relations, University of California.

Bruton, Garry D., Mike W. Peng, David Ahlstrom, Ciprian Stan, and Kehan Xu. 2015. "State-Owned Enterprises around the WORLD as Hybrid Organizations." *Academy of Management Perspectives* 29 (1): 92–114.

Buchmann, Claudia, Dennis J. Condron, and Vincent J. Roscigno. 2010. "Shadow Education, American Style: Test Preparation, the SAT and College Enrollment." *Social Forces* 89 (2): 435–61.

Burawoy, Michael. 1979. *Manufacturing Consent: Changes in the Labor Process under Monopoly Capitalism*. Chicago: University of Chicago Press.

Burt, Ronald S., and Sonja Opper. 2017. "Early Network Events in the Later Success of Chinese Entrepreneurs." *Management and Organization Review* 13 (3): 497–537.

Byun, Soo-yong, and Hyunjoon Park. 2012. "The Academic Success of East Asian American Youth: The Role of Shadow Education." *Sociology of Education* 85 (1): 40–60.

Carnoy, Martin. 1998. "National Voucher Plans in Chile and Sweden: Did Privatization Reforms Make for Better Education?" *Comparative Education Review* 42 (3): 309–37.

Carnoy, Martin, and Diana Rhoten. 2002. "What Does Globalization Mean for Educational Change." *Comparative Education Review* 46 (1): 1–9.

Carroll, Glenn R., and Michael T. Hannan. 2000. *The Demography of Corporations and Industries*. Princeton, NJ: Princeton University Press.

Chai, Huiqun 柴会群. 2006. "Kaoyanban 'jiaofu' jianghu lu zhongjie" 考研班"教父"江湖路终结 [The end of the wild career path of the "God Father" of the Chinese Graduate Examination Preparation]. *Nanfang zhoumo* 南方周末, August 17.

Chandler, Alfred D. 1993. *The Visible Hand: The Managerial Revolution in American Business*. Cambridge, MA: Belknap Press.

China Daily. 2016. "China's School Extracurricular Tutoring Market Size Reaches $115 Billion." Online version. December 29. https://www.chinadaily.com.cn/business/2016-12/29/content_27810429.htm.

China Statistical Yearbook 中国统计年鉴. 1980–2019. Beijing: Zhongguo tongji chubanshe.

Chung, Chi-Nien, and Xiaowei Luo. 2008. "Institutional Logics or Agency Costs: The Influence of Corporate Governance Models on Business Group Restructuring in Emerging Economies." *Organization Science* 19 (5): 766–84.

Clemens, Elisabeth S. 1993. "Organizational Repertoires and Institutional Change: Women's Groups and the Transformation of U.S. Politics, 1890–1920." *American Journal of Sociology* 98 (4): 755–98.

Clemens, Elisabeth S., and James M. Cook. 1999. "Politics and Institutionalism: Explaining Durability and Change." *Annual Review of Sociology* 25: 441–66.

Cyert, Richard M., and James G. March. 1963. "Chapter 3: Organizational Goals." In *A Behavioral Theory of the Firm*, 26–43. Englewood Cliffs, NJ: Prentice Hall.

Dang, Hai-Anh. 2013. "Private Tutoring in Vietnam: A Review of Current Issues and Its Major Correlates." In *Out of the Shadows: The Global Intensification of Supplementary Education*, edited by Janice Aurini, Scott Davies and Julian Dierkes, 95–128. Bingley, UK: Emerald Group Publishing Limited.

David, Robert J., Wesley D. Sine, and Heather A. Haveman. 2013. "Seizing Opportunity in Emerging Fields: How Institutional Entrepreneurs Legitimated the Professional Form of Management Consulting." *Organization Science* 24 (2): 356–77.

Davis, Deborah. 1999. "Self-Employment in Shanghai: A Research Note." *China Quarterly* 157: 22–43.

———. 2000. "Introduction: A Revolution in Consumption." In *The Consumer Revolution in Urban China*, edited by Deborah Davis, 1–22. Berkeley: University of California Press.

Deloitte China. 2010–19. *Report on the Education Industry in China*. (Author's note: Report titles vary depending on the year of publication). https://www2.deloitte.com/cn/en/pages/technol ogy-media-and-telecommunications/solutions/publications.html?icid=nav2_publications.

Dierkes, Julian. 2008. "Japanese Shadow Education: The Consequences of School Choice." In *The Globalization of School Choice*, edited by Martin Forsey, Scott Davies, and Geoffrey Walford, 231–48. Oxford: Symposium Books.

———. 2010. "Teaching in the Shadow: Operators of Small Shadow Education Institutions in Japan." *Asia Pacific Education Review* 11 (1): 25–35.

DiMaggio, Paul J. 1988 "Interest and Agency in Institutional Theory." In *Institutional Patterns and Culture*, edited by Lynn Zucker, 3–22. Cambridge, MA: Ballinger Publishing Company.

———. 1991. "Constructing an Organizational Field as a Professional Project: U.S. Art Museums, 1920–1940." In *The New Institutionalism in Organizational Analysis*, 267–92. Chicago: University of Chicago Press.

DiMaggio, Paul J., and Walter W. Powell. 1983. "The Iron Cage Revisited: Institutional Isomorphism and Collective Rationality in Organizational Fields." *American Sociological Review* 48 (2): 147–60.

Dollar, David, and Shang-Jin Wei. 2007. "Das (Wasted) Kapital: Firm Ownership and Investment Efficiency in China." IMF Working Paper 08/9 (January). www.imf.org.

Dougherty, Sean, and Richard Herd. 2005. "Fast-Falling Barriers and Growing Concentration: The Emergence of Private Economy in China." OECD Working Papers, 58, December 16, 2005. https://www.oecd-ilibrary.org/docserver/470526613141.pdf?expires=1635821650&id=id &accname=guest&checksum=0D8F84375A361423B211EA41FED48BE9.

Dunn, Mary B., and Candace Jones. 2010. "Institutional Logics and Institutional Pluralism: The Contestation of Care and Science Logics in Medical Education, 1967–2005." *Administrative Science Quarterly* 55 (1): 114–49.

Eyal, Gil. 2011. "Spaces between Fields." In *Pierre Bourdieu and Historical Analysis*, edited by Philip Gorski, 159–82. Durham, NC: Duke University Press.

Fei, Xiaotong. 1992. *From the Soil: The Foundations of Chinese Society*. Translated by Gary G. Hamilton and Wang Zheng. Berkeley: University of California Press.

Feige, Edgar. 1998. "Underground Activity and Institutional Change: Productive, Protective, and Predatory Behavior in Transition Economies." In *Transforming Post-Communist Political Economies*, edited by Joan M. Nelson, Charles Tilly, Lee Walker, and the National Research Council, 21–34. Washington, DC: National Academy Press.

Feng, Lun 冯仑. 2017. *Yeman shengzhang* 野蛮生长 [Savage growth]. Beijing: Zhongxin chuban jituan.

Fish, Robert J., Denise L. Parris, and Michael Troilo. 2017. "Compound Voids and Unproductive Entrepreneurship: The Rise of the 'English Fever' in China." *Journal of Economic Issues*. 51 (1): 163–80.

Fligstein, Neil. 1990. *The Transformation of Corporate Control*. Cambridge, MA: Harvard University Press.

Fligstein, Neil. 1996. "Markets as Politics: A Political-Cultural Approach to Market Institutions." *American Sociological Review* 61 (4): 656–73.

———. 2002. *The Architecture of Markets: An Economic Sociology of Twenty-First-Century Capitalist Societies.* Repr. ed. Princeton, NJ: Princeton University Press.

Fligstein, Neil, and Doug McAdam. 2012. *A Theory of Fields.* New York: Oxford University Press.

Fligstein, Neil, and Alexander F. Roehrkasse. 2016. "The Causes of Fraud in the Financial Crisis of 2007 to 2009: Evidence from the Mortgage-Backed Securities Industry." *American Sociological Review* 81 (4): 617–43.

Francis, Corinna-Barbara. 1999. "Bargained Property Rights: The Case of China's High-Technology Sector." In *Property Rights and Economic Reform in China*, edited by Jean C. Oi and Andrew G. Walder, 226–47. Stanford, CA: Stanford University Press.

Friedland, Roger, and Robert R. Alford. 1991. "Bringing Society Back In: Symbols, Practices and Institutional Contradictions." In *The New Institutionalism in Organizational Analysis*, edited by Walter W. Powell and Paul J. DiMaggio, 232–66. Chicago: University of Chicago Press.

Friedman, Milton. 1962. *Capitalism and Freedom.* Chicago: University of Chicago Press.

Gábor, Istvan. R. 1979. "The Second (Secondary) Economy: Earning Activity and Regrouping of Income outside the Socially Organized Production and Distribution." *Acta Oeconomica* 22 (3/4): 291–311.

Gallagher, Mary. 2005. "China in 2004: Stability above All." *Asian Survey* 45 (1): 21–32.

Geertz, Clifford. 1973. *The Interpretation of Cultures: Selected Essays by Clifford Geertz.* New York: Basic Books.

———. (1978) 2011. "The Bazaar Economy: Information and Search in Peasant Marketing." In *The Sociology of Economic Life*, edited by Mark Granovetter and Richard Swedberg, 119–24. Boulder, CO: Westview Press.

Giroux, Henry. 2002. "Neoliberalism, Corporate Culture, and the Promise of Higher Education: The University as a Democratic Public Sphere." *Harvard Educational Review* 72 (4): 425–63.

Glynn, Mary Ann. 2000. "When Cymbals Become Symbols: Conflict over Organizational Identity within a Symphony Orchestra." *Organization Science* 11 (3): 285–98.

Gold, Thomas. 1990. "Urban Private Business and Social Change." In *Chinese Society on the Eve of Tiananmen: The Impact of Reform*, edited by Deborah Davis and Ezra Vogel, 157–80. Cambridge, MA: Council on East Asian Studies, Harvard University.

Gordon, Amanda, and Ben Steverman. 2019. "Rich Parents Have Plenty of Ways to Game the U.S. Education System." *Bloomberg*, March 13, 2019.

Granovetter, Mark S. 1995. "Coase Revisited: Business Groups in the Modern Economy." *Industrial and Corporate Change* 4 (1): 93–130.

Greenwood, Royston, Mia Raynard, Farah Kodeih, Evelyn R. Micelotta, and Michael Lounsbury. 2011. "Institutional Complexity and Organizational Responses." *Academy of Management Annals* 5 (1): 317–71.

Guo, Hua 郭华, and Yang Zhao杨钊. 2008. "Beijing shi Xiaoxuesheng shijian anpai yu shengcun zhuangtai yanjiu" 北京市小学生时间安排与生存状态研究 [A study on the schedules and well-being of primary school students in Beijing]. *Jiaoyu kexue yanjiu* 教育科学研究, 11: 31–32.

Guthrie, Doug. 1999. *Dragon in a Three-Piece Suit: The Emergence of Capitalism in China.* Princeton, NJ: Princeton University Press.

Hamilton, Gary G. 2015. "What Western Social Scientists Can Learn from the Writings of Fei Xiaotong." *Journal of China in Comparative Perspective* 1 (1): 107–27.

Hannan, Michael T., and John Freeman. 1977. "The Population Ecology of Organizations." *American Journal of Sociology* 82 (5): 929–64.

————. 1989. *Organizational Ecology*. Cambridge, MA: Harvard University Press.

Haveman, Heather A., Jacob Habinek, and Leo A. Goodman. 2012. "How Entrepreneurship Evolves: The Founders of New Magazines in America, 1741–1860." *Administrative Science Quarterly* 57 (4): 585–624.

Haveman, Heather, Nan Jia, Jing Shi, and Yongxiang Wang. 2017. "The Dynamics of Political Embeddedness in China." *Administrative Science Quarterly* 62 (1): 67–104.

Haveman, Heather A., and Hayagreeva Rao. 1997. "Structuring a Theory of Moral Sentiments: Institutional and Organizational Coevolution in the Early Thrift Industry." *American Journal of Sociology* 102 (6): 1606–51.

Hsu, Greta, and Michael T. Hannan. 2005. "Identities, Genres, and Organizational Forms." *Organization Science* 16 (5): 474–90.

Hu, Huimin 胡惠闵, and Yin Yuxin 殷玉新. 2015. "Woguo jianqing zhongxiaoxue keye fudan de licheng yu sikao" 我国减轻中小学课业负担的历程与思考 [The reflection and advancement of reducing primary and secondary school academic burden in China]. *Quanqiu jiaoyu zhanwang* 全球教育展望 44 (12): 48–58.

Huang, Ruili 黄瑞黎. 2018. "Longzhao zai chouwen zhong de yiliao diguo: Putian xi yiyuan faji shi" 笼罩在丑闻中的医疗帝国：莆田系医院发迹史 [The medical empire clouded by scandals: The development history of the Putian network of hospitals]. *Niuyue shibao zhongwen ban* 纽约时报中文版, November 16, 2018. https://cn.nytimes.com/china/20181116/china-private-hospitals-putian/.

Huang, Yasheng. 2008. *Capitalism with Chinese Characteristics: Entrepreneurship and the State*. Cambridge: Cambridge University Press.

Hurun Report. 2020. "Hurun Global Education Rich List 2020." Hurun Research Institute. March 26, 2020. https://www.hurun.net/en-US/Info/Detail?num=8AF475DC1457.

Institute of International Education. 1980–1990. *Open Doors: Report on International Educational Exchange*. New York: Institute of International Education.

Johnson, Victoria. 2007. "What Is Organizational Imprinting? Cultural Entrepreneurship in the Founding of the Paris Opera." *American Journal of Sociology* 113 (1): 97–127.

————. 2008. "The Past in the Present." In *Backstage at the Revolution: How the Royal Paris Opera Survived the End of the Old Regime*, 15–36. Chicago: University of Chicago Press.

Kang, Yong, Lu Shi, and Elizabeth D. Brown. 2008. *Chinese Corporate Governance: History and Institutional Framework*. Santa Monica, CA: Rand Corporation.

Kellogg, Katherine C. 2011. *Challenging Operations: Medical Reform and Resistance in Surgery*. Chicago: University of Chicago Press.

Kiong, Tong Chee. 2005. "Feuds and Legacies: Conflict and Inheritance in Chinese Family Businesses." *International Sociology* 20 (1): 45–70.

Kipnis, Andrew. 2006. "Suzhi: A Keyword Approach." *China Quarterly* 186: 295–313.

Koo, Hagen. 2016. "The Global Middle Class: How Is It Made, What Does It Represent?" *Globalization* 13 (4) 440–53.

Kornai, Janos. 1997. "Reform of the Welfare Sector in the Post-Communist Countries: A Normative Approach." In *Transforming Post-Communist Political Economies*, edited by Joan M. Nelson, Charles Tilly, and Lee Walker, 272–98. Washington, DC: National Academy Press.

Koyama, Jill P. 2010. *Making Failure Pay: For-Profit Tutoring, High-Stakes Testing, and Public Schools*. Chicago: University of Chicago Press.

KPMG. 2011. *Education Industry in China*. Hong Kong: KPMG Partner Firm.

Kwok, Percy. 2001. "Local Knowledge and Value Transformation in East Asian Mass Tutorial Schools." *International Education Journal* 2 (5): 86–97.

———. 2010. "Demand Intensity, Market Parameters and Policy Responses towards Demand and Supply of Private Supplementary Tutoring in China." *Asia Pacific Education Review* 11 (1): 49–58.

Lafargue, Paul. 1972. *Marx and Engels through the Eyes of Their Contemporaries*. Edited by Institut Marksizma-Leninizma. Moscow: Progress Publishers.

Lawrence, Thomas B., Bernard Leca, and Tammar B. Zilber. 2013. "Institutional Work: Current Research, New Directions and Overlooked Issues." *Organization Studies* 34 (8): 1023–33.

Lee, Soojeong, and Roger C. Shouse. 2011. "The Impact of Prestige Orientation on Shadow Education in South Korea." *Sociology of Education* 84 (3): 212–24.

LEK Special Report 艾意凯特别报告. 2019. "2019 nian zhongguo jiaoyu shichang touzi zhanwang: jujiao jiaoyu keji" 年中国教育市场投资展望：聚焦教育科技 [Investment prospect in China's education market in 2019: A focus on education technology]. https://www.lek.com/sites/default/files/insights/pdf-attachments/China-Spotlight-EdTech_Chinese.pdf.

Lester, Richard K., and Michael Piore. 2004. *Innovation: The Missing Dimension*. Cambridge, MA: Harvard University Press.

Levin, Henry M. 2002. "A Comprehensive Framework for Evaluating Educational Vouchers." *Educational Evaluation and Policy Analysis* 24 (3): 159–74.

Levinthal, Daniel, and Hart E. Posen. 2007. "Myopia of Selection: Does Organizational Adaptation Limit the Efficacy of Population Selection?" *Administrative Science Quarterly* 52 (4): 586–620.

Li, David D. 1996. "A Theory of Ambiguous Property Rights in Transition Economies: The Case of the Chinese Non-State Sector." *Journal of Comparative Economics* 23 (1): 1–19.

Li, Haoyu 李好宇, Wang Kexin 王可心, Qiu Xun邱珣, and Wang Yujia王雨佳. 2015. *Peixun hangye zhe yinian* 培训行业这一年 [The supplemental education industry this year]. Beijing: Dianzi gongye chubanshe.

Li, Hongbin, Lingsheng Meng, Qian Wang, and Li-An Zhou. 2008. "Political Connections, Financing and Firm Performance: Evidence from Chinese Private Firms." *Journal of Development Economics* 87 (2): 283–99.

Li, Peilin. 2017. "China's Path to Overcoming the Double Middle-Income Traps." *China & World Economy* 25 (6): 28–44.

Li, Su 李肃. 2009. *Zhenxiang: Shei Tuidong le Zhongguo Gaige* 真相：谁推动了中国改革？ [The truth: Who has pushed forward China's reform?]. Beijing: Zhongguo fazhan chubanshe.

Lieberson, Stanley. 1991. "Small N's and Big Conclusions: An Examination of the Reasoning in Comparative Studies Based on a Small Number of Cases." *Social Forces* 70 (2): 307–20.

Lieberthal, Kenneth. 1992. "The 'Fragmented Authoritarianism' Model and Its Limitations." In *Bureaucracy, Politics and Decision Making in Post-Mao China*, edited by Kenneth Lieberthal and David M. Lampton, 1–30. Berkeley: University of California Press.

Lin, Le. 2020. "The Visible Hand behind Study-Abroad Waves: Cram Schools, Organizational Framing and the International Mobility of Chinese Students." *Higher Education* 79 (2): 259–74.

———. 2021 "Control and Consent in the Connected Age: The Work of Contractors on Transnational Online Education Platforms." *Socio-Economic Review* 19 (4): 1291–1313.

Liu, Sida. 2006. "Client Influence and the Contingency of Professionalism: The Work of Elite Corporate Lawyers in China." *Law & Society Review* 40 (4): 751–782.

Lü, Nan 吕楠. 2008. "Gaige kaifang sanshi nian zhongguo laodong hetongzhi de yanbian" 改革开放三十年劳动合同制的演变 [The thirty years' evolution of the labor contract institution since the reform and opening]. *Beijing shehui kexue* 北京社会科学 5: 10–17.

Lü, Xingwei吕型伟. 2005. "Women Jiujing Zai Tanqiu Shenme: Jianguo Hou Jichu Jiaoyu de Huigu"我们究竟在探求什么：建国后基础教育的回顾 [What are we pursuing—A reflection on the basic education after the founding of the people's republic of China]. *Jiaoyu Fazhan Yanjiu* 教育发展研究 3: 1–4.

Lu, Yuegang 卢跃刚. 2002. *Chaoji mache: Cong Shouda dao Chao xinxing de chuanqi* 超级马车：从首大到超新星的传奇 [The super carriage: The legends from Capital University to Supernova]. Beijing: Guangming ribao chubanshe. (Author's note: The organizations' names in the title have been changed to pseudonyms that are consistently used in the rest of the book.)

Luo, Yadong. 2006. "Opportunism in Inter-Firm Exchanges in Emerging Markets." *Management & Organization Review* 2 (1): 121–47.

Luo, Yonghao 罗永浩. 2010. *Wo De Fen Dou* 我的奋斗 [My struggle]. Kunming, China: Yunnan renmin chubanshe.

Lyons, Bruce, and Judith Mehta. 1997. "Contracts, Opportunism and Trust: Self-Interest and Social Orientation." *Cambridge Journal of Economics* 21 (2): 239–57.

MacArthur, Robert H., and Edward O. Wilson. 1967. *The Theory of Island Biogeography*. Princeton, NJ: Princeton University Press.

Mann, Michael. 1986. "Chapter One." In *The Sources of Social Power*. Cambridge: Cambridge University Press.

March, James G. 1991. "Exploration and Exploitation in Organizational Learning." *Organization Science* 2 (1): 71–87.

Maskus, K. E., and J. H. Reichman. 2004. "The Globalization of Private Knowledge Goods and the Privatization of Global Public Goods." *Journal of International Economic Law* 7 (2): 279–320.

Matsuoka, Ryoji. 2015. "School Socioeconomic Compositional Effect on Shadow Education Participation: Evidence from Japan." *British Journal of Sociology of Education* 36 (2): 270–90.

McPherson, Chad, and Michael Sauder. 2013. "Logics in Action: Managing Institutional Complexity in a Drug Court." *Administrative Science Quarterly* 58 (2): 165–96.

Medvetz, Thomas. 2012. *Think Tanks in America*. Chicago: University of Chicago Press.

Mehlum, Halvor, Karl Moene, and Ragnar Torvik. 2003. "Predator or Prey? Parasitic Enterprises in Economic Development." *European Economic Review* 47 (2003): 275–94.

Meyer, John W., John Boli, George M. Thomas, and Francisco O. Ramirez. 1997. "World Society and the Nation-State." *American Journal of Sociology* 103 (1): 144–81.

Meyer, John W., Francisco O. Ramirez, and Yasemin Nuhoğlu Soysal. 1992. "World Expansion of Mass Education, 1870–1980." *Sociology of Education* 65 (2): 128–49.

Meyer, John W., and Brian Rowan. 1977. "Institutionalized Organizations: Formal Structure as Myth and Ceremony." *American Journal of Sociology* 83 (2): 340–63.

Miao, Danguo 苗丹国. 2010. Chuguo liuxue liushi nian: dangdai zhongguo de chuguo liuxue zhengce yu yindao zaiwai liuxue renyuan huiguo zhengce de xingcheng, biange yu fazhan 出国留学六十年：当代中国的出国留学政策与引导在外留学人员回国政策的形成，变革与发展 [Studying abroad in sixty years: Contemporary China's policies for overseas study and the formation, change and development of the policies to guide people studying abroad]. Beijing: Zhongyang wenxian chubanshe.

Miles, Robert H. 1982. *Coffin Nails and Corporate Strategies*. Englewood Cliffs, NJ: Prentice Hall.

Ministry of Education of the People's Republic of China. 1997. *Regulations on Non-State Education*. Beijing: Gazette of the State Council of the People's Republic of China. http://www.gov.cn/gongbao/shuju/1997/gwyb199726.pdf.

Mok, Ka-ho. 1997a. "Privatization or Marketization: Educational Development in Post-Mao China." *International Review of Education* 43 (5-6): 547-67.

———. 1997b. "Retreat of the State: Marketization of Education in the Pearl River Delta." *Comparative Education Review* 41 (3): 260-76.

———. 1999. "Education and the Market Place in Hong Kong and Mainland China." *Higher Education* 37 (2): 133-58.

Mori, Izumi, and David Baker. 2010. "The Origin of Universal Shadow Education: What the Supplemental Education Phenomenon Tells Us about the Postmodern Institution of Education." *Asia Pacific Education Review* 11 (1): 36-48.

Morrill, Calvin. 2017. "Institutional Change through Interstitial Emergence: The Growth of Alternative Dispute Resolution in U.S. Law, 1970-2000." *Brazilian Journal of Empirical Legal Studies* 4: 10-36.

Naughton, Barry. 2007. *The Chinese Economy: Transitions and Growth*. Cambridge, MA: MIT Press.

———. 1992. "Organizational Dynamics of Market Transition: Hybrid Forms, Property Rights, and Mixed Economy in China." *Administrative Science Quarterly* 37 (1): 1-27.

Nee, Victor, and Sonja Opper. 2012. *Capitalism from Below: Markets and Institutional Change in China*. Cambridge, MA: Harvard University Press.

Ng, Yuk-Hang. 2009. "In Hong Kong, Cram School Teachers' Image Rivals Pop Stars." *New York Times* (online version), June 1, 2009. http://www.nytimes.com/2009/06/01/business/global/01iht-cramside.html?ref=globalbusiness&version=meter+at+6&region=FixedCenter&pgtype=&priority=true&module=RegiWall-Regi&action=click.

North, Douglass C. 1981. *Structure and Change in Economic History*. New York: W. Norton.

Oi, Jean C. 1992. "Fiscal Reform and the Economic Foundations of Local State Corporatism in China." *World Politics* 45 (1): 99-126.

———. 1995. "The Role of the Local State in China's Transitional Economy." *China Quarterly* 144: 1132-49.

Osrecki, Fran. 2017. "A Short History of the Sociology of Corruption: The Demise of Counter-Intuitivity and the Rise of Numerical Comparisons." *American Sociologist* 48 (1): 103-25.

Pache, Anne-Claire, and Filipe Santos. 2013. "Inside the Hybrid Organization: Selective Coupling as a Response to Competing Institutional Logics." *Academy of Management Journal* 56 (4): 972-1001.

Padgett, John F., and Christopher K. Ansell. 1993. "Robust Action and the Rise of the Medici, 1400-1434." *American Journal of Sociology* 98 (6): 1259-319.

Padgett, John F., and Walter W. Powell. 2012. *The Emergence of Organizations and Markets*. Princeton, NJ: Princeton University Press.

Page, Scott E. 2007. *The Difference: How the Power of Diversity Creates Better Groups, Firms, Schools, and Societies*. Princeton, NJ: Princeton University Press.

Pan, Philip P. 2001. "China's Test-Prep Tempest; As Scores Rise, U.S. Group Alleges Cheating." *Washington Post*, February 21, 2001, A01 Section.

Parish, William L., and Ethan Michelson. 1996. "Politics and Markets: Dual Transformations." *American Journal of Sociology* 101 (4): 1042-59.

Peli, Gabor. 2009. "Fit by Founding, Fit by Adaptation: Reconciling Conflicting Organization Theories with Logical Formalization." *Academy of Management Review* 34 (2): 343–60.

Peng, Mike W., and Yadong Luo. 2000. "Managerial Ties and Firm Performance in a Transition Economy: The Nature of a Micro-Macro Link." *Academy of Management Journal* 43 (3): 486–501.

Pianka, Eric R. 1970. "On R- and K-Selection." *American Naturalist* 104 (940): 592–97.

Polos, Laszlo, Michael Hannan, and Glenn Carroll. 2002. "Foundations of a Theory of Social Forms." *Industrial and Corporate Change* 11 (1): 85–115.

Portes, Alejandro, and Saskia Sassen-Koob. 1987. "Making It Underground: Comparative Material on the Informal Sector in Western Market Economies." *American Journal of Sociology* 93 (1): 30–61.

Qian, David D. 2010. "From TOEFL pBT to TOEFL iBT: Recent Trends, Research Landscape and Chinese Learners." In *English Language Assessment and the Chinese Learners*, edited by Liying Cheng and Andy Curtis, 95–111. New York: Routledge.

Qian, Ning 钱宁. 1996. *Liuxue meiguo: Yige shidai de gushi* 留学美国：一个时代的故事 [Studying in USA: The story of an era]. Nanjing: Jiangsu wenyi chubanshe.

Ragin, Charles C. 2009. "Introduction: Cases of 'What Is a Case?'" In *What Is a Case: Exploring the Foundations of Social Inquiry*, edited by Charles C. Ragin and Howard S. Becker, 1–17. Cambridge: Cambridge University Press.

Ragin, Charles C. 2014. *The Comparative Method: Moving Beyond Qualitative and Quantitative Strategies*. Oakland: University of California Press.

Ramus, Tommaso, Antonino Vaccaro, and Stefano Brusoni. 2016. "Institutional Complexity in Turbulent Times: Formalization, Collaboration, and the Emergence of Blended Logics." *Academy of Management Journal* 60 (4): 1253–84.

Roesgaard, Marie Hojlund. 2006. *Japanese Education and the Cram School Business: Functions, Challenges and Perspectives of the Juku*. Copenhagen: Nordic Institute of Asian Studies Press.

Romanelli, Elaine. 1991. "The Evolution of New Organizational Forms." *Annual Review of Sociology* 17: 79–103.

Rona-Tas, Akos. 1994. "The First Shall Be Last? Entrepreneurship and Communist Cadres in the Transition from Socialism." *American Journal of Sociology* 100 (1): 40–69.

Ruef, Martin. 2000. "The Emergence of Organizational Forms: A Community Ecology Approach." *American Journal of Sociology* 106 (3): 658–714.

Sachs, Jeffrey. 1991. "Poland and Eastern Europe: What Is to Be Done?" In *Foreign Economic Liberalization: Transformation in Socialist and Market Economies*, edited by Andreas Koves and Paul Marer, 235–46. Boulder, CO: Westview Press.

Schumpeter, Joseph A. 1976. *Capitalism, Socialism and Democracy*. New York: Harper.

Scott, W. Richard. 2002. "The Changing World of Chinese Enterprise: An Institutional Perspective." In *The Management of Enterprises in the People's Republic of China*, edited by Anne S. Tsui and Chung-Ming Lau, 59–78. Boston: Springer US.

Scott, W. Richard, and Gerald Davis. 2003. *Organizations and Organizing: Rational, Natural and Open System Perspectives*. 5th ed. Upper Saddle River, NJ: Pearson Prentice Hall.

Shane, Scott. 2000. "Prior Knowledge and the Discovery of Entrepreneurial Opportunities." *Organization Science* 11 (4): 448–69.

Shirk, Susan L. 1993. *The Political Logic of Economic Reform in China*. Berkeley: University of California Press.

Slaughter, Sheila, and Gary Rhoades. 2009. *Academic Capitalism and the New Economy: Markets, State and Higher Education*. Baltimore: Johns Hopkins University Press.

Smith, Wendy K., and Marya L. Besharov. 2019. "Bowing before Dual Gods: How Structured Flexibility Sustains Organizational Hybridity." *Administrative Science Quarterly* 64 (1): 1–44.

So, Alvin, and Yin-wah Chu. 2012. "The Transition from Neoliberalism to State Neoliberalism in China at the Turn of the 21st Century." In *Developmental Politics in Transition: The Neoliberal Era and Beyond*, edited by Chang Kyung-Sup, Kim Se-Kyun, and Ben Fine, 162–87. Macmillian's International Political Economy Series. London: Palgrave Macmillan.

Sobhy, Hania. 2012. "The De-Facto Privatization of Secondary Education in Egypt: A Study of Private Tutoring in Technical and General Schools." *Compare: A Journal of Comparative and International Education* 42 (1): 47–67.

Stark, David. 1989. "Bending the Bars of the Iron Cage: Bureaucratization and Informalization in Capitalism and Socialism." *Sociological Forum* 4 (4): 637–64.

———. 1996. "Recombinant Property in East European Capitalism." *American Journal of Sociology* 101 (4): 993–1027.

———. 2009. *The Sense of Dissonance*. Princeton, NJ: Princeton University Press.

Stevenson, David Lee, and David P. Baker. 1992. "Shadow Education and Allocation in Formal Schooling: Transition to University in Japan." *American Journal of Sociology* 97 (6): 1639–57.

Stinchcombe, Arthur. 1965. "Social Structure and Organizations." In *Handbook of Organizations*, edited by James G. March, 149–93. New York: Rand McNally.

———. 1997. "On the Virtues of the Old Institutionalism." *Annual Review of Sociology* 23 (1): 1–18.

Stromquist, Nelly. 2002. "The Twinning of Ideas and Material Conditions: Globalization, Neoliberalism, and Postmodernism." In *Education in a Globalized World*, 19–36. Lanham, MD: Rowman & Littlefield.

Su, Yiyi, Dean Xu, and Phillip H. Phan. 2008. "Principal–Principal Conflict in the Governance of the Chinese Public Corporation." *Management & Organization Review* 4 (1): 17–38.

Sun, Guoxiang 孙国祥. 2019. "Gaige kaifang yilai jingji xingfa jichu lilun shuping" 改革开放以来经济刑法基础理论述评 [A review on the fundamental theories of economic criminal codes since the reform and opening]. *Wuhan daxue xuebao (zhexue shehui kexue ban)* 武汉大学学报（哲学社会科学版）, no. 5.

Szelenyi, Ivan, and Eric Kostello. 1996. "The Market Transition Debate: Toward a Synthesis?" *American Journal of Sociology* 101 (4): 1082–96.

Tao, Xiping 陶西平, and Wang Zuoshu 王佐书. 2010. *Zhongguo minban jiaoyu* 中国民办教育 [Nonstate education in China]. Beijing: Jiaoyu kexue chubanshe.

Thompson, James D. 1967. *Organizations in Action: Social Science Bases of Administrative Theory*. McGraw-Hill College.

Thornton, Patricia H., and William Ocasio. 1999. "Institutional Logics and the Historical Contingency of Power in Organizations: Executive Succession in the Higher Education Publishing Industry, 1958–1990." *American Journal of Sociology* 105 (3): 801–43.

Thornton, Patricia H., William Ocasio, and Michael Lounsbury. 2012. *The Institutional Logics Perspective: A New Approach to Culture, Structure, and Process*. Oxford: Oxford University Press.

Tolbert, Pamela S., and Lynn G. Zucker. 1983. "Institutional Sources of Change in the Formal Structure of Organizations: The Diffusion of Civil Service Reform, 1880–1935." *Administrative Science Quarterly* 28 (1): 22–39.

Treisman, Daniel. 2000. "The Causes of Corruption: A Cross-National Study." *Journal of Public Economics* 76 (3): 399–457.

Trent, John. 2016. "Constructing Professional Identities in Shadow Education: Perspectives of Private Supplementary Educators in Hong Kong." *Educational Research for Policy and Practice* 15 (2): 115–30.

Tsai, Kellee S. 2007. *Capitalism without Democracy: The Private Sector in Contemporary China.* Ithaca, NY: Cornell University Press.

Tsang, Mun C. 2000. "Education and National Development in China since 1949: Oscillating Policies and Enduring Dilemmas." *China Review* 579–618.

Tsiplakides, Iakovos. 2018. "Shadow Education and Social Class Inequalities in Secondary Education in Greece: The Case of Teaching English as a Foreign Language." *International Journal of Sociology of Education* 7 (1): 71–93.

Turner, Ralph. 1960. "Sponsored and Contest Mobility in the School System." *American Sociological Review* 25 (6): 855-67.

21st Century Education Research Institute 二十一世纪教育研究院. 2012. "Beijing shi 'xiaoshengchu' zexiaore diaocha" 北京市 "小升初"择校热调查 [An investigation on Beijing's fever over the choice of secondary schools by elementary school students]. In *Zhongguo jiaoyu fazhan baogao* 中国教育发展报告 [China education development report]. Beijing: Shehui kexue wenxian chubanshe.

Vaughan, Diane. 1999. "The Dark Side of Organizations: Mistake, Misconduct, and Disaster." *Annual Review of Sociology* 25: 271–305.

Ventura, Alexandre, and Sunhwa Jang. 2010. "Private Tutoring through the Internet: Globalization and Offshoring." *Asia Pacific Education Review* 11 (1): 59–68.

Vogel, Ezra F. 1990. *One Step Ahead in China: Guangdong under Reform.* Cambridge, MA: Harvard University Press.

Walder, Andrew G. 1995. "Local Governments as Industrial Firms: An Organizational Analysis of China's Transitional Economy." *American Journal of Sociology* 101 (2): 263–301.

Wang, Haijian 王海舰. 1993. "Haidian: Shehui liliang banxue qunxing cuican" 海淀：社会力量办学群星璀璨 [Haidian: Full of shining stars in education with the support of societal resources]. *Zhongguo chengren jiaoyu* 中国成人教育, March 20–24, 1993.

Wang, Shanmai 王善迈. 2011. "Minban jiaoyu fenlei guanli tantao" 民办教育分类管理探讨 [Exploring the classified management of private education]. *Jiaoyu yanjiu* 教育研究 383: 32–36.

Wang, Xiaozong 汪孝宗, Zhao Ji 赵吉, and Zhao Na赵娜. 2010. "Zhongguo Kaoyan peixun diyi'an kaishen, jie Kaoyan peixun shichang you duo luan" [The No. 1 lawsuit in the Chinese Graduate Exam test preparation is underway, revealing how messy the Chinese Graduate Exam market is]. *Zhongguo Jingji Zhoukan* 中国经济周刊, July 6, 2010. http://www.china news.com/edu/2010/07-06/2383897.shtml.

Wang, Yiwei 王义伟. 2003. "Chao xinxing chuanqi" 超新星传奇 [The legend of Supernova]. *Guanli kexue wenzhai* 管理科学文摘 3: 25-7. (Author's note: The organization's name in the title has been changed to a pseudonym that is consistently used in the rest of the book.)

Wank, David L. 2001. *Commodifying Communism: Business, Trust, and Politics in a Chinese City.* Cambridge: Cambridge University Press.

Warner, Malcolm, and Keith Goodall. 2010. *Management Training and Development in China: Educating Managers in a Globalized Economy.* London: Routledge, 180–81.

Weber, Max. 2011. *Methodology of Social Sciences*. Edited by Alan Sica. New Brunswick, NJ: Routledge.

Wen, Hua. 文华 1983. "Minban xuexiao shi zhili kaifa de yizhong hao xingshi: Beijing minban xuexiao qingkuang diaocha" 民办学校是智力开发的一种好形式：北京民办学校情况调查 [Nonstate schools are a good approach for developing intelligence: A investigation on Beijing's nonstate schools]. *Qianxian* 前线 10: 31–33.

Werder, Axel V. 2011. "Corporate Governance and Stakeholder Opportunism." *Organization Science* 22 (5): 1345–58.

Williamson, Oliver E. 1975. *Markets and Hierarchies*. New York: Free Press.

———. 1981. "The Economics of Organization: The Transaction Cost Approach." *American Journal of Sociology* 87 (3): 548–77.

———. 1993. "Opportunism and Its Critics." *Managerial and Decision Economics* 14 (2): 97–107.

Wu, Handong 吴汉东. 2018. "Zhongguo zhishi chanquan falv bianqian de jiben mianxiang" 中国知识产权法律变迁的基本面向 [The Basic Dimensions of the Evolution of China's Intellectual Property Laws]. *Zhongguo shehui kexue* 中国社会科学 8: 108–25, 206–7.

Wu, Liao 吴聊. 1998. *Tuofu tingli de xianwai zhi yin* 托福听力的弦外之音 [The undertone of the TOEFL Listening Test]. Beijing: Shijie zhishi chubanshe.

Wu, Xiaogang, and Yu Xie. 2003. "Does the Market Pay Off? Earnings Returns to Education in Urban China." *American Sociological Review* 68 (3): 425–42.

Wu, Yongkui 吴永奎. 2007. "Gaoxiao peixun jigou renzhong daoyuan" 高校培训机构任重道远 [There is still a long way to go for SEOs affiliated with state universities]. *Ershiyi shiji yingyu jiaoyu* 二十一世纪英语教育 69. https://paper.i21st.cn/story/29665.html.

Xu, Dean, Jane W. Lu, and Qian Gu. 2014. "Organizational Forms and Multi-Population Dynamics: Economic Transition in China." *Administrative Science Quarterly* 59 (3): 517–47.

Xue, Haiping 薛海平, and Ding Xiaohao 丁小浩. 2009. "Zhongguo chengzhen xuesheng jiaoyu buxi yanjiu" 中国城镇学生教育补习研究 [A study on the supplementary education and training of China's urban students]. *Jiaoyu yanjiu* 教育研究 6 (1): 39–46.

Xue, Haiping 薛海平, and Fang Chenchen方晨晨. 2019. "Woguo yiwu jiaoyu kewai buxi: xianzhuang yu qushi" 我国义务教育课外补习：现状与趋势 [Supplemental education for our country's compulsory education: Current status and trends]. *Jiaoyu jingji pinglun* 教育经济评论 4 (4): 75–97.

Yan, Shipeng, Fabrizio Ferraro, and Juan (John) Almandoz. 2018. "The Rise of Socially Responsible Investment Funds: The Paradoxical Role of the Financial Logic." *Administrative Science Quarterly* 64 (2): 1–36.

Yang, Dongping 杨东平. 2009. "Wo weishenme fandui aoshu" 我为什么反对奥数 [Why do I oppose Math Olympiad?] *Sina* (blog), April 19, 2009. http://blog.sina.com.cn/s/blog_492471c80100cqcr.html?tj=1.

———. 2018. "Yingshi jiaoyu de 'juchang', shei lai dang bao'an" 应试教育的"剧场"，谁来当保安 [In the theater for exam-oriented education, who should be the security guards?] Lecture given at the conference for releasing the *Research Report on the Issue of "Reducing Academic Burden" for K-12 Students*. https://www.sohu.com/a/224988260_100974.

Yao, Zelin 姚泽麟. 2016. "Zeren zhuanyi, jixing xinren yu bianyuan shengcun: 'Putianxi' beihou de zhidu genyuan" 责任转移，畸形信任与边缘生存："莆田系"背后的制度根源 [Shifting responsibilities, twisted trust and survival on the periphery: The institutional root of the Putian system]. *Wenhua zongheng*文化纵横 (4): 104–11.

———. 2017. *Zai liyi yu daode zhi jian: dangdai zhongguo chengshi yisheng zhiye zizhuxing de shehuixue yanjiu* 在利益与道德之间：当代中国城市医生职业自主性的社会学研究 [Between interest and morality: A sociological study on the professional autonomy of urban physicians in contemporary China]. Beijing: Zhongguo shehui kexue chubanshe.

Yi, Joseph. 2013. "Tiger Moms and Liberal Elephants: Private, Supplementary Education among Korean-Americans." *Society* 50 (2):190–95.

York, Jeffrey G., Timothy J. Hargrave, and Desirée F. Pacheco. 2016. "Converging Winds: Logic Hybridization in the Colorado Wind Energy Field." *Academy of Management Journal* 59 (2): 579–610.

Yuan, Cheng, and Lei Zhang. 2015. "Public Education Spending and Private Substitution in Urban China." *Journal of Development Economics* 115: 124–39.

Zhang, Jianjun, and Hao Ma. 2009. "Adoption of Professional Management in Chinese Family Business: A Multilevel Analysis of Impetuses and Impediments." *Asia Pacific Journal of Management* 26 (1): 119–39.

Zhang, Jun 张军. 2005. *Ziben xingcheng, touzi xiaolv yu zhongguo de jingji zengzhang: shizheng yanjiu* 资本形成，投资效率与中国的经济增长：实证研究 [An empirical research on capital formation, efficiency of investment and China's economic growth]. Beijing: Qinghua daxue chubanshe.

Zhang, Ran 张冉, and Yao Jinju 姚金菊. 2017. "Gongli xuexiao jiaoshi youchang buke de falv guizhi: meiguo jingyan jiqi dui zhongguo de qishi" 公立学校教师有偿补课的法律规制：美国经验及其对中国的启示 [Legal regulations for tutoring with reward among public school teachers: US experience and implications for China]. *Beijing daxue jiaoyu pinglun* 北京大学教育评论 15 (2): 63–76.

Zhang, Wei. 2014. "The Demand for Shadow Education in China: Mainstream Teachers and Power Relations." *Asia Pacific Journal of Education* 34 (4): 436–454.

Zhang, Wei, and Mark Bray. 2017. "Micro-Neoliberalism in China: Public-Private Interactions at the Confluence of Mainstream and Shadow Education." *Journal of Education Policy* 32 (1): 63–81.

Zhang, Yu. 2013. "Does Private Tutoring Improve Students' National College Entrance Exam Performance?—A Case Study from Jinan, China." *Economics of Education Review* 32 (1): 1–28.

Zhang, Yu 张羽, Huang Zhenzhong黄振中, and Li Manli李曼丽. 2014. "Beijing 'Kengban' shi zexiao jiqi dui jichu jiaoyu shengtai de yingxiang" 北京"坑班"式择校及其对基础教育生态的影响 [The seat-occupying school choice policy in Beijing and its influence on elementary education ecology]. *Jiaoyu fazhan yanjiu* 教育发展研究 2: 28–37.

Zhang, Yuan. 2002. *Yingyu ye paoxiao: Paoxiao Yingyu beihou de gushi* 英语也咆哮：咆哮英语背后的故事 [English can also be roaring: The stories behind Roaring English]. Beijing: Wenhua yishu chubanshe. (Author's note: The organization's name in the title has been changed to a pseudonym that is consistently used in the rest of the book.)

Zhang, Yueyun, and Yu Xie. 2016. "Family Background, Private Tutoring, and Children's Educational Performance in Contemporary China." *Chinese Sociological Review* 48 (1): 64–82.

Zhao, Dingxin. 2001. *The Power of Tiananmen: State-Society Relations and the 1989 Beijing Student Movement*. Chicago: University of Chicago Press.

———. 2015. *The Confucian-Legalist State: A New Theory of Chinese History*. New York: Oxford University Press.

Zhong, Jiandu 钟剑都. 2012. "Shei lai jianguan xiaowai peixun jigou" 谁来监管校外培训机构 [Who is going to supervise SEOs?] *Zhongguo jiaoyu bao* 中国教育报, October 16, 2012. http://www.moe.gov.cn/jyb_xwfb/moe_2082/s6236/s6880/201210/t20121022_143536.html.

Zhou, Xueguang. 2000. "Economic Transformation and Income Inequality in Urban China: Evidence from Panel Data." *American Journal of Sociology* 105 (4): 1135–74.

Zhou, Xueguang 周雪光. 2017. *Zhongguo guoji zhili de zhidu luoji* 中国国家治理的制度逻辑 [The institutional logic of governance in China]. Beijing: Shenghuo dushu xinzhi sanlian shudian.

Zuckerman, Ezra W. 1999. "The Categorical Imperative: Securities Analysts and the Illegitimacy Discount." *American Journal of Sociology* 104 (5): 1398–438.

Zuckerman, Ezra W., Tai-Young Kim, Kalinda Ukanwa, and James von Rittmann. 2003. "Robust Identities or Nonentities? Typecasting in the Feature-Film Labor Market." *American Journal of Sociology* 108 (5): 1018–74.

Index

ABCKID, 219n2
Abolafia, Michel Y., 192
absconding, 184
adaptation, 19, 139, 164, 166, 169, 196. *See also* selection-adaptation debate
administrative/ownership structure of SEOs: coevolutionary process of management and opportunistic practices in the 2000s and 2010s, 137–39 (*see also* managerial revolution); corporate control/operation of SEOs, 40, 120–22; cross-region expansion (*see* cross-region expansion); family control structures, 38, 138, 141, 145–46, 171–73; franchise model, 146–49; initial public offerings (IPOs) (*see* initial public offerings (IPOs)); SEOs as formal or informal organizations, 23–24; state regulation of, 118–19. *See also* ownership
affiliated transactions, 120, 171, 217n5
Alibaba, 219n7
ambiguity: conflict at Supernova and, 172–73; illegitimacy discounts and, 26–27; one-dimensional, 22–23, 26; options for cross-region expansion and, 147–49; state regulation and, 120–21; supplemental education organizations (SEOs) and, 5–6; takeaways regarding, 191–93; theories of, 12, 22, 34; two-dimensional (*see* two-dimensional ambiguity); of the US rideshare industry, 191–92
Ansell, Christopher, 187, 192
anxiety, 3, 125–26, 129–30, 187–90, 206n12
Arrow Education, 182–83, 186

Baker, David P., 8
Barron's, 63, 94
Beijing: K–12 submarket in (*see* K–12 submarket); TOEFL/GRE submarket in (*see* TOEFL/GRE submarket)

Beijing Student Movement of 1989, 47, 212n9
Berlitz, 2
Blue Ocean: failed IPO of, 185; family founding and management at, 145; family members as management at, 141; informal economy used by, 52–53; as market leader, 123; opportunism by a manager at, 181; opportunistic practices by, 26, 56–57, 184; opportunistic practices used against, 149; slow track of the coevolutionary process/managerial revolution at, 138, 140; teachers at, 72; teachers' opportunistic actions at, 75–76; teaching by founders, absence of, 80; transition from family to professional management, failure of, 137–38
Blue Wings, 53, 80, 184–85
Bray, Mark, 8
bribing, 58
Brittain, Jack, 193
Burawoy, Michael, 215n14

Capital University: donors to, 43; first-generation teachers at Supernova from, 72, 93; as market leader in the early-to-mid-1980s, 47; reputation of, 48; Su Leidong as struggling student and faculty member at, 101; Su Leidong's departure from, 43, 56, 96, 211–12n2
Capital University SEO, 47–48, 50
Central College of Foreign Languages, 47, 97
Central College SEO, 47–48, 50
Chandler, Alfred, 137, 139, 218n3
chedan, 97. *See also* performative pedagogy
China: institutional change in, 196–98; institutional environment for employment relationships, 69–70; market transition and marginal entrepreneurs in, 31–33; new institutionalism applied to, 197; rise of the private sector in,

China (*cont.*)
accounts of, 219–20n1; supplemental education industry in, exponential growth and impacts of, 2–5 (*see also* supplemental education organizations (SEOs))
Chinese culture. *See* culture/cultural explanation/cultural factors
Chinese Graduate Exam submarket: bargaining power of early teachers in, 72; Blue Ocean as market leader in, 123 (*see also* Blue Ocean); teachers' opportunistic practices in, 75–76
chuishui, 97. *See also* performative pedagogy
competition: among opportunist SEOs, 37; dynamics under two-dimensional ambiguity, 34–35; theories of ambiguity and, 34
conflict. *See* intraorganizational conflict
Confucianism, 10, 189
Cornerstone: embeddedness in the state education system, level of, 92–93; family founding and management at, 145; informal economy used by, 52, 54; as a market leader in Beijing's TOEFL/GRE submarket, 50; opportunistic practices by, 60, 94
corporate control, contrasting conceptions of, 140
corruption, 2, 29, 161, 174, 192, 212n9, 220n4
cross-region expansion: centralized model for, 143–45, 156–57; decentralized model for, 155–59; difficulties of without successful managerial revolution, 146–49
crystallization/crystalized, 92, 97, 215n5
cultural capital, 189
Cultural Revolution, 32, 45
culture/cultural explanation/cultural factors, 10, 64, 68, 189–190, 194, 198, 206n16
customers. *See* students

Dai Bin, 150–51, 170, 172, 174
danwei, 32, 70, 212n2
deadlock, 38, 170, 175, 178, 186
Deng Xiaoping, 28, 30, 45, 54
Doo & Cool Education Inc.: centralized model for cross-region expansion, 143–45; corporate control at, 140; domestic and global investment by, 166; fast track of the coevolutionary process/managerial revolution at, 138–43; founding of, 121–22, 142; IPO of, 168–69; K–12 pedagogy at, 132–34; seat-occupying classes and, 131, 134; Supernova and, comparisons of, 145, 155–57, 163–64; teachers at, 71
Duan Ping, 110–12, 148, 180–81
duanzi, 97. *See also* performative pedagogy
dumping classes, 68, 75, 77, 88, 214n2
Duvell: background of founders of, 122; corporate control at, 140; fast track of the coevolutionary process/managerial revolution at, 138–42;

K–12 pedagogy at, 133; withdrawal from stock markets by, 186

economy/economies: informal (*see* informal economy); rise of the private sector, accounts of, 219–20n1; transition economies, opportunists and, 30–31
education: evolution of in China, 45–46; higher education, expansion of, 119; malaise of the Chinese education system, 126; marketization of, 119–20; neoliberal policies in, 208n27; overseas, expansion of demand for, 45–47; reform policy agenda, demand side impact of, 124–27; the state and, 50–52 (*see also* state, the); supplemental education organizations (SEOs) (*see* supplemental education organizations (SEOs))
Education Act of 1995, 121
Educational Testing Service (ETS), 62–64, 95
Education Industry, supplemental education organizations (SEOs). *See* supplemental education organizations (SEOs)
embeddedness, 92–93, 96–97, 187
English Excellence, 123
entrepreneurs: institutional, 195–96; marginal (*see* marginal entrepreneurs); opportunistic practices following the first IPO wave, 183–84; opportunistic practices when seeking investment, 180–83; part-time entrepreneurs as SEO founders, 25–26; power dynamics between teachers and, 68–69, 88–89; responses to teachers' opportunistic practices by, 78–82; seat-occupying classes and, 130–31; state regulations of 1997 and, 119; taming teachers, and market-based teacher evaluation, 82–85; taming teachers, and specialized teaching and the coteaching model, 85–88; two-dimensional ambiguity of SEOs and, 51. *See also* names of specific supplemental education organizations (SEOs)
exit-and-entrepreneurship, 70, 78, 80, 82, 87–88

Falcinelli, Chris, 1
family business, 18, 79–80, 137–38, 149–51, 181
Fei, Xiaotong, 198
Feng Lun, 20, 30–31
field theory, 196
financial revolution in the Education Industry. *See* global finance of SEOs; initial public offerings (IPOs)
Fligstein, Neil, 11, 187, 190, 195, 211n9
Focus Educational Services, 2
formality, two-dimensional ambiguity and, 23–24
formalization, 16, 38–39, 138, 162–63, 166, 171, 176, 178, 186, 194, 196–97, 207n23, 217–18n1, 219n5
franchise model, 146–49
Freeman, John, 193, 209n40

ganqing, 58
Gao Wenbo, 137, 181
Geertz, Clifford, 198
getihu, 32, 51
global finance of SEOs, 165–67; formalization and
    opportunism, the contradiction of, 178–80;
    initial public offerings (IPOs) (*see* initial public
    offerings (IPOs)); listing on overseas stock
    markets as an institutionalization process,
    167–69; opportunism and failures of, 185–86;
    seeking investment, opportunistic practices
    and, 180–86; Supernova's IPO as an adaptation
    process, 169–70 (*see also* Supernova's IPO)
globalization, 8–10
Gong Ming, 80
Goodman, Leo A., 31
Gordon, Amanda, 1
growing out, 24
guanxi, 196–97
Guthrie, Doug, 11, 217n1

Habinek, Jacob, 31
Hannan, Michael T., 209n40
Haveman, Heather A., 31
Hercules Education, 130–31
hold-up, 75, 77, 214n7
Huang, Yasheng, 32
hukou, 57, 213n20

illegitimacy discounts, 26–27
imprint, 118, 141, 164, 166, 216n2
informal economy: definition of, 207n21; intellec-
    tual SEOs and, 54–55; opportunist SEOs and,
    52–55; opportunists in, 35; as a social source
    of two-dimensional ambiguity, 24–26; two-
    dimensional ambiguity of SEOs and the, 50–52
initial public offerings (IPOs): of Arrow Educa-
    tion, 182; the contradictions of for SEOs, 178–
    80; newly established SEOs and, 39; number of,
    2005–2018, 168; as a selection and institution
    process, 166–69; by Supernova (*see* Supernova's
    IPO)
innovation and opportunism, overlap between, 29
institutional change: with Chinese characteristics,
    196–98; opportunism and, 195–96. *See also*
    organizational change(s)/theory
institutional complexity, 21–22
institutional entrepreneurs, 195–96, 220n8
institutionalization, 6, 16, 19, 35, 39–40, 164, 166–
    69, 186, 193, 197–98, 207n23, 219n5
institutional logic perspective, 21
institutional work, 195, 220n8
intellectual property laws, 64
intellectual SEOs, 48–49; the informal economy
    and, 54–55; negotiating with state officials, fear

of, 65; opportunistic practices, limited use of,
    55–56, 62–64, 82; state education system re-
    sources, access to, 52–53; state regulation and,
    66, 71; student recruitment by, 59; teachers in,
    71–72; teaching by founders and family mem-
    bers, absence of, 80
International English Language Testing System
    (IELTS), 123
interorganizational-model competition, 196
intraorganizational conflict, 38–39, 166, 186
isomorphism/isomorphic pressure/isomorphic
    process, 11, 166, 186, 219n6

Japan, 7, 9, 25, 126, 147
Jin Yong, 103, 216n15
Johnson, Victoria, 216n2
juku(s), 206n6, 206n15, 213n9

Kang Chun, 150, 170
Kaplan, 2
Kellogg, Katherine C., 31
Key Worldwide Foundation, 1–2
Korea, Republic of (South), 8, 10, 205n3, 206n12,
    215n7
Kostello, Eric, 32–33
K–12 submarket, 117–18; education reform, de-
    mand side impact of, 124–27; expansion of and
    the rise of market leaders, 132–35; market size
    of K–12 after school tutoring compared to total
    number of students in formal education, 3; old
    and new opportunistic practices in, 127–32;
    participation rate among K–12 students, 135
Kumon, 2, 9
kung fu, 60, 137, 216n15
Kunlun Consulting, 170–71, 176
Kwok, Percy, 7–8

Le-We-Me, 166
Lingua Fun, 122, 219n2
Li Su, 36–37
Li Yan, 121–22
local governments, dealing with, 157–59
locking in, 215n5
Long Weiping, 60–61, 80
Luo, Yadong, 28, 31
Lu Yuegang, 90–91

malfeasance, 29, 211n13
managerial revolution, 137–39; cross-region ex-
    pansion and, 143–45; dimensions of, 139–40;
    the exception track, 138–39, 149–64; the fast
    track, 138, 140–43; the slow track, 138, 145–49
managers/management: opportunistic practices
    by, 181–83. *See also* administrative/ownership
    structure of SEOs

Mann, Michael, 20

marginal entrepreneurs: barefoot doctors as, 35–36; China's market transition and, 31–33; definition of, 31, 207n22; embeddedness in the state education system, impact of, 92–94; highly marginal and moderately marginal, distinction between, 32; new generation of, 122; as opportunistic market leaders, 44; opportunist SEOs and, 49–50; patterns regarding, 33

marketability: single-dimensional ambiguity and, 22–23; two-dimensional ambiguity and, 23–24

markets: Chinese approach to, 40; opportunistic practices used to enter, 56–59

Marx, Karl, 90

mass teaching model, 92, 97; components of, 105–7; crystallization of, 107; difficulty of implementing, 124; evolution of performative pedagogy, 101–5; nonteaching services not needed in, 133; performative pedagogy as the core, 97–100, 124 (*see also* performative pedagogy); phased out in K–12 submarket, 134–35; at Roaring English, 110–12; student performance and, 110; Supernova's dominance and, 107–10, 123–24

Math Olympiad Culture Corporation, 121

Math Olympiad Web, 121, 131

Ma Tiannan: departure from Seven Swords, 80; embeddedness in the state education system of, 92–93; experience before founding Pioneers, 56; opportunistic practices as a teacher by, 78; reorientation of teaching by, 94, 96–97; responses to teacher's opportunistic practices, 79; Su Leidong and, comparison of level of embeddedness by, 96–97; teacher evaluation implemented by, 83

McAdam, Doug, 195

medical system, state-run, 191

Mercury, 78

meritocracy, 10, 189

methodology: anonymity, issue of, 209–10n42; case selection, 12–14, 209nn40–41; data collection, 14–16; six key SEO cases, 14; snowball sampling method, 14

middle class/middle-class families, 10, 127, 130, 189, 206n12

minban, 208n30. *See also* nonstate organizations

Nasdaka English, 123

Nee, Victor, 11, 30, 40, 207n18

neoliberalism, 7–8

new institutionalism/theory, 11–12, 21–22, 37, 195–97

noncompete clause, 70, 76

noncompliance/noncompliant practices, 15, 28–29, 31, 44, 47, 55, 62, 65, 94, 269, 278. *See also* opportunism/opportunistic practices

Non-State Education Promotion Act, 119–21, 140, 142, 147, 213n14

nonstate organizations: business-state ties, significance of, 21–22; disadvantages faced by, 55; under one-dimensional ambiguity, 26; opportunists and, 34–35 (*see also* opportunism/opportunistic practices); opportunist SEOs (*see* opportunist SEOs); under two-dimensional ambiguity, 26–27

Nova Academy: ambiguity and the founding of, 23–24; founding as an intellectual SEO, 49–50; the informal economy and, 54–55; marketing strategy of, 59; Su Leidong and, 56–57, 76, 81, 213n13; teachers at, 71–72; teachers' opportunistic practices at, 78, 82; teaching by founders and family members, absence of, 80

one-dimensional ambiguity, 22–23, 26

Opper, Sonja, 11, 30, 40, 207n18

opportunism/opportunistic practices: by branch school presidents, 159–62; coevolution of institutionalization and, 40; conceptualizing/theorizing, 27–29; controlling the market with force, 59–61; definitions of, 211n10; embezzling tuition revenue, 139; franchises and, 147–49; innovation and, overlap between, 29; institutional change and, 195–96; institutionalization and/of, 193, 197; in the K–12 submarket, 127–32; malfeasance, predation, corruption, and, 29; the managerial revolution at Supernova and, 162–64; market entry by bending rules, 56–59; market formation and, 6–7; in the power dynamics between teachers and entrepreneurs, 68–69; prevalence across industries and countries, 206n16; recruiting student with fraudulent information, 61–62; reemergence of old tricks following the first IPO wave, 183–84; r-K theory and, 193–94; seat-occupying classes, 129–31; securing investment and, 180–86; social conditions and, 30–31; state regulation and, 36–37, 64–66, 190–91; takeaways regarding, 191–93; targets of, 5; by teachers, 70, 73–78; by teachers, entrepreneur's responses to, 78–88; types of, 28–29; using test materials without permission, 62–64. *See also* noncompliance/noncompliant practices

opportunists: competition between, 35–36; nonstate, state-affiliated organizations and, 36; selection and adaptation of, 37–39

opportunist SEOs, 49–50; embeddedness in the state education system, impact of, 92–94; the informal economy and, 26, 52–55; the managerial revolution and (*see* managerial revolution); market-based teacher evaluations by, 83–85; opportunistic practices used against teachers, 80–82; opportunistic practices used to maneuver ambiguity, 55–64; pedagogy and the competition between (*see* pedagogy); state regulation circumvented by, 122; state regulation turned to the advantage of, 64–66; state relations and, 196; taxation, evasion/reduction of, 64–65; teaching by founders and family members, 80

organizational change(s)/theory: competition dynamics under two-dimensional ambiguity and, 34–37; cultural explanations, 10, 198; Darwinian versus Lamarckian, 194; directions of, 39–40; economic explanations, 10–11; field theory, 196; interorganizational-model competition, 196; literature on expansion, privatization, and marketization, 7–11; micro-level organizational ecology theory, 193–94; new institutional perspective on, 11–12, 21–22, 37, 195–97; r- and K-strategies, 193–94; selection-adaptation debate, 37–39. See also institutional change

organizational repertoires, 5, 23–25, 207n21

organizations: with clear or ambiguous ownership and marketability, 22; models of SEOs in Beijing, 47–49; nonstate (see nonstate organizations)

ownership: one-dimensional ambiguity and, 22–23, 26–27; two-dimensional ambiguity and, 23–24, 27. See also administrative/ownership structure of SEOs

Padgett, John, 187, 192

part-time entrepreneurs as SEO founders, 25–26

pedagogy: coteaching, 86–88, 106; "English training camps" model, 112; evolution of and opportunistic practices in, 90–92; general model, 85–86; for K–12 classes, 132–35; mass teaching model (see mass teaching model); performative (see performative pedagogy); specialized, 86; from teaching English to coaching test-cracking, 94–97; transition from general model of teaching to coteaching model, 86–88; Western model, 123

Peng, Mike, 31

performative pedagogy: coteaching model and, 106; entertaining discourses/elements/performances, 17, 96–97, 101, 104–5; as entertainment, 99–100; evolution of, 101–5; large class sizes and, 107; market-based teacher evaluation and, 106–7; motivational discourse/elements/stories, 17, 91–92, 96–97, 101, 104–6, 109–112, 215n7, 216n16; nationalist comments/discourse/jokes, 17, 96–97, 99, 109–112, 216n11, 216n16; at Roaring English, 111; as the taken-for-granted model for teaching TOEFL/GRE classes, 124. See also chedan; chuishui; duanzi; xianpian

Pioneers: embeddedness in the state education system, level of, 92–93; family founding and management at, 145–46; opportunistic practices by, 56; responses to teacher's opportunistic practices, 79, 93–94; state education system resources available to, 52; taming of teachers

by, 82–83; teaching by founders and family members, 80; transformation of TOEFL/GRE training at, 92, 94, 96–97; varying fortunes in Beijing's TOEFL/GRE submarket, 50, 124

population ecology, 37, 193–95

predation, 29

predatory practices, 29–30, 35, 55

private economy/private sector, 187, 208n25, 213n19, 219–20n1

professional associations, 70, 220n3

professionalization, 38–39, 170, 175, 186, 197, 220n3

public goods, 8, 24, 191, 208n26, 210n4, 220n1

pulling students away, 75–77, 81, 88, 180, 183, 214n2

Qian Ning, 90

Questing School: general model at, 85; graduate students hired as teachers at, 72; informal economy, lack of participation in, 54; intellectual SEO, as example of, 48–50; Ma Tiannan at, 78; teachers' opportunistic practices at, 78, 82; teaching by founders and family members, absence of, 80

Ragin, Charles C., 208n34

r- and K-strategies, 193–94

Regulations on Non-State Education, 118–19

residency-based admission policy, 125–26, 129

Roaring English: competition faced by, 123; failed IPO of, 185; family founding and management at, 145–46; franchise model adopted by, 146, 148; as opportunist SEO in the spoken English submarket, 110–12; slow track of the coevolutionary process/managerial revolution at, 138, 140

Rona-Tas, Akos, 33

Scholastic Aptitude Test (SAT), 123

Scholastic Times, 111, 148–49

Schumpeterian tradition, 29

Scott, W. Richard, 197

Sea Dragon, 60–61, 66, 80

seat-occupying classes, 129–31

selection, 19, 164, 166–67, 169, 186

selection-adaptation debate, 37–39, 193–94

SEOs. See supplemental education organizations (SEOs)

Seven Swords: embeddedness in the state education system, level of, 92–93; enrollment around 1990, 49–50; exit-and-entrepreneurship practiced against, 82; graduate students hired as teachers at, 73; informal economy used by, 52, 54; Ma Tiannan at, 78; opportunistic practices by, 60, 63; opportunistic practices used against teachers, 80, 94

Singer, Rick, 1–2

skipping classes, 75, 77

social conditions/sources: anxiety and, 189–90; opportunism and, 30–31; two-dimensional ambiguity and, 24–26

socialist public goods. *See* public goods

socially marginal individuals, 32–33. *See also* marginal entrepreneurs

Song Jian, 181, 185

specialty health-care industry, 24, 30, 35–36

spoken English submarket, 110–12, 123. *See also* Roaring English

Spotlight Education, 169

Stark, David, 213n11

state, the: ambiguity of regulation of nonstate education, 120–21; anxiety, as a cause of, 188–89; demand side impact of education reform, 124–27; early regulation of SEOs, 4; local governments, dealing with, 157–59; opportunistic practices, attempts to regulate, 64–66, 190–91; opportunistic practices hidden to regulators, 36–37; regulation of nonstate education, 118–19; regulations and sanctions aimed at curtailing opportunism, 35; as a social source of two-dimensional ambiguity, 24–26; two-dimensional ambiguity of SEOs and, 50–52

state fragmentation, 27, 64

state governing logic, distinct, 26–27

state neoliberalism, 7–8

state retreat, 7, 189

state SEOs: affiliation with host institutions, 47–48; the informal economy and, 55; opportunistic practices, limited use of, 55–56, 62–64; state education system resources, access to, 52–53; state regulation and, 66, 71; state relations and, 196

Steverman, Ben, 1

Stinchcombe, Arthur, 43, 117, 216n2

students: demand side impact of education reform, 124–27; evaluation of teachers by, 82–85; expansion of in China's higher education system, 119; participation rate in SEO classes by, 3; performative pedagogy, popularity of (*see* performative pedagogy); recruiting, 59, 61–62; residency-based admission policy, 125–26, 129; retention of in the K–12 submarket, 133–34; Supernova's reputation among, 58–59; two-dimensional ambiguity of SEOs and, 51

Su Leidong: "advertisement war" described by, 59–60; bodyguard hired by, 61; Capital University, departure from, 43, 56, 96, 211–12n2; Capital University SEO, reputation and popularity of, 48; colleagues from Capital University, 72; decentralized approach to branch schools by, 155; encouragement of teachers by, 112; family control, moving away from, 150–51, 171–76; family members, reliance on, 54; on founders of other SEOs, 54; hiring standards used by, 103; informal relations maintained by, tension

between corporate formalization and, 162–63; the IPO and, 178; Kunlun Consulting and, 170; the mass teaching model and (*see* mass teaching model); Ma Tiannan and, comparison of level of embeddedness of, 96–97; moderate degree of embeddedness in the state education system of, 93; opportunistic practices against and by, 76–78, 81, 160–62; opportunistic practices used to enter the market, 56–59; origin as an SEO entrepreneur, 43–44; personal teaching style of, 101; on recruiting students, 61–62; reorientation of teaching by, 94–97; responses to teacher's opportunistic practices, 78–79, 85, 87; state regulation of SEOs, disgruntlement with, 119; Supernova Corporation, initial shareholding in, 171; teacher evaluations implemented by, 83–84; teachers' class preparation practices rarely monitored by, 143; transition in K–12 submarket, 134–35

Supernova: adaptation, as a case of, 38–39; complicated structure of, 47; corporate control at, 140; dominance of, mass teaching and, 107–10, 123–24; Doo & Cool and, comparisons of, 145, 155–57, 163–64; elements of classes, 91; embeddedness in the state education system, level of, 93; exception track of the coevolutionary process/managerial revolution at, 138–40, 149–50, 194 (*see also* Supernova, managerial revolution at); family members as management at, 141, 145, 151, 171–73; founder of, 43–44 (*see also* Su Leidong); founding of Supernova Corporation, 171; as a generalist SEO competing with specialists, 136; informal economy used by, 52, 54; in the K–12 submarket, 127–28, 134–35; as a market leader in Beijing's TOEFL/GRE submarket, 50, 91; mass teaching model at (*see* mass teaching model; performative pedagogy); opportunistic practices and, 26, 56–63, 139, 183; responses to teacher's opportunistic practices, 93–94; second and third generation teachers at, 101–3; significance of as a key case, 13; specialized teaching and coteaching model implemented by, 86–88; star teachers at, 74; state education system resources available to, 52; student enrollment in, 37, 108; taming of teachers by, 82–88; teacher pay at, 84, 106; teachers at, 71–73, 143; teachers' opportunistic practices at, 76–78, 183; teaching by founders and family members, 80; transformation of TOEFL/GRE training at, 92, 94–97

Supernova, managerial revolution at, 149–50; decentralized model for cross-region expansion, 155–59; family control, moving away from, 150–51, 171–73; opportunism by branch school presidents and Su's responses, 159–62; promotion of managers from within, 151–54; senior managers, exodus of, 163–64; Su's informal relations and corporate formalization, tensions between, 162–64

Supernova Corporation, 155, 162, 171

Supernova's IPO, 38–40, 166–67; as an adaptation process, 169–70; exhaustion of trust and organizational deadlock, 173–75; family conflict as a catalyst for, 171–73; origin of the idea, 170–71; other SEOs imitating, 167–69; professionalization of financial management as a catalyst for, 175–77; as a turning point for the SEO industry, 179–80; venture capital and going public, 177–78; VIE structure, establishment of, 176–77

supplemental education organizations (SEOs): administrative/ownership structure of (*see* administrative/ownership structure of SEOs); alternative names for, 205n2; ambiguity and, 5–6; anxiety, as a cause of, 188; boom in, overseas studies and, 46–47; competition dynamics under two-dimensional ambiguity in, 34–35; the context and the competitors, 45–50; cross-region expansion, 36–37; evolution of, 117–18 (*see also* K–12 submarket); foreign, 123; formalization process in, the rise of managers and, 138 (*see also* managerial revolution); founders of, 25–26, 122 (*see also* entrepreneurs); global finance of and initial public offerings (IPOs) (*see* global finance of SEOs; initial public offerings (IPOs); Supernova's IPO); intellectual (*see* intellectual SEOs); IPOs by (*see* initial public offerings (IPOs)); list of with data characteristics, 203–4; local protectionism and nepotism in, 147; the managerial revolution and (*see* managerial revolution); market leaders after the early 2000s, 123; opportunist (*see* opportunist SEOs); organizational models in Beijing's TOEFL/GRE submarket of, 47–55; organizational repertoires of, 25; registration and operation of, changes in the policy and institutional environment for, 118–23; shift from "remedial" to "remedial" and "enrichment" classes, 134; social conditions for opportunism present in, 30; social sources of two-dimensional ambiguity and, 24–26; state (*see* state SEOs); state fragmentation and, 27; teachers and, 69–73 (*see also* teachers); two-dimensional ambiguity and, 23–24, 50–51; underdeveloped market institutions and, 27; in the United States, 1–2, 9, 25. *See also names of specific supplemental education organizations (SEOs)*

supraorganizational changes/forces/pressure, 7, 12, 19, 34, 166

Sylvan Learning Centers, 9

Szelenyi, Ivan, 32–33

Taurus Global, 178

taxation: evasion/reduction of by opportunist SEOs, 64–65; two-dimensional ambiguity and, 27

teachers: bargaining power of, 69–73, 84–85, 142–43; collective preparation by, 143; competition between, 87; exit-and-entrepreneurship by, 70, 78, 80, 82, 87–88; at intellectual SEOs, 48–49; market-based evaluation of, 82–85, 106–7; opportunistic practices of, 70, 73–78, 94; pay at Supernova, 84, 106; power dynamics between entrepreneurs and, 68–69, 88–89; responses of employers to opportunistic practices by, 78–82, 93–94; second and third generation teachers at Supernova, 101–3; star, 74, 85; at state SEOs, 48; stealing of by franchisees, 148–49

teaching. *See* pedagogy

test-cracking skills, 94–97

TOEFL/GRE submarket: alternative approaches in, 29; bargaining power of teachers in the 1980s and early 1990s, 69–73; boom in demand, overseas study and, 46–47; dominance of Supernova in, 107–10, 123 (*see also* Supernova); organizational models of SEOs in, 47–49; pedagogy in (*see* pedagogy); shift in top SEOs in, 47, 49–50; teachers' opportunistic practices in, 75–78; test materials used without permission in, 62–63

transition economies, opportunists and, 30–31

two-dimensional ambiguity: characteristics of, 26–27; competition dynamics under, 34–37; development trajectory of industries under, 39–40; dimensions of, 23–24; illegitimacy discounts under, 26; opportunistic practices used to maneuver, 55–64; social sources of, 24–26; of supplemental education organizations (SEOs), 23–24, 50–51; taxation and, 27, 65; three models of supplemental education organizations (SEOs) under, 47–55

Uber, 191–92

underdeveloped market institutions, 27

United IELTS: backgrounds of founders of, 122; family founding and management at, 145–46; franchise model adopted by, 146; IPO by, 168; withdrawal of stock markets by, 186

United States: ambiguity of rideshare industry in, 191–92; college admission bribery case, 1–2; overseas Chinese students in, 1980–90, 46; predatory practices in the nineteenth century, 29; supplemental education organizations (SEOs) in, 1–2, 9, 25

variable interest entity (VIE), 167, 169, 176, 183, 219n7

Wank, David I., 40

Wei An, 150–51, 170, 172, 174

Werder, Axel V., 28

Whooshing Education, 183

Williamson, Oliver E., 27–28

World Trade Organization (WTO), 122–23
Wu, Xiaogang, 33
wuxia, 103, 216n15

xianpian, 97, 104. *See also* performative pedagogy
Xie, Yu, 33

Yang Dongping, 117, 130, 135, 188–89
Yuan Shikai, 81, 214–15n9

Zhang, Wei, 7–8
Zhao, Dingxin, 194
Zuckerman, Ezra W., 210n6

Made in United States
North Haven, CT
19 September 2024

57593417R00143